THE
WALL STREET
GURUS

THE WALL STREET GURUS

HOW YOU CAN PROFIT FROM INVESTMENT NEWSLETTERS

PETER BRIMELOW

MINERVA BOOKS
WASHINGTON, D.C.

Grateful acknowledgment is made to the following for permission
to reprint from previously published material:

Harper & Row: Specified excerpt from *The Money Masters* by John Train.
Copyright © 1980 by John Train. Specified excerpt from
The Intelligent Investor by Benjamin Graham. Copyright © 1973 by
Harper & Row, Publisher, Inc. Reprinted by permission of
Harper & Row, Publishers, Inc.

The Putnam Publishing Group: Excerpt reprinted by permission of
the Putnam Publishing Group from *Rogues to Riches*:
The Trouble with Wall Street, by Murray Teigh Bloom.
Copyright © 1972 by Murray Teigh Bloom.

St. Martin's Press, Inc.: Excerpt from *The Book of Granville*:
Reflections of a Stock Market Prophet, by Joseph E. Granville
with William Hoffer. Copyright © 1984 by Joseph E. Granville and
William Hoffer, St. Martin's Press, Inc., New York.

Simon & Schuster, Inc.: Excerpt from *Where Are the Customers' Yachts?*
by Fred Schwed, Jr. Copyright 1940 by Fred Schwed, Jr.
Copyright renewed 1967 by Harriet Wolf Schwed.

W. W. Norton & Company, Inc.: Excerpts from
A Random Walk Down Wall Street, Fourth Edition, by Burton G. Malkiel.
Published by W. W. Norton & Company, Inc., 1985.

Library of Congress Cataloging-in-Publication Data
Brimelow, Peter, 1947–
The Wall Street gurus.

Includes index.
1. Investment advisors. 2. Investment analysis.
I. Title.
HG4621.B69   1986   332.6   85-28153
ISBN 0-9620125-1-3

FOR MAGGY

Thou art all fair, my love.
—Song of Solomon 4:7

Acknowledgments

I am quite inadequate to the task of thanking all the people who over several years have helped feed my fascination with investment letters. Many of their names are to be found in the text; I am grateful to everyone who appears there, even James Dines. Dogs may not thank their fleas, but perhaps a flea can thank the investment letter industry, its friends and relations.

Some special acknowledgments must be attempted. This book simply could not have been undertaken without the support of Alan Abelson, editor of *Barron's*. Similarly, Bob Bleiberg, publisher and editorial director of *Barron's*, has been most kind. My debt to Mark Hulbert is obvious on every page; my debt to my brother John, Director of International Research at Keane Securities Company in New York, is less easily expressed. Kiril Sokoloff, whose highly regarded letter *Street Smart Investing* does not figure in these pages only because of its recent origin and deliberate exclusiveness, provided assistance and encouragement at a crucial point.

I want also to take this opportunity to thank one of North America's outstanding journalists, Neville J. Nankivell, editor-in-chief of the *Financial Post* of Toronto, Canada. The extent of my obligation to him may be judged by the fact that his recruiting abilities provided me with both a career and a wife.

At an early stage in this project, after Harry Schultz was good enough to mention it in his *International Harry Schultz Letter*, I was contacted by one of the investment letter industry's more remarkable figures, Lester A. Euell of Daytona Beach, Florida. Euell, whose wide experience has included associations with the *Granville Market Letter* and the *Drew Odd-Lot Studies*, told me that he is "the world's leading authority on newsletters and on technical analysis," a claim that I certainly have no wish to dispute, and offered me the benefit of his knowledge and insight. He has been most generous, and I am grateful.

I am also grateful, alphabetically, to: Ralph Acampora; Rebecca Ashe; Michael Baybak and his colleagues at Michael Baybak & Company; Arthur Behrstock; Teresa Bucher and her staff at the *Financial Post* library; Noel T. Casey; Connie Clausen and Guy Kettlehack at Connie Clausen Associates; Kate Dalton; Adrian Day; Darienne L. Dennis; Richard A. Donnelly, Floyd Norris and other friends at *Barron's*; A. Carlyle Dunbar; Dr. Clifford L. Egan; Jason Epstein, Derek Johns, Kate Trueblood and Sandy Schoenfein at Random House; Gerald Gold; Charles Grayson; Dr. Daniel L. Gressel; Al Krause; Hyman R. Hirsch; Andrew J. Hutchings; Kermit Lansner, editor-in-chief of *Financial World*; Dr. Melvin S. Levine; Neil Lovatt; Frederick A. Lynn; John O'Sullivan; Andrew H. Massie; Professor Henry G. Manne; Kathryn B. McGrath, Mary McCue and their colleagues at the Securities and Exchange Commission; William P. Sarubbi; Dawn Schultz, Ivan Shaffer; Donald R. Storey; John Train; Donna Westemeyer; Joel Wittenberg.

Others judged it best to remain anonymous and some, to whom I apologize, have undoubtedly been missed. All errors of fact and judgment are of course my own.

In conclusion, I want most humbly and earnestly to thank my wife Margaret, to whom this book is dedicated, for coming with me on the great journey of life.

Contents

THE
WALL STREET
GURUS

CHAPTER ONE

Introducing
Investment Letters

Full many a gem of purest ray serene
The dark unfathom'd caves of ocean bear.

—THOMAS GRAY, "Elegy Written in a Country Church-
yard"

Wall Streeters are a fair people, as Samuel Johnson once said
about the Irish: they never speak well of one another. Thus they
are particularly disinclined to praise the investment letters that
are published by independent observers of the financial scene,
sometimes thousands of miles from Harry's Bar and the joys of
lower Manhattan. In fact, they often know surprisingly little
about them.

Investment letters? You mean like Joe Granville's?

Well, yes. He's one of them. Most stockbrokers do know
about the flamboyant editor of the *Granville Market Letter*, because of the panic his widely publicized predictions of imminent
crashes and rallies caused among their clients in 1980 and 1981.
More recently, the managers of some mutual funds have been
apprised of the existence of "telephone switch" letters by the
tidal waves of money that arrive out of nowhere when one of
these letters recommends their fund to its subscribers, only to

depart equally abruptly when it signals a sell. In 1984, as much as $600 million was reported to have moved on one command from Dick Fabian's *Telephone Switch Newsletter*. A few Wall Streeters may even recall dimly that for several years in the late 1970s almost all the bank and insurance company portfolio managers who were tracked in the quarterly *Pension & Investment Age* Performance Evaluation Report (PIPER) were ignominiously beaten by a small Missouri bank, Citizens Bank of Chillicothe, which attributed its success to following an investment advisory service, Arnold Bernhard's *Value Line*.

Nah, we never read them. They're just promoters, charlatans. And they're always bullish/bearish.

The particular allegation selected depends on the age of the speaker. In the 1970s, some advisories like *The Dines Letter* and the *International Harry Schultz Letter* constantly warned about the dangers of inflation and became fixed in many Wall Streeters' minds as "gold bugs" and "gloom-and-doomers." But in the 1960s, when the postwar bull market was reaching its peak, the common accusation had been that the popular letters were always optimistic, trying to boost their circulations.

Actually, investment letters cover the gamut. Some are bulls, some bears; some are rapidly trading hares, others are tortoises that hold positions for years; some are popular, some are scholarly; some are promotional, others are monastically reclusive, never advertising and depending on a group of loyal subscribers to renew and spread the word. A few letter writers are Byronic loners, who might well be hearing voices in the air, but others preside over research departments comparable in size and sophistication with many on Wall Street.

Yeah, well anyway they're always wrong.

You mean, like Wall Street firms?

[Rueful grunt.]

The exact timbre of this grunt depends on how well the market has done that day. But most Wall Streeters are secretly all too well aware of the fact that their clients don't have much to show for their high-priced efforts. The clients themselves keep bleating plaintively about it, and, adding insult to invest-ment loss, a plague of professors has broken out with an entire academic theory explicitly asserting that the market cannot be beaten over the long haul—the "Efficient Market Hypothesis." It has proved embarrassingly difficult to refute.

But this book is about new evidence that apparently does refute the Efficient Market Hypothesis. This evidence suggests that the market can be beaten. Some investment letters have beaten it.

Sure, for a year or so. But not over the long run.

Evidence of the highest quality has been collected since June 1980. Enough letters have beaten the market over that pe-riod to deserve serious study. Strongly suggestive evidence ex-tends much farther back.

On a risk-adjusted basis?

This Wall Streeter has been to business school. The profes-sors have got at him. The answer is yes, but read the book.

If they're so smart, how come they're not rich? [Snigger.]

Some of them are. *Forbes* magazine estimated in 1984 that Arnold Bernhard of *Value Line* was worth over $400 million. But let's concede that in many ways he's an established Wall Street figure. A consciously un–Wall Street type, Charles Allmon of *Growth Stock Outlook,* is worth $4 million, not counting his own-ership interest in the business, which is very substantial. Good enough?

No. They made their money selling advice, not acting on it.

That's not necessarily true. To take one clear-cut example: Al Frank ran up $8,006.51 to more than $200,000 between March 1977 and June 1985. That's an increase of more than 2,500 percent. It's his own money and he prints the results in his *Prudent Speculator,* which as late as 1983 was selling all of seventy-five copies, making him very little money indeed.

Look. If people really knew how to beat the market, they wouldn't sell the secret in a newsletter for a lousy few hundred bucks.

Yes they would, for important reasons that will become clear. Read the book.

[Another voice:] *Geez—do I really have to read another book about business in my spare time, just because some guys can beat the market?*

This is a very understandable question. It happens, however, that the investment letter industry contains about as weird a set of characters as you could hope (or would hope) to meet. A strong personality is a professional requisite for investment advisors. They have to have one to survive in a business that can be cruelly testing and dramatic. Charisma helps, too. Moreover, the investment letter phenomenon says something about the turbulent nature of American society, and it casts an eccentric light on the history of recent times. Investment letters, in other words, can be fun.

"Books about Wall Street fall into two categories," wrote Fred Schwed, Jr., in 1940 in his great book about Wall Street *Where Are the Customers' Yachts?*, "which may respectively be called the admiring, or 'Oh, my!' School, and the vindictive, or 'Turn the Rascals Out' School. Needless to say, the former were all written formerly, and the latter, latterly, the dividing line being around October 1929."

This book attempts to invent a third category. It might perhaps best be described as the "They May Be Rascals—But They're Our Rascals" School. Admiring books are still sometimes written about the Wall Street establishment, but over the years there has been a relentless battering of the advisory services. Two titles that succinctly expressed the financial press's attitude were Murray Teigh Bloom's *Rogues to Riches* and John L. Springer's *If They're So Smart, How Come You're Not Rich?*, both published in 1971. Essentially, critics of the investment letters have argued that the advisors are ignorant (they may have no formal education or experience in investments), incompetent (their investment record can be bad), dishonest (they can lie about their records) jerks (jerks). All of which can be true. It's also true of many of the inhabitants of the rest of the investment industry, of course, but they at least look respectable. Journalists are often more conventional than they like to admit.

Not that journalists are alone in applying a more demanding standard to investment advisors. In 1975 the Securities and Exchange Commission prosecuted Thomas L. Phillips, publisher of *The Retirement Letter,* because he was cashing subscription checks as they came in and employing the money immediately in his business. The SEC thought he should hold the subscription revenue in escrow, not touching it until he had mailed out the last copy for which he had been paid. This may sound a nice idea at first, but what Phillips was doing was actually standard business practice for every commercial publisher, such as Dow Jones *(Wall Street Journal)* or McGraw-Hill *(Business Week).* The case was thrown out of court, in one of the SEC's rare defeats prior to 1985. Similarly, the disapproval often expressed of some letters' heavy advertising overlooks the fact that the selling of many consumer products, such as soap powder, routinely involves vast promotional expenses.

The premise of this book is that if you want truffles, you hire a truffle hound. You do not ask it to dine with you and you do not want to see its pedigree, although you know that breeding counts. You do not forget that it can bite, that it might have fleas and may not be housebroken. You keep it in a kennel and on a leash. You just require that it find truffles. And some of the investment letters can find truffles.

In mid-1985, the U.S. Supreme Court unexpectedly ruled in *Lowe* v. *Securities and Exchange Commission* that the SEC did not have the power to require investment letters to register with it, as it had been doing for nearly half a century. SEC officials were stunned. One spokeswoman commented that the decision would "put the burden on the consumer to . . . not believe everything he sees in print."

Ultimately, however, that's where the burden always was. *Caveat emptor,* let the buyer beware, has been the practical reality of business for rather a long time, yet commercial life has somehow been able to proceed.

Truffles, anyone?

CHAPTER TWO

Investment Letters: The Case for the Defense

It is happy for man that he does not know what the morrow is to bring forth; but, unaware of this great blessing, he has, in all ages of the world, presumptuously endeavoured to trace the events of unborn centuries, and to anticipate the march of time. He has reduced this presumption to a study. He has divided it into sciences and systems without number, employing his whole life in the vain pursuit. Upon no subject has it been so easy to deceive the world as this.

—CHARLES MACKAY, *Extraordinary Popular Delusions and the Madness of Crowds* (1841)

People will endeavor to forecast the future and make agreements according to their prophecy. Speculation of this kind by competent men is self-adjustment of society to the probability.

—OLIVER WENDELL HOLMES, in a U.S. Supreme Court decision

By the dawn's early light—or at any rate at the distressing hour when Wall Streeters are clawing their way in from the suburbs and financial journalists are still asleep—a beautiful Chinese woman in a loose shift sits drinking coffee and reading in an apartment full of her own artwork high above Manhattan's East Side. Tina Sheff is already at work. She is a designer and her

American husband, Don, is a wealthy entrepreneur who runs a photography correspondence school; they have the quintessentially metropolitan hobby of collecting interesting people and holding amusing dinner parties. However, what absorbs Tina Sheff right now is a long way from art or wit. Tina manages her own investment portfolio. She trusts neither banker nor broker, but makes decisions herself after studying a selection of the independent investment letters that have proliferated across America in recent years.

"It's a very tough game—basically very tough," she says. "But it's a little more interesting than the Las Vegas game. You learn about the real world and you have a chance to do well." Tina has subscribed to many different investment letters over the years, depending on the state of the market. Recently, she has relied most heavily on Dick Fabian's *Telephone Switch Newsletter*, which is designed for investors in mutual funds and attempts to warn them of major market moves so that they can shift from stocks into cash and back again. Tina credits Fabian with inspiring them to get into the market in August 1982, when one of the greatest rallies in history was beginning, and out again in early 1984, just before they embarked on a trip of Egypt, when the market had stalled and showed signs of going into a tailspin. ("I finally got the *Wall Street Journal* in Cairo and saw how far down the market was . . . he saved us!") Tina Sheff's childhood in wartime China has given her an intense aversion to inflation and a respect for the traditional hedge, gold. Despite the steady erosion in the metal's price since 1980, she still subscribes to *Hard Money Digest* just as a precaution. For a portfolio she manages for her family overseas, who are taxed on income but not capital gains, she subscribes to the *Value Line OTC Special Situations Service*, from which she culls smaller fast-growing companies that she intends to hold for three to five years to give them a chance to appreciate. ("You have to gamble—otherwise there's no chance.") And, finally, she takes *Personal Finance*, which provides all-round advice on investments, taxes and developing trends.

At the same gray hour in another city some 400 miles to the northwest of New York, one investment letter editor's working day is just ending—briefly. Like a restless vampire with staring eyes, beard and wild hair, Ian McAvity has been prowling all night long through his silent Victorian townhouse in Toronto's gentrified Cabbagetown area, a silent tumult of conflicting memories, ideas and reflections. Periodically, he has been stopping to consult one of his cats, all Siamese crossbreeds perfectly accustomed to the nocturnal creative frenzies every two weeks at the deadline for McAvity's investment letter *Deliberations*. McAvity is a technical analyst. He specializes in the arcane and controversial art of predicting the future direction of financial markets by studying their trading action, including the patterns formed by their past price movements when traced on a chart, rather than the traditional "fundamental" analysis that focuses on corporate earnings and prospects. To save time laying out his letter, he types his comments directly on to the page around that issue's charts, growing noticeably more acerbic as he runs out of space. His white cat helps by sitting beside the electric typewriter, watching intently. She is convinced that once she has figured out the mechanism, she will be able to halt it in midsentence, just as with the old manual typewriter, by inserting a paw.

In a few hours, letters printed and envelopes stuffed, McAvity will be driving the short distance across the U.S. border to Buffalo. There, reflecting the patriotic pride in the efficiency of Canada's postal service that is part of every Canadian's national heritage, he will mail to the great majority of his several thousand subscribers who live in the United States or abroad. Next, without rest, McAvity will head for the airport and yet another of his many speaking engagements at an investment conference in New Orleans, Chicago or perhaps Los Angeles. He will catch up with his reading on the plane.

It's a grueling schedule. McAvity is paler and paunchier than the exuberant, squash-playing, tanned, bearded, long-haired Viking-like figure of some years ago, when in his early thirties he was one of the fastest-rising stockbroker-analysts on the continent. In those days his individuality was expressed by always being the only man in any office not wearing a tie. But leaving the brokerage business to become his own boss seems to have satiated that compulsion. It has calmed down considerably the iconoclastic lifestyle McAvity adopted when his first marriage broke up and he left his hometown of Montreal for Toronto. *Deliberations* has made him famous among his peers in the (North) American investment world. And it is the flagship of a business that can not only accommodate his independence but also make him rich.

Deliberations costs $215 a year. A thousand subscribers mean $215,000 gross revenue, ten thousand subscribers, $2,150,000, even before speaking fees and other emoluments. And the rule of thumb in the investment letter industry is that, depending on accounting methods, half or even three-quarters of that gross could be profit. Several of today's best-known investment letters were literally begun "on the kitchen table," in industry jargon, with no more expenditure than labor and a few hundred dollars for printing and mailing to a list of friends. Now they are flourishing enterprises, sometimes developing money management and even investment banking arms. Their proprietors have created a substantial capital asset out of midnight oil. The American Dream of From Log Cabin to White House must now be supplemented by From Kitchen Table to Financial Institution.

Tina Sheff and Ian McAvity are specimens, exotic but not exceptional, from the seething investment letter subculture. This little-known industry has quietly become one of the most energetic expressions of American pluralism. At any one time, depending on how inviting the financial markets look, somewhere from 500,000 to over a million Americans subscribe to investment letters. A year's subscription usually costs $150–$300, but can range from $39 (like Max Bowser's *The Bowser Report*, specializing in low-priced stocks) to $1,365 (the complete weekly *Mansfield Stock Chart Service*) or even higher. And many investment letter subscribers buy more than one. Tina Sheff's selection, for example, was costing her $546 a year, excluding any short-term trials she might be sampling. Some particularly rugged individuals have been known to get as many as forty investment letters—incredible until you consider that $5,000–$10,000 annually is not much to pay for advice on managing a portfolio that may amount to millions, and that for tax purposes any expenditure on market letters can normally be deducted from income as a legitimate business expense.

Investment letters blossom with favorable stock markets like desert flowers after a rainstorm, and some of them have even shorter lives. They bloomed in the strong markets of the 1950s, wilted steadily into the sharp break of 1961, and flourished again as the market peaked in 1966–8, fading thereafter as it headed into the 1974 low. In the aftermath of the great 1982–3 bull market, perhaps 1,000–1,500 investment letters had sprouted. Most of them were kitchen-table affairs with handfuls of clients. But about 400 letters were serious, well-established operations, and of these two or three dozen accounted for the great bulk of readership. Howard Ruff's $145-a-year *Financial Survival Letter* and KCI Publications' $65-a-year *Personal Finance* achieved circulations of 150,000 and 200,000 respectively. These were aimed at popular audiences. More specialized and expensive letters aimed at heavier-breathing investors, such as Dr. Martin Zweig's *Zweig Forecast* ($245) and Stan Weinstein's *Professional Tape Reader* ($250), reached the 15,000–20,000 level. And after every rainstorm, there are more desert flowers. Both in quality and quantity the investment letter industry has changed out of recognition in the last forty years.

Typically, an investment letter consists of several eight-and-a-half-by-eleven-inch pages, often printed, sometimes typed and reproduced by the offset process, occasionally just Xeroxed. They arrive by mail every two, three or four weeks. Some investment letters also put out special bulletins if the market does anything dramatic at awkward moments between deadlines, as it is obnoxiously inclined to do; increasingly, letters are supplemented by telephone hotlines, numbers that anxious subscribers can call to get recorded remarks about the market's latest gyrations.

Wall Street and the financial press have tended to view the investment letter industry with distaste. Partly this is because the entrepreneurs who publish investment letters are often ruthless competitors. "If you haven't heard of me, ask your broker," trumpeted *The Worden Tape Reading Studies*' Don Worden in a famous and very effective direct-mail solicitation back in 1963. "If your broker hasn't heard of me, *ask yourself about your broker!*" The brokerage industry naturally felt that quite enough mutinous customers were asking themselves awkward questions already, and Worden's incitement was particularly irritating because he had actually started in the business only a couple of years earlier. (Later in the 1960s, his operation did become the best-known technical service around, perhaps not surprisingly.) Investment letters are equally disrespectful of major media news judgment. They regard it as axiomatic that the appearance of a story on the cover of a national magazine means that the trend thus celebrated is about to end, as when *Business Week*'s August 19, 1979, "Death of Equities" cover story appeared just before the market began to revive, or when its May 9, 1983, "Rebirth of Equities" marked the stalling of the 1982–1983 rally. This does not help their popularity. Dogs do not love their fleas, particularly dogs that view themselves as gad-flies.

Outsiders often complain about the investment letter industry's strident salesmanship. So do insiders. The favorite example of an overpromoted service among its older, more established competitors was the Aden sisters' *Aden Analysis*, which in the early 1980s rocketed up to a circulation of some 20,000 largely on the strength of a widely publicized prediction that the gold price would fall (right) and then rebound to $4,888 an ounce (. . . wrong). This was no doubt unfair to Mary Anne and Pamela Aden, who seemed knowledgeable enough and were by no means alone in their view of gold. By contrast, the industry vote for the title of most-deserving underpromoted service would probably go to *The Polymetric Report*, an intense computer-based survey of U.S. and Canadian stocks published from Toronto by a gentle, self-effacing Welshman, Picton Davies.

Not even their best friends would deny that investment letter proprietors can be relentless, almost lunatic, self-promoters. In the early 1980s Joseph E. Granville achieved genuine superstar status, certified by his being the first—and so far only—technical analyst to get his picture on the front page of the New York *Times*. As the stock market staggered in apparent accordance with his predictions, the circulation of his $250-a-year *Granville Market Letter* soared to a high somewhere over 14,000, producing a 1981 gross income reported—by himself, and somewhat implausibly—to be over $10 million. Granville was constantly on the road, traveling a million miles in four years to speak at "seminars" all over the country, and by this time he had them turned to a high pitch. He would never share the platform with anyone except for occasional special guests like a tame chimpanzee, named "Dwarfman" in honor of the syndicated financial columnist Dan Dorfman, or an iguana named "Greenspan" for the noted Wall Street economist and former Chairman of the President's Council of Economic Advisers Alan Greenspan. In Tucson once, Granville began by walking across a swimming pool on a plank hidden just below the surface, then telling the assembled multitude, "And now you know!" In Atlantic City he had himself carried into a seminar in a coffin under a shroud of ticker tape, eyes shut and martini in hand, before resurrecting himself, drunk as it turned out, before the audience of nearly a thousand. In Minneapolis, when asked how he could keep close to the market while traveling so much, he dropped his tuxedo pants to reveal boxer shorts printed with stock quotations that he successively identified, finally pointing to his crotch with the delighted cry of "And here's Hughes Tool!" Granville seminars usually began with a rendition of "The Bagholder Blues," a song he had written himself to memorialize the plight of Wall Street and its clients, a.k.a. "bagholders." Granville's sell signal on January 6, 1981, telephoned at midnight to subscribers who had paid an additional $500 for his Early Warning Service, precipitated a record-volume 23-point collapse on the New York Stock Exchange. In one day some $45 billion was wiped off share values, three times the dollar amount lost on Black Tuesday, the worst day of the Great Crash of 1929.

Granville was unmistakably a throwback to a once-familiar type: the traveling Yankee snake-oil salesman. He is a lean, ravaged-looking man whose quick, emphatic gestures and full head of hair belie his age (he was born in 1924 and remembers his banker father losing money in the 1929 Crash). At lunch with the editors of *Barron's* in 1982, joking in his rasping voice about his visit to the visitors' gallery above the New York Stock Exchange, when he stood until the attention of all the traders was focused on him and then turned his thumb down to a chorus of boos, Granville appeared entirely sane, if slightly sadistic. It was really a way, he explained, of testing market sentiment. Only when the professionals were too demoralized to protest would all the selling be over and a rally be about to start. But around this time Granville also said repeatedly that, as he told a Vancouver audience, "I'll never make another major mistake in the stock market." It was the stock market equivalent of announcing immortality. And about this he was not joking. A fellow investment letter editor, Stan Weinstein, ventured to question him on the notion in the privacy of an hotel elevator. He emerged dazed to report only a glare and a ferocious reaffirmation.

The investment letter industry was collectively appalled.

They were already terrified that Granville's antics would bring retribution upon them all in the form of crusading congressmen and regulatory officials inspired by the inevitable injury to naïve but vocal investors. This latest excess, however, violated sacred industry traditions. It was worse than a crime—it was a clear-cut call.

And it was wrong. In the middle of 1982, Granville fell off his flying trapeze. He completely missed the 1982 rally and remained bearish as the Dow Jones Industrial Averages went from 776 to over 1,280. The *Granville Market Letter*'s circulation plunged to well below 2,000. By 1985, he had moved from Florida to Kansas City, the home of his new wife, Karen, and seemed to have virtually vanished from public view under expensive quarrels with the Internal Revenue Service, his brokers and his son and ex-business partner, Blanchard Granville. But he was not extinct. As the stock market had moved sideways through 1983 and 1984, other analysts had begun to decide that the bear trend was reasserting itself. And Granville, who has never been totally committed to one side of the market or the other, did score something of a coup by making perhaps the clearest prediction of the market's sharp upward stab in August 1984, while continuing to maintain that the longer-run trend was down. Joe Granville had been down before in his long career, several times, and had always come back. No one was eager to count him out.

Even paranoids have enemies, and even snake-oil salesmen sometimes have snakes. Or oil. Beyond the hoopla, the reason for Granville's popular success was that in the several years prior to 1982 he had indeed been generally accurate on the market's direction. And he had not hesitated to say when he thought it was about to fall, something Wall Street, with its direct interest in sales and commissions, has been notoriously reluctant to do.

Moreover, Granville's activities should be set in perspective. Exactly parallel with his rise, Wall Street was itself evolving a remarkably similar figure of its own: Dr. Henry Kaufman, chief economist of Salomon Brothers, one of the most powerful investment banking firms in the country. Kaufman's periodic pronouncements on interest rates had been hair-raising but sadly accurate throughout the late 1970s, as the prime rate reached levels unprecedented in history. And Kaufman too became a certified celebrity, making regular appearances on the nightly network news. By the time he came to make his annual forecast at the beginning of 1982, his public utterances were highly orchestrated affairs, obviously designed for maximum impact.

First, after the markets closed, Kaufman journeyed around Manhattan unveiling his views to the banks and investment fund managers who were Salomon's institutional clients. So great was his reputation at this time that these presentations were reportedly greeted in respectful silence, with almost no questions from the floor. Then, early the next morning before the markets opened, journalists and television cameras were summoned to a simple breakfast in one of the Salomon dining rooms, on a mezzanine below which the firm's traders could be seen gathering at their desks, baying and salivating at the electronic ticker that stretched along a wall. Kaufman is a small, rotund man with eyes that seem to vanish behind his bifocals. He looks like the cartoon character Mr. Magoo, except for a fleeting, tentative smile and an impressively regal manner once at the podium. On that January morning, Kaufman said interest rates were going back up, inflation would be high and there wasn't going to be no economic recovery. The stock market, which dislikes higher rates partly because much trading is done on borrowed money, promptly crashed 17 points.

There are, of course, considerable differences between Granville and Kaufman. Kaufman is a card-carrying Ph.D.-possessing economist. He is a leading exponent of the "flow-of-funds" forecasting technique, which means that he estimates the amount of borrowing governments and corporations will have to do in each year, balancing it against the funds available and tracing its effect through the various levels of the economy. A thick expository booklet printed on elegant bond was supplied to the milling scribes, causing one guest, the long-retired dean of flow-of-fund forecasting, Sydney Homer, to twitch his hoary mustache and reflect quietly that he remembered when it could all be done on one sheet of paper.

But the fact is that Kaufman's method is not as scientific as it looks. The basic building blocks of his technique are government statistics, and these are revised not once but many times, so that substantial changes are still being made to figures that were first released ten years ago. The variations are so great as to render calculations that anyone cared to base on these figures at least questionable if not worthless. (Nor is this problem unique to economic forecasters. Wall Street analysts who follow oil company stocks regularly predict the oil price after elaborate computations of supply and demand, but the actual world consumption of oil in any year since the late 1950s is still uncertain.) And Kaufman, like Granville, was wrong. Later in the year, when it became obvious that his scenario was not working out, Kaufman did reverse himself and predict lower interest rates. The stock market responded with a day even bigger than the one that occurred after Granville's sell signal twenty months before. And on August 19, 1982, the *Wall Street Journal*'s Thomas Petzinger reported:

> When Henry Kaufman gets an idea, is it ethical for his employers to quietly act on it? . . .
> Traders at the Chicago Board of Trade say Salomon Brothers, a unit of Phibro Corp., piled up a huge position in futures on treasury bonds—totaling $400 million in face value by some accounts—and only then let the rest of the world in on Mr. Kaufman's thinking.*

Bond prices rise when people expect interest rates to fall, and the profits are even more dramatic for anyone holding the futures, which are essentially rights to buy a bond at a certain price some months forward. By contrast, Joe Granville says he doesn't trade on his own recommendations at all, before or after he makes them. And although throughout this period the regulatory authorities were certainly watching him with rapt attention, they have never contradicted this claim. Yet Kaufman has never been exposed to anything like the opprobrium hurled at Granville.

There are at least two morals to be extracted from this story. Firstly, the investment business, on whatever level it operates, is inherently susceptible to charisma. Secondly, as *Barron's* editor Alan Abelson observed some years ago, on

---

*Salomon Brothers would not confirm the rumored transactions, although they are not prohibited by current law.

Wall Street it's easier to peddle high-class junk than low-class junk.

The failings of Wall Street and of the established economic authority generally have been crucial to the rise of the investment letter industry. Investment letters really came to prominence in an era of unprecedented error on the part of the economic establishment: the Great Inflation that occurred in the years after World War II and culminated (or so everyone hopes) at an annualized rate of over 20 percent in 1980. Leading investment letter writers were just quicker to see the implications of inflation than were most institutional investors, policy makers and academic economists. These letter writers urged their readers to buy gold, the historic refuge against inflation. For years they were known derisively as gold bugs. The insult became progressively easier to absorb as the metal's price rose from $35 an ounce in 1968 to a 1980 high of over $870. Gold mine stocks were even more consoling. For example, Hartebeestefontein rose from the equivalent of $1 to over $100. Significantly, and quite contrary to stereotype, many of the famous investment letter gold bugs like Harry Schultz of the *International Harry Schultz Letter*, Harry Browne of *Harry Browne's Special Reports* and Vern Myers of *Myers' Finance and Energy*, were also remarkably quick to bail out of precious metals as they peaked, and to say with varying degrees of urgency that the age of inflation might be over.

The investment world turned upside down in the 1970s, and inflation had a lot to do with it. The *Wall Street Journal*'s Alfred E. Malabre supplied a classic commentary on the subject in a column that appeared in the newspaper on August 20, 1973. In my left hand in the pink trunks, he said in effect, Dr. Robert H. Parks, chief economist of Blyth Eastman Dillon, one of New York's most important securities firms. On my right hand in the camouflaged trunks, Dr.—well, make that "Dr."—Harry D. Schultz, proprietor of the *International Harry Schultz Letter*, which is published from whatever country Schultz happens to be visiting that month, a long list from which his native United States has been conspicuously absent for some time. Dr. Parks' credentials were impressive: a bachelor's degree from Swarthmore; a master's and doctorate from the University of Pennsylvania; professorships at two colleges. "Dr." Schultz's credentials were also impressive, although in not quite the same way. He had once told the *Wall Street Journal* that his Ph.D. came from St. Lawrence University in upstate New York. But officials there said they had no record he had received a degree of any kind or indeed that he had ever attended their institution at all. Schultz did seem to have spent a couple of years at City College of Los Angeles, but his major had been journalism, not economics. (At the time, Harry Schultz was also claiming a D.Sc., but you get the idea.)

Parks had been predicting business expansion—good for the stock market—and had endorsed international financial agreements aimed at eliminating gold from the world monetary system with a report ringingly entitled "King Gold Is Dead!" Schultz had been pessimistic about United States prospects and had advocated diversification out of the dollar and into European securities and South African gold mining shares. Score at the time of writing: Schultz ahead on points—his European stocks were up 20 percent at a time when United States markets had slumped; his South African selections were up some 200 percent. For the future, Parks remained cheerful ("this expansion may turn out to be one of the longest in U.S. history") whereas Schultz ("Civilization, as we know it, is crumbling . . . a strong dollar is nowhere in sight") was growing positively apocalyptic. In fact, there was a severe recession, a very sick stock market, a sliding dollar and unsubdued inflation. Final score: Schultz by a knockout.

Malabre emphasized that his purpose was not to disparage Parks, who represented the best thinking on Wall Street (and today heads his own firm—Blyth Eastman Dillon having joined the long list of famous Wall Street names to be swallowed by a competitor, in this case Paine Webber). Indeed, Malabre volunteered, he himself had written very nastily three years earlier about the best-selling book *How You Can Profit From the Coming Devaluation* by Harry Browne, who had spent even less time in college than Harry Schultz (two weeks—Browne says he used to fall asleep in class). Malabre had dismissed Browne's forecast of inflation, dollar devaluation and escalating gold prices. He had been particularly sarcastic about Browne's recommendation that investors obtain a "rural retreat" because in an inflationary collapse food supplies to the cities might be disrupted. "Now in New York City in the summer of 1973," Malabre concluded, "we haven't nailed down that country hideaway. But we've been extra-friendly with a family that grows tomatoes and squash in their backyard out on Long Island . . . As for appraising business and financial prospects—the thing that pays the bills in our household—we're saving up to buy our first crystal ball, if the price doesn't go completely out of sight."

This is not a laughing matter, so it naturally calls for a joke:

> There was a man who took his large estate to the investment counsel, and emerged looking a little dazed.
> "What did they tell you?" asked his friend.
> "They told me to sell everything and put all the money, except for $3,500, in government bonds."
> "What did they tell you to do with the $3,500?"
> "They told me to give it to them."

The point of this joke is not simply the high cost of professional management—most investment counselors charge some three-quarters of 1 percent of the funds under their care each year, regardless of performance, so that the estate in question here would be some $460,000. It's the investment advice given: *buy government bonds.* That was universally agreed by all the best people to be the sound, safe, prudent thing to do in 1940, when the story first appeared in Fred Schwed's witty exposé of Wall Street, *Where Are the Customers' Yachts?* Yet from World War II, the bear market in bonds was virtually continuous for over thirty-five years. Because bonds yield a fixed proportion of their face value each year, bond prices fall when interest rates rise until the yield approximates returns available elsewhere. Even when investors held their bonds to maturity, and got back the full face value, inflation had eroded its purchasing power. Bonds issued in the 1940s, when interest rates were around 2 percent, retained only 20 percent to 25 percent of their purchasing power when they matured in the 1970s. This has been one of the greatest financial catastrophes of history, on a scale quite comparable with the 1929 Crash. And it affected not just the public but America's great institutional investors—the Prudentials and Chase Manhattans. They all bought bonds in vast quantities all the way down the thirty-year slope.

This was by no means the investment establishment's only misjudgment. It is of course an open secret that much of the over $100 billion lent by American banks to the Third World and the Communist bloc is never coming home again. And institutional investors under the guidance of leading investment banks like Merrill Lynch poured a total of $8.3 billion into the Washington Public Power System, which in 1983 produced the largest default in United States financial history, leaving the bondholders the proud possessors of little more than a large hole in the ground in a remote area of Washington State.

Anyone can make a mistake . . . or two. But the public was invited to participate directly in these mistakes over a remarkably long time. For example, a generation of Americans was urged by campaign committees of corporation presidents and local notables to buy, as a patriotic duty, U.S. Savings Bonds ("a piece of America"). These paid a fixed interest rate lower than the current inflation rate. The presidents and notables would never have considered them for themselves. Similarly, the savings accounts offered by commercial banks, thanks to regulation by a friendly federal government, were actually forbidden to pay interest that would compete with prevailing rates, let alone attempt to compensate for inflation. This was fine with the banks, of course, since they got to turn around and lend the money out at the higher rate. All by itself, this regulation probably inflicted the single largest financial loss ever suffered by the trusting American public. Eventually, money market funds, which are mutual funds investing only in obligations that are so short-term they are virtually equivalent to cash, squeezed through a loophole in the law and began to offer the public higher rates for their savings. The banks quickly persuaded the regulators to ease up. But as late as April 1981, Americans had some $362.9 billion deposited in bank savings accounts and earning a mere 5.5 percent, whereas the yield on the $115.66 billion in money market funds was 14.1 percent. This amounted to a loss by the public at an annual rate of over $31 billion.

And then there is the continuing saga of "whole life" life insurance. Whole life, the favored vehicle of the insurance industry, consists of an insurance component and a forced-savings component, as opposed to "term life," which is the insurance component alone. The insurance companies collect a fee to manage these forced savings far more substantial than the measly

0.75 percent charged by investment counselors, and they accordingly pay their salesmen very well to push whole life. Moreover, in an era of inflation, the actual value of the final payout on any life insurance policy is often nowhere near what the purchaser expected when he bought it years before. Andrew Tobias, in his searching look at the insurance industry, *The Invisible Bankers*, quotes the example of oil economist Walter Levy's father: he took out a policy in Germany in 1903 and after twenty years of faithful payments cashed it in and bought—a single loaf of bread. Inflation in America hasn't been quite that bad, of course. Here, twenty-year life insurance policies are worth quite a number of loaves of bread.

That's why people listened to Joe Granville when he told them to sell short into market declines—to sell stock for future delivery in the hope it can be bought cheaper later, the riskiest form of speculation—and when he dismissed caution as a sign of ignorance. He derided the principle that responsible fiduciary management meant conservatism, the so-called "prudent man rule," as "the prudent and poor man rule." And his audiences knew just what he meant.

Complaints about establishment investment advice are not new. Way back in 1932, an independently wealthy amateur statistician named Alfred Cowles read a paper called "Can Stock Market Forecasters Forecast?" to a joint meeting of the American Econometric Society and the American Statistical Association. Cowles' answer: no. He argued that the results of a number of forecasters and money managers over a period including the Great Crash were actually worse than would have been expected from pure chance. In 1944, another Cowles study published in *Econometrica* magazine concluded that, with one modest exception, no leading investment service could be shown to outperform the market. David Dreman in his book *Contrarian Investment Strategy* listed fifty-one surveys going back to 1928 in which investment managers had been asked to name their favorite stocks for the next year. In thirty-nine cases, their choices underperformed the market. In one particularly colorful example, some 2,000 top money managers attending *Institutional Investor* magazine's 1970 conference voted for a company called National Student Marketing. It fell 95 percent in five months. In assessing the contempt that the investment establishment affects to feel for the investment newsletters, when it deigns to notice them at all, it is salutary to remember Professor Burton G. Malkiel's summary, in stinging italics, of the current consensus among academic authorities on investing:

> *No scientific evidence has yet been assembled to indicate that the investment performance of professionally managed portfolios as a group has been any better than that of randomly selected portfolios.*

Members of the investment establishment can't help being mistaken. Powerful institutional forces make them do it. The most obvious such forces affect the brokerage houses. On Wall Street, brokerage houses are known collectively as the "sell side," because their function is to sell securities to individuals and also to the big investment institutions, who are collectively called "the buy side." Brokers are rewarded by commissions on each sale and also by fees and other goodies when they persuade a corporation to "go public" and sell shares in itself to outside investors. They are not rewarded on how well these investments work out. Satisfied customers may return, but this is a longer-term and more general consideration than the extra commission a firm may be offering its salesmen in any given week to unload a particular block of stock, or "product," as it is chillingly described. Trading is an end in itself to brokers. Thus the archetypal Wall Street story that gave Fred Schwed his title in 1940 and was already ancient:

> . . . an out-of-town visitor was being shown the wonders of the New York financial district. When the party arrived at the Battery, one of his guides indicated some handsome ships riding at anchor.
> He said, "Look, those are the bankers' and the brokers' yachts."
> "Where are the customers' yachts?" asked the naïve visitor.

The divergence of interest between broker and client comes close to an outright conflict when the firm's investment banking arm flexes its bicep. This department specializes in the financing needs of corporations, raising money for them by selling stocks or bonds. The corporations want to sell these instruments for the highest price. Investors want to buy them at the lowest. The brokerage house . . . brokers between the two. The possible conflict is particularly acute in the case of the brokerage house's research department. In theory, this is supposed to be full of analysts researching away to provide investors with the best possible advice. But the brokerage house gets paid only if investors trade. So there is little incentive to issue general sell recommendations that will drive them out of the market completely, particularly since few investors have the stomach to go short. Predicting interest rate increases is especially delicate, because brokerage houses are compelled by the nature of the bond market to carry large inventories of bonds and consequently can lose money if rates rise. Additionally, as a practical matter it is difficult for a brokerage house research department to be critical of the prospects for stock issued by its firm's corporate clients. In fact, it is not easy for them to be critical of corporations at all, because managements get resentful and can refuse to talk further. Accordingly, many analysts will only make sell recommendations verbally. And since they will not take phone calls except from large institutional clients, this is an example of how the system discriminates against smaller investors. It also explains why research departments persist in publishing reports describing stocks as "holds," although logically, unless it is being held to qualify for capital gains tax treatment, a stock can only be a buy or a sell—if it's going sideways, you would be better off in interest-earning cash. Some Wall Streeters protest that "hold" means you think the stock may go up, but not strongly enough to justify the trouble (and commission costs) of buying it if you don't already own it. But basically it's a code word for "sell," particularly in the charming variant "a weak hold."

Investment analysts on Wall Street are really closer to copywriters on Madison Avenue, composing unusually prolix advertisements for an esoteric product, than they are to scientists or doctors. They also have a distinct (if rarely noted) resemblance to airline stewardesses. Until recently, the federal government regulated airlines closely and did not allow them to compete directly on fares or flight frequency. Instead, the airlines attempted to lure passengers by promising movies, drinks and friendly female attendants. This brandishing of ancillary benefits is a characteristic feature of what economists call "nonprice competition," which tends to occur between members of a price-fixing cartel. The New York Stock Exchange was precisely such a cartel, requiring member firms to charge a uniform commission on trades until compelled to desist in 1975 by a combination of government pressure and client rebellion. Voluminous research, comforting even if indeterminate in value, was —and is—a way for brokerage houses to attact business without cutting prices.

Negotiated commission rates have taken time to bite, but the brokerage industry is slowly rationalizing along more economically efficient lines. The salaries and bonuses of investment analysts are probably lower now in real terms than those of the "superanalysts" who attracted attention in the 1960s bull market—"the go-go years." And the public can trade through no-frills discount brokers who charge about 70 percent less than the "full-service" brokers. Less research is being done by brokerage houses, but a number of independent research services have emerged, selling to institutions that pay them with so-called "soft dollars" by directing commission business to one of perhaps several brokerage houses that have agreed to compensate the service with cash, usually several thousand dollars a year. For example, Richard J. Hoffman, formerly portfolio strategist for Merrill Lynch & Company, the largest U.S. broker, now markets his views through the Autranet brokerage house, which specializes in such arrangements, and grossed an estimated $1 million in 1983. One of the services he has offered undertakes to give nothing but sell recommendations on stocks.

This incidentally exposes another cause of the investment letter explosion: it is in part a parallel development to soft-dollar research, but on the retail rather than the wholesale level and charging smaller sums of cash—"hard dollars." Many newsletter subscribers are actually retail brokers, who often feel oppressed and manipulated by the large brokerage houses for whom they work, not without reason, and prefer to develop their own sources of investment ideas.

In contrast to the brokerage houses, institutional investors are paid a fee for managing their clients' money, and have no reason to want a high volume of trading as such. But they have other problems. The most commonly cited is the hippopotamus-entering-small-pool argument: Many institutional investors simply have too much money under management to do other than buy and hold boring, heavily traded stocks that they can accumulate without splashing the price upward. While there is some evidence that the stock market is surprisingly liquid, clearly Prudential Insurance Company, with around $100 billion under management has less room for maneuver than the small investor. A less obvious problem is that institutional investors, as large organizations, turn out to be just as vulnerable to the irrationalities of crowds as any other collection of individuals. The "two-tier market" of the early 1970s, when the shares of a small group of big, strong, fast-growing companies nicknamed the "Nifty Fifty" were bid up completely out of line with other stocks and subsequently crashed to 10 percent to 15 percent of their peak prices, was a classic speculative mania to be ranked with the Dutch Tulip Craze and the South Sea Bubble. Yet it was entirely the product of buying by the most respectable institutional investors, buying they indignantly defended at the time as being patently, perfectly, prudent.

The self-interest of the institutional investor, as with the broker, is only indirectly served by successful management of clients' accounts. What the institutional investor really wants is more accounts, and more management fees. The greater the extent to which the investment process appears complicated, the more easily will the institutional investor be able to intimidate critics and persuade them that he is necessary. Hence the larger institutions' interest in computers and the esoteric mathematical techniques deriving from what is collectively known as Modern Portfolio Theory. Fear of firing for a mistake that can be traced to him is much more real to the professional money manager than the hypothetical advantages of bold risk taking. It is tempting and indeed rational for him to make for the center of the herd and hide behind the fashionable consensus, regardless of whether or not he agrees with it. (Several money managers, such as Capital Guardian, actually lost clients for eschewing the Nifty Fifty when all the best people endorsed them.) Similarly, mutual funds will stay fully invested even when they think the market is going down because they know people are reluctant to pay them a management fee just to hold their money in cash, irrespective of the result.

Institutional investors are bureaucracies, and are motivated by bureaucratic incentives. It takes time to assemble all the appropriate committees whenever an analyst changes his mind about a stock, and the ultimate decision may well be contaminated by personalities and power struggles. Overall investment strategy is centralized, and individuals within the organization plod along, focusing on whatever affects them personally. Analysts become totally absorbed in the interesting game of estimating corporate earnings, although this is several steps removed from predicting stock performance. Sometimes they go completely native, identifying with the industries they follow: when Professor Arthur Laffer, in a speech to the 1982 annual meeting of the National Association of Petroleum Investment Analysts, predicted that oil prices would fall, he was booed. (He was also correct.) Bank regulation and pension legislation have infused legal concepts of procedure and responsibility into what is allegedly a risk-taking activity, so that much research is really designed to document prudent management rather than to determine investment truths. "When the bank examiner came to our offices," says a veteran of one bank's trust department, "he would pick up our research files *and weigh them.* Now you know why institutional research reports are hundreds of pages long."

As with the military, the professional turbulence of Wall Street masks the fact that it is in many respects a highly traditional occupation. Some of those commuters from New Jersey are coming along the same railroads that their great-grandfathers used a century ago, heading for jobs that, give or take telephones and computer terminals, have remained essentially unchanged—one of very few American ways of life of which this can be said. And although the wheeler-dealers, superanalysts and assorted other promotional types attract public attention, the bulk of America's savings are in the hands of institutions where soberly suited people talk quietly, refer to their employer as "We" (as in "We don't do things that way") and regard with suspicion subordinates who stay in the office past 5 P.M. Wall Streeters, rumors to the contrary, are human. Prestige matters to them, and personal contacts remain vital even if they are nowadays more often made through the business school meritocracy than the prep school patriciate. This is a natural and, in a business that requires mutual trust, perhaps an unavoidable development. Even the statistically sophisticated Alfred Cowles, when asked in 1970 what he did with his family's own money, replied "Basically, we're advised by

Brown Brothers-Harriman . . . Averell Harriman was a class-mate of mine at Yale." But it is not necessarily an environment conducive to new ideas.

Investment letter writers are the guerrillas of the financial industry—the irregular troops of Wall Street. They cannot rely on the social status and accumulated momentum of the long-established Wall Street institutions: they have to create their own status by force of personality, like the leaders of partisan bands or charismatic religions. They live off the country: their income is derived only from selling their advice ("say for pay"). They face considerable dangers: mistakes mean disgruntled sub-scribers and dropping circulation, and can even put the letter out of business. But the investment letter business can accom-modate individuals who either would not or could not find a niche on Wall Street. Both Joe Granville and Jim Dines began their careers at major brokerage houses but left amid uproar; one of the best-known letter proprietors, Tom Holt of the *Holt Investment Advisory,* is a Chinese immigrant who taught himself about investing in New York public libraries in the early 1950s, but was unable to break into Wall Street until given a job by Arnold Bernhard's *Value Line* service.

And these individuals, whatever else can be said about them, do have ideas. Their letters have been quicker than Wall Street to examine not just investing in gold but the whole area of technical analysis. THE INSTITUTIONAL EDGE, read the headline of a New York *Times* story on November 25, 1985, about a com-puterized service that Salomon Brothers had spent seven years developing for its institutional investor clients.

By virtue of its size, an institution that invests in the stock market gets daily access to research material that the average citizen never sees . . .

For any stock being studied, the computer separates the trades—as quickly as they take place—into two categories: those of 10,000 shares or more—presumably done by big, powerful insti-tutions—and those of less than 10,000 shares.

In each of the two categories, the computer then looks at the value of trades that took place on an uptick (meaning the price moved up from the last sale) and the value of the trades that took place on a downtick (meaning that the price moved down). The value of the downtick trades is then subtracted from the value of the uptick trades. (Trades that did not cause a price movement are discarded.)

If the number is positive, it means money is going into the stock. If the number is negative, the stock is being sold. Sometimes, the big institutions sell, pulling out their money, while the little investor keep on buying.

This, under the name of "tick volume," was exactly what Don Worden was supplying to average citizens in his investment letter more than twenty years earlier. Much the same is true in fundamental analysis, supposedly the institutions' forte. For example, a recently fashionable idea is that the ratio of a company's sales revenues to its shares says something about its health. Charles Allmon's *Growth Stock Outlook* has quietly been employing it for years.

Not all individuals and ideas will eventually become respectable. But you never know.

Meanwhile, back in the academy, a view has been developed of the investment process that renders irrelevant all dispute between establishment and radicals, technicians and fundamentalists. This is the Efficient Market Hypothesis. It essentially maintains that stock prices respond so quickly to information that it is simply not possible, consistently and over the longer term, to pick stocks that will appreciate faster than the general stock market. There is, of course, chilling evidence for this proposition. Naturally, Wall Street hates the idea, and has gone grinding on trying to outguess the market. But by 1983 the Efficient Market Hypothesis had established itself in the nation's business schools so strongly that *Fortune* magazine's Dan Seligman was able to quote the confession of a concerned proponent, Michael C. Jensen of the University of Rochester: "It's dangerously close to the point where no graduate student would dare send off a paper criticizing the hypothesis." This has resulted in the curious spectacle of two respectable professional groups going about their daily rounds firmly believing that the animating assumption of the other is hogwash.

More recently, however, there have been signs that the Efficient Market Hypothesis may not be completely airtight.

These so-called "anomalies" take the form of evidence that a few money managers and market strategies have indeed been able to achieve consistently above-average results. For all its idiosyncrasy, the investment letter industry provides some of these anomalies. One of the best known is the long-standing ability of the *Value Line Investment Survey* service to rate hundreds of stocks in order of their performance potential with far more success than it ought to have enjoyed according to the theory. But there are others who have not been recognized.

This subject will be examined further in chapter 4. But it is worth noting at this stage that the several investment letters that will be cited there for superior performance employ totally different techniques, and even regard each other with distinctly unsporting skepticism. Any study of the investment letter phenomenon inevitably confirms the wisdom of the policy enunciated (in a different context) by another prominent guerrilla some years ago: let a hundred flowers bloom.

CHAPTER THREE

Investment Letters: Their Life and Times

There is nothing new under the sun and least of all in the stock market.

—"LARRY LIVINGSTONE" (JESSE LIVERMORE), IN EDWIN LEFEVRE's *Reminiscences of a Stock Operator* (1923)

The panic following Joe Granville's sell signal in early 1981 had a parallel more than half a century before: the Babson Break of September 5, 1929. After reaching the record peak of 386.10 on the Dow two days earlier, stock prices had suddenly plunged on heavy volume when Roger Babson, speaking at his own Annual National Business Conference in New England, was quoted on the Dow Jones financial news service as predicting an imminent crash. In retrospect, this was a haunting moment for a whole generation of Americans. Those price levels would not be seen again until nearly ten years after World War II. After the Babson Break, the market lurched on for a couple of months, trying to stabilize and then slipping again amid such reassuring establishment noises as Yale professor Irving Fisher's immortal claim that stocks had reached "what looks like a permanently high plateau." But then it went over the edge of Black Thursday, October 24. The Great Crash had begun. By July 8, 1933, the Dow was at 40.56, a drop of nearly 90 percent.

Who was Roger Babson? John Brooks, in his elegant history of the era *Once in Golconda*, reports that he was "a not especially well-known, and hitherto even less influential, financial adviser operating far from Wall Street—a frail, goateed, pixyish-looking man [based in] Wellesley, Massachusetts . . . his earlier warnings had been roundly ignored. He was, in fact, widely thought of as something of a nut."

This is perhaps somewhat unfair to Babson. By 1929 he was already a wealthy financier and a polymathic entrepreneur, the proprietor of the *Babson's Reports* advisory service and publisher of an investment letter with an astonishing 25–35,000 circulation. Back in 1904, Babson had heard an address in which the black leader Booker T. Washington explained his strategy of encouraging his students at the Tuskegee Institute to specialize in particular skills—carpentry, pecan planting—on the theory that possessing any speciality no matter how insignificant would give them a comparative advantage when they returned to their communities. Babson took Washington's advice. He had enjoyed a brief, turbulent career on Wall Street, but now he founded his Babson Statistical Organization in Wellesley to focus solely on providing objective statistics and analysis on public corporations to brokers and institutional investors. Shortly afterward, he started a lower-priced research service aimed at small investors—what is now known as the "retail" business. One of its features was the "Babsonchart." This early form of composite indicator tracked many forms of economic activity, consolidated them to establish the underlying trend and attempted to forecast the future by analogy with Newtonian physics, specifically the second law of motion ("action and reaction are equal and opposite"). Babson had a lifelong fascination with Newton, reflecting his engineering education at the Massachusetts Institute of Technology.

In the course of his hyperactive life, Babson held interests in several other investment services, including parts of what subsequently became the much-loved Wall Street institutions Moody's Investors Service and Standard & Poor's Corporation, both of which primarily supply basic reference material to individual and institutional investors; and the National Quotations Bureau, which maintains the "pink sheets" listing market-makers in over-the-counter (OTC) stocks. He founded three colleges and two still-flourishing communities named "Babson Park," one near Wellesley to which he tried to attract competing investment services to form what he called a "statistical community," a sort of think tank; and the other in central Florida. The *Oil/Energy Statistics Bulletin* is still published from Babson Park, Massachusetts, the survivor of a once-major service, *Spear & Staff Publications*. And Babson's first-hand experience of the 1920s Florida land boom and bust was one reason he kept saying the stock market was describing a similar parabola. Even after the Crash, his critics argued that he was right only because he repeated his message until it eventually came true. But the fact remains that a plateau is not a parabola.

To be fair to the financial establishment, Babson was a decidedly unusual character. He had strong views about practically everything, from diet to religion. He was insatiably curious about new inventions. He funded research into the possible use of gravity as an energy source. He believed that the central Midwest would play a pivotal role in a future reorganized America, just as Joe Granville after he shifted his headquarters to Kansas City began to claim that it would someday be the U.S. capital. After a bout with tuberculosis Babson developed the habit of working outdoors even in winter, dictating to a secretary who sat swaddled in blankets, wearing gloves and typing with the aid of metal prongs. He never drank or smoked, and in 1940 ran for President on the Prohibitionist Party ticket. Needless to say he lived to be ninety-two, dying in 1967. *Babson's Reports* is still controlled by the Babson family and published from Wellesley Hills. Its present treasurer, Allan Brackett, relates that his first job in the organization in the years just before Babson's death was to look into this new-fangled nuclear power industry, the latest area to attract the old man's restless eye.

It is typical of the investment letter industry that Babson was able to develop his impressive business without Wall Street's knowledge, and to some extent in conscious rebellion against it. It is also significant that this happened in the 1920s. Modern capital markets with real public participation had emerged only with the bond drives of World War I. They lasted only some fourteen years before the Great Crash and the imposition of government regulation during the New Deal. The combined shock seems to have been so severe that some patterns of activity, like mass-circulation investment letters, took decades to reestablish themselves.

Of course, the conventional wisdom during the Depression was that the free-wheeling unregulated markets of the 1920s had led to speculation, manipulation, the exploitation of small investors, the 1929 stock market crash and perhaps even the the economic crisis itself. This was the theme of the Senate Banking and Currency Committee hearings, where a number of stock market figures were publicly keelhauled as a prelude to the introduction of legislation establishing the federal Securities and Exchange Commission in 1934. There is, however, a revisionist version of the history of the 1920s that should be mentioned, as it is dear to the hearts of many of today's leading investment letters. According to this view, the New Deal's intervention in both the economy and the financial markets was based on a misunderstanding of free-market processes, and the Banking Committee's image of irresponsible cigar-chomping tycoons debauching the economy was as fanciful as the contemporaneous claims by another Senate inquiry headed by Senator Gerald Nye that "munitions kings" were responsible for World War I. This elemental dispute continues burbling in the background, the SEC's regulation of investment letters being merely one manifestation of it.

The investment letter industry commonly claims a collateral lineage reaching back to Thomas Paine during the American Revolution. But strictly speaking, what Paine wrote were polemical pamphlets, a literary form that was highly developed in eighteenth-century England. A closer contemporary equivalent to these pamphlets is perhaps the series of books by investment letter writers that in recent years have unexpectedly erupted to best-sellerdom, such as Harry Browne's *How You Can Profit From the Coming Devaluation* (1970) and *How You Can Profit From a Monetary Crisis* (1974), Howard Ruff's *How to Prosper During the Coming Bad Years* (1979) and Douglas Casey's *Crisis Investing* (1979).

There is, however, a definite parallel between today's investment letters and the newspapers appearing in the eighteenth century. In those days, newspapers were basically small-format digests of information, often compiled and commented upon by one hardworking hand, deriving most of their revenues from high subscription prices rather than from the sale of space to advertisers. Their psychology was very different from that of the modern media corporation, which is frequently run by accountants and superannuated salesmen and to some extent has gravitated into the business of erecting a high-class species of advertising billboard. With the newsletter phenomenon, the newspaper business has come full circle. Benjamin Franklin lives.

In the nineteenth century the immediate ancestor of the *Wall Street Journal* was a newsletter. *The Customers' Afternoon Letter* was begun in 1883 by Charles Dow and Edward Jones (with their partner Charles Bergstrasser, now memorialized only by "& Co.") to summarize and supplement the financial bulletins their service had been delivering by hand in the Wall Street area since the previous year. Only in 1889 did *The Afternoon Letter* mutate into the *Wall Street Journal* and begin accepting advertisements.

And even then it retained key similarities with modern investment letters: like many of them, it developed and published its own market indices, the friendly Dow Jones Industrial and the Dow Jones Transportation Averages, and it featured the ruminations of Charles Dow, and later William Peter Hamilton, on what the gyrations in these indices meant. Between them the two men invented the "Dow Theory." This holds that the movements of the overall stock market can be analyzed into three categories: the *primary trend*, lasting for one or more years; the *secondary reaction*, lasting for weeks or months; and the *minor movement*, lasting for days or weeks. Normally, a primary bull or bear market is divided into three stages or "legs" by secondary reactions, which can retrace up to two-thirds or even more of the preceding move. In order to decide when the market has changed direction, Dow Theorists compare the action of the two Dow Jones averages. When one average makes a new high in a given period, and the other follows suit, a buy signal has been given and confirmed. New lows on both averages signal a sell. The Dow Theory was first expounded in 1900, and over the years interpreting it has become an art form. It has been particularly favored by investment letters, and several have named themselves after it—for example, the venerable *Dow Theory Fore-*

casts and Richard Russell's *Dow Theory Letters*—thus compelling the *Wall Street Journal* to point out endlessly that they have No Connection with itself.

Along with most establishment opinion, William Peter Hamilton greeted Babson's warnings with something less than gratitude. He denounced Babson's "notorious inaccuracy" and mocked him as "the sage of Wellesley." But within a month, Hamilton himself was expressing severe reservations about market trends in a celebrated editorial, "The Turn of the Tide." Ironically, according to the survey by Alfred Cowles, Hamilton's own record between 1904 and 1929 had failed to outperform the market—although Cowles noted with heroic understatement that had Hamilton actually stayed short from October 1929 until the survey date in 1932, "his performance would, of course, have shown a heavy superiority." Hamilton, however, was already a sick man, and in December 1929 he died. The *Wall Street Journal* stopped editorializing about the Dow Theory after Hamilton's death. Nowadays it will not even accept advertisements from investment letters.

But *Barron's*, the *Journal's* sister paper, does both. *Barron's* is a weekly tabloid review of all financial markets, read primarily by independent investors. It occupies a unique strategic position at the intersection of establishment journalism and the investment letter underworld and is practically the only place where advertising investment letters pays. As a reward for this, it suffers the indignity of having its investment letter advertisements regularly inspected by other investment letters as a possible backdrop for a favorite forecasting ploy, the invocation of Contrary Opinion. This is essentially the axiom that the majority is always in the wrong. Investment letters do not hesitate to apply it to each other. *Smart Money's* Yale Hirsch has cited the publication of a record-size, advertisement-bloated *Barron's* as evidence that a bear market is about to begin; *The Zweig Forecast's* Marty Zweig has developed an entire index measuring market sentiment by what proportion of *Barron's* investment advisory advertisements are bullish or bearish.

Banks and brokerage houses have been sending out letters on economic and market conditions since the 1850s, but independent investment letters in their present form seem to have originated around the last decade of the nineteenth century. According to one authority, perhaps the first letter to build up a paid subscription of its own was put out in about 1895 by a Danish immigrant called Carsten Boe; another letter, *Ridgely's Financial Forecasts*, began in 1902. Early in the twentieth century, a number of services apart from Babson's developed substantial circulations, often commenting on general business conditions as much as on the financial markets. A prominent example was the St. Louis-based *Brookmire's Economic Service*. A direct descendent of this breed is United Business Service Company's *United Business and Investment Report*, founded in 1919 (and once owned by Roger Babson). Prominent services begun in this era included Richard D. Wycoff's *Trend Letter*, the *Wetzel Market Bureau*, the *Van Strum Financial Service*, the Alexander Hamilton Institute's *Business Conditions Weekly*, Thomas Gibson's *Forecasts* and—still publishing, although merged in 1985 with *The Predictor* —the *Tillman Survey*.

One long-forgotten feature of the expanded public participation in the stock market of the 1920s was a vogue for astrology. The popular seer Evangeline Adams put out a financial newsletter at fifty cents a month that reportedly reached a circulation of over 100,000. She even claimed among her private consultation clients investment banker J. Pierpont Morgan, industrialist Charles Schwab and film star Mary Pickford. Although she told New York radio station WJZ on Labor Day, 1929, that "the Dow Jones could climb to heaven," Adams actually anticipated Black Thursday, even predicting its worst hour. That evening she had to hold mass audiences in the waiting room of her studio above Carnegie Hall to accommodate the demand for private consultations. She told everyone that the market would recover in the next two days, and in fact it did stabilize briefly. Then, after her clients left, she ordered her own stock sold at the Friday opening. Adams' letter did not survive the Crash, and the same fate befell the mass-circulation Langham & Liggett service. But Edgar Cayce, perhaps an even more prominent psychic than Ms. Adams, was credited by his followers with foreseeing the Crash in its entirety. For the fee of $25, Cayce would consult the "universal consciousness" and give "life readings" for individuals without the formality of meeting them. In 1939 he performed this feat for the fifteen-year-old Joseph Granville. Cayce announced that Granville had been reincarnated four times and was "inclined to be dramatic." Now, in the early 1980s, with the caution of deer reentering a burned-out forest, astrologers are occasionally to be seen tiptoeing along Wall Street once again.

While the investment letter industry was beginning to sprout, the first inside-Washington business-oriented political-intelligence letter, the *Whaley-Eaton Service*, was founded in 1918. Its great rival, the *Kiplinger Washington Letter*, appeared in 1923. By 1940 these newsletters had a circulation of 6–7,000 and 30–40,000 respectively. They had been credited by Frederick Lundberg in a long article in *Harper's* magazine with causing "a revolution in journalism," and had provoked President Franklin Delano Roosevelt to complain repeatedly about troublemaking "tipster sheets."

The devastation of the stock market world by the Great Crash was so complete that in effect an entire generation did not show up for work on Wall Street—or if it did, there was no one there to hire them. The dramatic rise of so many young men as analysts and portfolio managers during the go-go years of the 1960s was partly due to the fact that there were no middle-aged men between them and the generation just entering retirement.

The investment letters suffered during the Depression too. And their lives were greatly complicated by the New Deal's invention of the Securities and Exchange Commission, with powers to register and regulate that were reinforced by the Investment Advisors' Act of 1940. The new agency took the position that it had authority not just over brokers and investment managers who actually handled their clients' money, but also over investment letters that merely carried their editors' opinions. Indeed, SEC officials often said that they believed their jurisdiction ought to extend to the financial press itself. However, they were never bold enough to act on this belief, although they did bring an unsuccessful experimental action against the *Wall Street Transcript*, a magazine specializing in the recycling of brokerage house research.

How much this sort of regulation benefits investors is an interesting question. For example, in 1947 the eighty-three-year-old proprietor of the F. N. Goldsmith Financial Service, Frederick N. Goldsmith, admitted that the "inside information" he claimed to possess was largely derived from studying the popular "Bringing Up Father" comic strip. Goldsmith said the strip contained encoded information about the market. When a character's cigar was drawn with two puffs of smoke, the market would go up in the second hour . . . and so on. The authorities put him out of business. But Goldsmith had been publishing his letter since 1916, and was able to submit in his defense many testimonials from satisfied clients, including several Wall Street professionals. Again, in the mid-1970s the SEC fought a prolonged campaign to convince Colonel Edward Crosby Harwood, a particularly recalcitrant gold bug and founder of the American Institute for Economic Research, that he should recognize its existence and fill out the forms it had decreed for money managers. During this dispute, the SEC caused over $100 million of mainly gold-related assets belonging to Harwood's counseling clients to be frozen in the midst of a severe market decline, and at one point even attempted to have them liquidated on the grounds that gold was clearly an improper investment. In fact, of course, by recommending gold, Harwood had involved his clients in one of the great bull markets of all time, and many of them bitterly protested against being "protected" by the SEC in this fashion, but to no avail.

Whatever the economic and legal merits of regulation, there can be no doubt that conducting a business under a regulatory agency equipped with the considerable discretionary powers of the SEC was quite different from what is normally thought of as life under a rule of law. The investment letter editors were genuinely afraid. They were also afraid of the SEC's equivalents at the state government level to whom they were arguably also subject. For one thing, just paying the fees to register with them all would have cost an estimated $100,000 by the mid-1980s. The issue came to a head when the SEC attempted to deny the registration of the *Lowe Investment & Finance Letter*'s Christopher Lowe because of the fact that he was a convicted felon. Backed by an impressive range of supporters including the American Civil Liberties Union, Lowe claimed that this violated his constitutional right to freedom of speech. In 1985 the Supreme Court ruled 8–0 that the SEC had no jurisdiction over investment letters. Of course, they remain subject to a variety of statutes, including the stringent mail fraud provisions.

Despite the Depression and the SEC, investment letters continued to develop. Technical analysis in its modern form was fermenting quietly in the 1930s, with seminal books by Richard W. Schabacker (*Stock Market Theory and Practice*, 1930; *Technical Analysis and Market Profits*, 1932), and Harold M. Gartley (*Profits in the Stock Market*, 1935). The Dow Theory was refined further in Robert Rhea's *The Dow Theory* (1932). Reader reaction to Rhea's book was so strong that although bedridden as a result of a war wound, he launched his own letter, *Dow Theory Comment*, which was subsequently taken over by Perry Greiner and is now published by Michael MacGuire.

Also in the 1930s there appeared perhaps the earliest recorded specimen of the professionally charismatic investment advisor, many of whose characteristics would recur in his spiritual heirs forty years later. Lawrence Lee Bazley Angas was a fiercely mustachioed English ex-military man who shrewdly insisted on always being addressed by his former rank of Major. He had written books in England whose splendidly portentious titles (*The Coming Collapse in Rubber, The Coming Rise in Gold Shares*) were also to find echoes in the 1970s, and he was imported to the United States by the Brookmire service. But he soon struck out on his own, putting out at various times his own letters and a number of other books, including the highly successful *Investment for Appreciation* (1936). Major Angas specialized in hiring hotel space and holding one-shot investment conferences and high-priced consultations, complete with exclusive interviews with awed journalists, an activity that became an important part of the investment advisor business once again in the 1970s. Exceptional in that era, Angas was particularly interested in monetary policy and credit conditions, and like his later imitators he mixed into his product a good dose of philosophizing about capitalism, a subject about which few were prepared to be philosophic at that time. In his old age, Angas moved to a converted hotel he had bought in the remote settlement of Saxtons River, Vermont, somewhat to the surprise of his fellow letter editor and Brookmire alumnus Humphrey B. Neill (*Neill Letters of Contrary Opinion*), who lived there on the homestead his family had occupied for generations. Angas wrote a book on golf, and was occasionally seen spontaneously directing traffic in the little town. Jim Fraser, a former colleague of Neill's whose *Contrary Investor* letter continues this curmudgeonly Vermont tradition, remembers five Cadillacs standing neatly parked outside Angas's house. None of them worked. Angas lived alone, surrounded by his voluminous papers, and in 1973 he died as a result of injuries received in a fire.

The end of World War II was a curious moment in the history of American business. There was widespread expectation of a renewed slump, implying such a dire outlook for the stock market that, for example, as late as 1951 the New York *Journal of Commerce* felt able to drop its stock quotation section. This turned out to be a classic blunder, materially contributing to the paper's eclipse by the *Wall Street Journal.* Although the wartime rally stalled in 1946, the ensuing bear market was mild, and after reaching a bottom in the low 160s in 1949 the Dow began a purposeful advance that was interrupted only by pauses for breath, alarming as they appeared at the time, until on February 9, 1966, it burst through the 1,000 barrier, hung momentarily in the air at 1,001.11, and fell back, to close below. By this time the stock market would was not merely resuscitated but positively rampant.

Garfield Drew's *New Methods for Profit in the Stock Market,* published in 1948, was the first successful stock market book of the new generation. It inspired Drew, Harvard '26 and a salesman with United Business Service, to begin his own investment letter the following year. His speciality was studying the behavior of small investors ("odd-lotters," who cannot afford to buy a round lot of 100 shares), using statistics that, ironically, were a by-product of the SEC's surveillance activities. In essence, Drew concluded that small investors were right on trends but tended to get overexcited and miss turning points, so that excessive odd-lot enthusiasm spelled danger. This respect for the professional over the amateur was something of a feat of objectivity for Drew, who said his early experiences on Wall Street had disgusted him with the financial establishment and who gloried in the independence of his base in Newton Center, Massachusetts. *The Drew Odd Lot Studies* was a powerful factor in the 1950s, with a circulation peaking at 4–5,000 in 1959. But thereafter the odd-lotters reformed themselves—or more likely the pattern of market participation changed. Drew sold his service in 1973 and told Lester A. Euell, its ultimate owner, that he had concluded his life's work was outmoded.

Also in 1948, E. George Schaefer brought out his *Dow Theory Trader* letter. Schaefer further refined Dow's work and popularized a number of technical innovations, such as the 200-day moving average, which contrasts each day's current price with the rolling average of the previous 200 days, providing a measure of the underlying market trend. Schaefer has become a legend in the investment letter community. His calls were unusually long-term and remarkably accurate. He was bullish on the stock market from 1949 to 1966, when the Dow peaked, and bearish thereafter. He recommended gold as it began to rise in the late 1960s and put out a sell signal in 1974, whereupon the metal's price broke sharply and it decisively entered its mid-1970s period of eclipse. At this point Schaefer fell to his death from an apartment window in his hometown of Indianapolis.

The verdict of suicide was not well received by the rapidly burgeoning tribe of gold investors, a notoriously suspicious lot. It is worth noting that throughout Schaefer's career, his perspective had brought him into apparently continual conflict with his clients. They tended to want him not just to stand there long-term but to do something short-term, disregarding the fact that his long-term stands turned out to be right. Schaefer's major book, *How I Helped More Than 10,000 Investors to Profit in Stocks* (1960), contains a lot of pitiful whimpering about the cruel psychological torture inflicted upon innocent advisors by their ignorant but irate subscribers. And hell hath no fury like a gold bug scorned, although Schaefer's death certainly diverted their attention, and many still allege foul play. Schaefer's experience has had important consequences in the investment letter industry. A number of its denizens have concluded darkly that they must predict, frequently and confidently, or perish. Accuracy is less important than action.

Franklin Roosevelt's attacks on "tipster sheets" displayed his usual street-fighting polemical technique, always an impressive attribute in one of such patrician birth and gentle upbringing. He was of course being totally unfair to the Washington letters. They did not recommend stocks at all. But the New Deal legislators, as part of their general concern with establishing fairness in the marketplace, were easily impressed by the possibility that investment letters might accept payoffs to "puff" stocks, or engage in "scalping" by taking a position in a stock before recommending it to clients—colloquially known as slipping a "zinger" to the "mooches" or "suckers."

This does happen. As recently as December 1984, the SEC announced that the *Penny Stock Letter* had signed a consent decree in an action brought in connection with the payment of a fee to promote Belgium Standard, a Canadian-based company traded over-the-counter in the United States. However, it was a much more frequently heard allegation during the golden age of tip sheets in the fifties and early sixties. Many of these letters were associated with Canadian mining groups. At that time Canadian mining stocks were being pushed hard by "boiler rooms" full of salesmen telephoning into the United States, often working in collusion with promoters who were doing their best to manipulate prices. On some days the volume of trading on the Toronto Stock Exchange exceeded that in New York, although of course the average price of the stocks, and hence the total value of trading, was much lower. Investment letters are particularly suited to wild, speculative markets with huge retail interest, and the Canadian mining market was a whopper. It attracted worldwide attention. Looking back on those happy days in the fifties from the vantage point of 1970, a particularly enterprising Canadian letter writer called Peter Jeffrey explained his weekly routine to the writer Murray Teigh Bloom as follows:

> Sunday night I'd fly from New York to Lisbon on Pan Am. Monday morning, I'd connect with TAP to Tangier, where I'd write the *American & Foreign Bank Letter.* Monday night to Madrid and play. They have interesting broads there. Tuesday morning to Zurich for writing *Richtung* ("Direction"). Originally, the private bank that published it had a long German name for it, but I got them to change. I wrote it in English and they'd translate it. Wednesday, I'd fly to Paris or London for a little playing around. Wednesday night or Thursday morning I'd fly back to New York. Then to Toronto, where I'd write the *Jack Elder Letter.* From Toronto to Detroit, where I'd write the *Cronenburg Report.* Then to New York Saturday morning for fooling around. On Sunday I'd do just the lead on the *Dynamics Letter,* which my elder brother, Grant, and I ran. In the afternoon I'd write the *Owen K. Taylor Letter,* and then Sunday night I'd start all over again with

the flight to Lisbon. I did this for a year and I probably made $200,000 that year. The only reason I had to quit was they were flying the piston planes that year, still. With the jets, I might still be doing that crazy schedule.

But the pistons used to shake the hell out of you. I was flying 500,000 miles a year. I had to quit because my asshole fell out. Literally. Early in 1960 I was in Mount Sinai Hospital in New York with a fistula cyst in my ass. I blame the shaking piston planes, but, you know, it could just as easily have been the damn cabs to and from the airports. In all, then, 1959 was my *anus mirabilis*, so to speak.

Some investment letters were certainly involved in manipulations. Dick Angle of *The Canadian Forecaster* even found himself embroiled with a Canadian subsidiary of the Magaddino organized crime family of Buffalo. While acting as a witness for the prosecution in a resulting trial, one of the longest series in Canadian legal history, Angle was obliged to admit that he had recommended stocks that he secretly controlled. He said it was "the general way things are done on the Street." (Bay Street, that is, Canada's Wall Street.) Angle's story was particularly poignant, since he was originally a Kansas City grain trader who had driven nonstop to Toronto looking for revenge after being zinged by a boiler room promotion, only to be seduced by the sinful ways of the small city.

Eventually, American protests about the general way things were done on Bay Street stimulated the Ontario authorities to tighten regulation. This choked off the mining market, and also most of the Canadian letters. It also, not coincidentally, choked off mine finding. The most important Canadian development in recent years, Hemlo, was a product not of the Toronto market but of the more liberal Vancouver Stock Exchange. The lawyers had made a desert and called it a fair market.

By the early 1960s the investment letters that were to dominate the scene until the present day were beginning to appear. Richard Russell's *Dow Theory Letters* was founded in 1959; Don Worden's *Worden Tape Reading Studies* in 1961; James Dines' *The Dines Letter* in 1962; Joe Granville's *Granville Market Letter* in 1963;

Harry Schultz's *International Harry Schultz Letter* in 1964; Charles Allmon's *Growth Stock Outlook* in 1965. Joe Granville's book *A Strategy of Daily Stock Market Timing for Maximum Profit* was a big best seller in 1960, and its catalogue of technical market indicators directly inspired the founding the next year of *Indicator Digest*, whose principal, Samson Coslow, was a prominent song writer *(Cocktails for Two, My Old Flame)*. Now under the direction of Coslow's associate, Jack Maurer, an accountant with an extensive show business practice, *Indicator Digest* has served a sort of audition function for the rest of the industry. It has discovered, and subsequently lost amid scenes of variegated drama, such future advisory stars as *Professional Investor's* Bob Gross, *Professional Tape Reader's* Stan Weinstein, *Smart Money's* Yale Hirsch, *Market Vantage's* Bill Chidester, *Scientific Market Analysis's* Dr. Irving Reich and *Justin Mamis' Insights'* Justin Mamis.

(Show business and the stock market, particularly technical analysis, have long had an intriguing affinity for each other. Al Jolson, star of the first talkies, is said to have suggested the name "oscillator" for the graphic method used to represent technical indicators such as the numbers of advancing stocks versus the number declining, a measure of market momentum, whose fluctuation around a zero line reminded him of the action of a metronome. The movie director Frank Capra *(It Happened One Night, Mr. Smith Goes to Washington)* once sold mining stocks door-to-door, a common practice before the advent of the SEC. Richard Ney, ex-husband of Greer Garson and her costar in *Mrs. Miniver*, has written best sellers alleging manipulation by the New York Stock Exchange's market-making specialists *(The Wall Street Jungle, The Wall Street Gang)*, and now publishes his own technical letter, *The Ney Report*. Howard Ruff was once a professional singer and Richard Russell's daughter Betsy is a film actress. The association has not always been happy. The comedian Eddie Cantor was among several entertainment personalities wiped out in 1929. "They told me to buy common stocks for my old age," he said. "And it worked. Within a week I was an old man!")

At the end of the 1960s, it was becoming plain that the stock market was in trouble again. In fact, after first hitting the 1,000 barrier on the Dow Jones Industrial Average in 1966, it was not to break decisively through it for another sixteen years. Although the Dow did struggle up to 1,067 in 1973, it then collapsed precipitously. By the time the Dow subsided below 600 in 1974, many on Wall Street (and in Washington, in that Watergate year) were on the verge of real panic. The carnage among the smaller stocks not included in the Dow was even worse. On the American Stock Exchange, which specializes in junior companies, the average stock was down some 90 percent from the mid-1960 highs.

Conspicuously keeping his head amid all this was Richard Russell of the *Dow Theory Letters*. Russell had been unrelievedly bearish since 1966, and many people were beginning to think he had got stuck in that position. But on December 20, 1974, he put out a special issue announcing that, although on December 6 the Dow Industrials had broken through the previous low made in October and reached 577.6, the Dow Transportation Average had not made a new low, and therefore had not confirmed the bearish primary trend. The odds were better than fifty-fifty, Russell concluded, that the bear market was over. This turned out to be one of the outstanding calls of recent market history. The market rebounded fiercely in early 1975. On January 27 both the Dow Industrial and Transportation Averages surpassed the highs they had made in November, and Russell announced a Dow Theory confirmation of the bullish primary trend, noting that the sheer power of the advance and the simultaneous signal was unprecedented and that an epochal turning point had occurred. Within months the Dow was over 800. For the next several years, it was convalescent, working its way to the 1,000 level in 1976 and 1981 and the relapsing.

While the stock market was sick, the investment letter business naturally showed sympathetic symptoms. In a 1977 study for a curious major publisher, George H. Wein, president of the Select Information Exchange subscription agency, estimated that this underground industry had been quietly selling some 550,000 long-term subscriptions in 1968, a figure that declined to 460,000 in 1972 and 439,500 in 1977. However, Wein thought that the letters had been able to persuade this hard core of readers to pay higher prices, so that the industry's total revenues had increased from an estimated $45 million in 1972 to $56 million in 1977. (Wein says now that total long-term subscriptions reached a peak at about 800,000 in 1983 and are currently about 750,000, with another perhaps 2.5–3 million short-term subscriptions taken out each year.) The investment letters had stood up to the 1970s fairly well. The cost of New York Stock Exchange seats had fallen from over half a million dollars in 1969 to a mere $35,000 in 1977, at which point they were some $20,000 cheaper than New York taxi medallions, the value of which had doubled in the same period.

As in the 1930s, despite market conditions the investment letter industry continued to develop. Edson Gould's *Findings and Forecasts* was founded in 1970 and rapidly emerged as a powerful force. Gould was perhaps the first letter writer to become a modern media phenomenon. This was widely credited to astute handling by Steven Greenberg, chairman of Anametrics, Inc., the advisory firm that published his letter. Gould seemed a veritable "Market Methuselah" compared to the whiz kids of the just-deceased go-go era. He was sixty-nine when *Findings and Forecasts* began, and had spent his entire career on Wall Street, starting at Moody's and finishing by writing a market letter for the investment counseling firm of Arthur Wiesenberger & Company. At $500 a year, *Findings and Forecasts* was primarily aimed at an institutional clientele. Anametrics had a money management division, and at one point even floated an Edson Gould Fund. But in the later 1970s, Gould suffered ill health and seemed to find increasing difficulty in calling short-term market trends. His letter's circulation fell off sharply from its peak of above 2,000. Greenberg was engaged in a bewildering variety of other pursuits, such as investor relations work for companies like Commodore International and Bally and interests in Wendy's franchises and Manhattan's Roxy Roller Disco. Eventually, he decided to close *Findings and Forecasts* and sell off Anametrics' money management operation completely. Gould retired to his farm in Pennsylvania, again.

Gould, however, was no mere creation of publicity. "There is literally no other Advisor in this business that could disturb us if he (or she) were of a different opinion as to the direction of the primary trend," wrote *Professional Investor*'s Robert T. Gross in one of his periodic surveys of the industry published in 1977. Gould was primarily a technical analyst, happiest when drawing parallels with market patterns in previous eras. But he also watched economic trends, particularly monetary conditions, which he believed were inextricably linked to inflation, rejecting the then fashionable view that it was the result of greed or perversity and could be squashed by direct price controls. He minimized the importance of corporate earnings: "They're not real. They're what some accountant thinks they are." He preferred instead to watch dividend yield. Of the several technical concepts popularized by Gould, some are now rarely used—for example, his "speed resistance lines," an attempt to project parameters for future stock price movements according to different proportionate extrapolations of their recent rate of change. Others have passed into the language, for example, his Three-Step Rule of market moves: "Expect three steps, but be prepared for a fourth."

Gould's reputation was boosted by a series of extremely prescient long-term calls. In a famous February 1963 study entitled *The Next 400 Points,* he had compared the postwar bull market with that of the 1920s. Only two of his expected three steps had by then occurred in the postwar version, he pointed out. Therefore, despite widespread contemporary pessimism, he asserted that the market was good for another 400 points on the Dow and would top out at 1,066 in July 1966. It actually reached 1,001 in February 1966. Gould then began to look for a bear market that would last eight years ("one-third the previous advance") and also move in three or four stages. In the early 1970s he was repeatedly quoted as saying that the bear market would end in the 550–650 range late in 1974. It bottomed at 570 in December 1974. At that point Gould was quoted as expressing skepticism that a strong market could begin for some years, although he did say that the Dow could test 1,000 in 1975 or 1976. "There are four prerequisites for a sustained bull market," he told *Business Week*'s William G. Shepherd in 1974. "You need ample credit at a cheap price, a pent-up demand for goods, favorable cost-price relationships—attractive potential profit margins in other words—and a deflated debt structure." None of these conditions existed at that time, he said. But, he told another interviewer, "if you want a long-term projection, the Dow average in the 1980s will be up in the stratosphere. Who knows, perhaps 3,000, 4,000 or 5,000."

Although the investment letter audience survived the 1970s relatively well, the overall numbers concealed some radical shifts. Don Worden dates one such shift to "the month Nixon resigned"—August 1974. Abruptly, the bottom fell out of Worden's business. He needed $45,000 a month to break even, and all of a sudden less than $15,000 was coming in. Worden had been publishing a $240-a-year weekly technical stock market service, with ancillary products like do-it-yourself chart books and paper, which he says as many as 60 percent of his subscribers bought. These individuals were clearly working on their own charts and were generally spending a lot of time on their investments. What had happened was that the bear market had finally broken their hearts. They gave up, and never came back. In retrospect, of course, this turned out to be only months from the final lows. The stock market never promised you a rose garden, or even a bear garden.

After 1974, Worden also noticed a dramatic change in the kind of people attending investment conferences, the clan gatherings of the investment letter subculture, where editors and subscribers get to inspect one another. Previously, the average age of the audience had been close to sixty—people who had the money and the leisure to play the market. Subsequently, the average age dropped to the forties. Inflation and the resulting instability in the financial markets had eaten right through the normal speculative crowd and was biting into the working and saving middle classes, forcing them to the conclusion that taking risks was the only form of prudence available in that financial environment.

Worden's personal solution to the problem illustrates the great resilience of investment letters—and their proprietors. He cut away most of his overhead, the thirty employees and the building named after himself in Fort Lauderdale, Florida, and moved to Chapel Hill, North Carolina. He had children, and thought the way of life there was better anyway. By eliminating frills, dropping his price and reducing his publishing frequency to once a month, he was able to salvage a modest but profitable lower-profile business. He experimented with a letter for options trading, a rapidly expanding area in the mid-1970s, before consolidating his operations in to the *Worden Report* in 1983. Recently, most of his attention has been focused on another burgeoning new area: computer technology for investors. In late 1984 he began marketing *Telchart*, a service combining software and data-bank access so that subscribers could keep up-to-date charts via their personal computers.

The investment letter industry's general response to the stock market malaise showed equal flexibility. It began to develop in another direction: gold. Inflation soared in the late 1970s and the gold price reacted with increasing vehemence, finally peaking at over $870 in 1980. It was literally a golden age for those letter publishers like Jim Dines and Harry Schultz who had long been interested in the yellow metal, and for those adroit enough to move in to exploit crisis. *Harry Browne's Special Reports* began in 1974, Howard Ruff's *Ruff Times* (subsequently *Howard Ruff's Financial Survival Report*, now *Howard Ruff's Financial Success Report*) began in 1975; and there were many others, often specializing in "hard assets," "collectibles" like stamps, coins and precious stones, whose popularity was a sign of increasing doubts about the dollar.

Out of the inflation imbroglio emerged one of the central institutions of the investment letter community: the National Committee for Monetary Reform and its super-colossal Annual Investment Conference, held every fall in New Orleans. NCMR was the brainchild of James U. Blanchard, a young Southern schoolteacher and part-time coin dealer, who ran it from the wheelchair to which he was confined as result of an automobile accident. It has expanded into an empire with many provinces, including a personal finance magazine, *Wealth*, and three newsletters of its own: *Market Alert*, sent free to clients of NCMR's coin-dealing affiliate; the Aden sisters' *Aden Analysis*; and Robert J. Ringer's *The Tortoise Report*, which, according to one reference book's deadpan description, "gives readers the advantage of receiving input" from the best-selling author of *Winning Through Intimidation*, *Looking Out for #1*, and *Restoring the American Dream*.

Blanchard held the first NCMR New Orleans conference in 1974. In return for a registration fee of several hundred dollars, it offered its audience not just gold experts but a smorgasbord of speakers from all across the investment spectrum to complement their hard-money predilections. This formula proved an enormous success, particularly in the mid-1970s when gold was weak. And as gold peaked in the fall of 1980, NCMR attendance reached an astonishing 8,500, amid scenes of evangelical fervor. On its tenth anniversary, with the price of gold slowly deteriorating, NCMR attendance had slipped below

2,000. But this was still an impressive showing, given that travel and hotel bills must have put the total cost per person well above $1,000, even if it was tax deductible. New Orleans' cavernous Rivergate Conference Center was filled with the stoical buzzing of gold bugs who, while wounded, were definitely not yet slain.

By this time the main topic of NCMR debate had become: was inflation dead? And would it be followed by disinflation (slowing price rises) or downright deflation (price declines, possibly precipitous)? A schism occurred in the hard-money movement. Those like Harry Schultz and Harry Browne who were prepared to contemplate the end of inflation and to trade gold were opposed by those, like Howard Ruff, the Aden sisters and Ian McAvity, who believed that the inflation cycle would just come round again. This was not necessarily reactionary stubbornness: most conventional academic economists were equally puzzled by inflation's nonreappearance on cue in the early 1980s. But an important straw investment letter writer in the wind at recent NCMR conferences could well be Charles Allmon of *Growth Stock Outlook*. Everyone listened to his presentations with scrupulous care. Allmon has the old-fashioned investment philosophy that if you buy stock in small, well-managed companies and let them go to it, their increasing earnings will show up in higher stock prices, just like the textbooks say. Significantly, in 1983 and 1984 he was also named Speaker of the Year by a rival conference organization, Charles Githler's Investment Seminars Inc., which is noted for cold-eyed analysis of the results of its audience polls. It seemed as if, after an inflationary binge and hangover, the American economy might be returning to its last, at last. And investors, and investment letters, were following it.

The Monetary Reform in which Blanchard's Committee is interested is of course a return to the gold standard. This public-spirited concern with questions of policy and philosophy is characteristic of the investment letter industry as it has emerged in the 1980s. Many letters espouse ferociously right-wing attitudes. They stand in total opposition to the works of American liberalism right back to the New Deal, and above all to government intervention in the economy and to the monetization of the federal debt, which they loosely describe as "Keynesian-ism." Frequently, their ideological inspiration is the classical, laissez-faire type of liberalism that has been so thoroughly dispossessed in this century that it has been deprived even of its name and has been obliged to accept the cumbersome sobriquet "libertarianism." This is certainly the case with Blanchard's NCMR group. They even provided the forum for the last speech made just before her death by the Objectivist novelist Ayn Rand (*Atlas Shrugged, The Fountainhead*), bringing her to New Orleans by private rail car. But investment letters also regularly display a more traditional conservatism, as when Harry Schultz's *International Harry Schultz Letter* devoted much space in the last years of the Carter Administration to documenting the military threat from the Soviet Union, complete with a 1,000-day countdown to a Soviet demand for U.S. unconditional surrender, which Schultz maintained would occur early in a second Carter term. (For the record, though, it should perhaps be noted that there are no racist or fascist investment letters.)

There is little that seems inherently conservative about the investment letter format. Eliot Janeway of *The Janeway Letter* has always flaunted his connections with Democratic politicians. Charles Stahl of *Green's Commodity Comments* is a longtime critic of the gold standard despite actively trading the metal, and identifies himself as a liberal Republican, an even more endangered political species. There is an investment letter for blacks (*The Puryear Money Report*) and one for homosexuals (the *Lambda Financial Advisor*). The Lowry family's *Good Money* actually recommends investments on their "social responsibility" and contribution to "change." It offers a specially discounted rate to low-income subscribers and nonprofit organizations.

But from a cultural standpoint, the investment letter phenomenon has been unmistakably linked to the revival of American conservatism, from its low point in 1950, when the critic Lionel Trilling made his celebrated observation that in the United States "liberalism is not only the dominant but even the sole intellectual tradition . . . there are no conservative or reactionary ideas in general circulation," to 1980, and the election of Ronald Reagan. For much of this period, Trilling's remark remained quite accurate for America's major media. The investment letters constituted a kind of conservative *samizdat*.

When Reagan became governor of California, his victory

was attributed to the fact that people like the Joads, the Oklahoma dustbowl family that was forced to join California's migrant fruit pickers in John Steinbeck's Depression novel *The Grapes of Wrath*, had become wealthy and conservative during the state's wartime and postwar booms. In the 1970s, Joads all over the country were reading Howard Ruff's political sermons in *Ruff Times* and brooding about the connection between what inflation was doing to their savings and its effect on the nation's integrity. Against this background, the presidential election of 1980 is less surprising. Experienced Washington observers were deceived about the strength of the Reagan movement because of the very pluralism and diversity of American society that makes it possible for newsletters to find markets.

The Joads still don't think much of Eastern bankers, though. In 1983 a last-minute lobbying campaign partly organized by Howard Ruff's Free the Eagle Political Action Committee stimulated thousands of threatening communications from Joads to their congressmen and stalled bipartisan legislation to increase United States contributions to the International Monetary Fund, causing great alarm among debtor nations (and their creditors, who looked to the IMF to bail them out). And regardless of Reagan, Joads also show a continuing suspicion of U.S. governments and their financial policies. When the radical libertarian Republican congressman Ron Paul lost his race for the Republican Senate nomination in Texas in 1984, his first step was to found an investment letter—called, conservatively, *Ron Paul's Investment Letter*—prophesying economic disaster because of unchecked federal spending.

Ultimately, the investment letter phenomenon is neither conservative nor liberal, but deeply American. Investment letters have not developed to anything like the same extent in countries like Britain, where there is a coherent social elite and finance has remained the exclusive preserve of a select priesthood that regards it as an esoteric rite to which outsiders cannot possibly contribute. In America, by contrast, there is a large, educated and enterprising population that believes in the value of self-help. It is unimpressed by, indeed often actively hostile toward, the Eastern financial and social establishments. The same uncritical faith in education that has produced universal high schools, degree courses in Home Economics and McDonald's Hamburger University drives polyester-clad Middle

Americans to attend investment conferences, where they sit dutifully through long sessions, take copious notes—and learned about gold back in 1970. "It doesn't work in Britain," says Harry Schultz, an experienced conference-holder and an Anglophile without illusions. "They're all too conceited to be taught anything."

In the 1980s, newsletters can finally be seen to have been the extreme edge of the "revolution in journalism" that Frederick Lundberg described over forty years before. Its slogan has been specialization. Subscribers (and advertisers) have been willing to pay a premium to get exactly what they want. Like deer beset by wolves, the great general-interest magazines, *Life, Look, Saturday Evening Post, Collier's*, have been brought down by more numerous, more narrowly focused magazines. Henry Luce's marketing strategy for *Fortune*, brought out in the Depression year of 1930 as a "magazine for millionaires" and priced at $12 annually—which some comparisons suggest is equivalent to $120 today—ironically had more in common with modern investment letter concepts than with his mass-market creation, *Time*.

The investment letter phenomenon is only a part of a much broader upsurge of newsletter publishing. Technical change is partly responsible. Personal computers chew cheerfully through the clerical and mechanical aspects of the business, previously a forbidding chore. Direct-mail techniques have been developed into a science—partly by conservatives seeking to raise money for their Political Action Committees—and this allows newsletters to locate their audience efficiently. (Advertising in newspapers is generally too expensive for noninvestment letters.) Newsletter publishing itself is evolving into a sophisticated profession. It even has its own self-help and Washington lobbying group, the Newsletter Association. Only a quarter of its 900-odd members are financially oriented, according to executive director Frederick D. Goss. The rest focus on travel, health and "every type of industry imaginable." Investment letters are the most expensive of the "consumer letters" aimed at individuals. But some specialized business letters cost hundreds and even thousands of dollars a year. A similar organization, the Newsletter Clearing House in Rhinebeck, New York, services nonprofit and in-house letters and publishes—inevitably—*The Newsletter on Newsletters.*

The newsletter with the largest circulation is probably Roger Tyndall's *The Contest Newsletter,* published in Fernandina Beach, Florida. It keeps its readers up to date on every possible competition they can enter. *The Contest Newsletter* costs $12.95 a year. More than 1.5 *million* people subscribe.

Their idea of a good competition apparently does not include the stock market.

CHAPTER FOUR
Measuring Investment Letter Performance

Concerning these predictions we are about to ask:
1. *Are they pretty good?*
2. *Are they slightly good?*
3. *Are they any damn good at all?*
4. *How do they compare with tomorrow's weather prediction you read in the paper?*
5. *How do they compare with the tipster horse-race services?*

—FRED J. SCHWED, JR., *Where Are the Customers' Yachts?*

Philosophy will clip an angel's wings.

—JOHN KEATS, *Lamia*

Late one frosty Washington night in January 1983, Mark Hulbert returns from dinner to the pristine Capitol Hill townhouse he occupies alone with his eight possessions, seven of which are directly employed in his monthly *Hulbert Financial Digest* investment letter performance-monitoring service. He frowns, and stops talking in midsentence. An untoward event has injected itself into his life, where such things are not permitted. A computer has mutinied. It stares at him defiantly, protruding a rude tongue of incompleted printout.

With his beard, glasses, curly hair, cheerful demeanor and

open-necked shirts no matter how cold the weather, Hulbert looks like the recently graduated philosophy student he is. (Haverford '77, Oxford '79, son of a professor of botany at Kansas State University.) But there's a hidden Hulbert, as the numerous investment letter writers who have tried to shake him off their trail can attest. With a growl, he leaps at the recalcitrant machine. He forces it to disgorge pages of information. He inspects them for an hour, nose an inch from the paper, mouth down-curving like that of an angry Jove. Finally, he reprograms his way around the problem. Only then do his surroundings swim back into this consciousness, and his natural amiability returns with a grin.

The *Hulbert Financial Digest* became an instant institution in the investment letter subculture as soon as it appeared in September 1980. Hulbert was then twenty-five. The previous fall he had attended NCMR's New Orleans conference with a fellow ex-Yank at Oxford, James Davidson, head of the National Taxpayers' Union, a lobbying group invented by Davidson to press for, among other things, a constitutional amendment requiring a balanced federal budget. California governor Jerry Brown was trying this idea on for size prior to making his bid for the Democratic presidential nomination. Hulbert and Davidson were to brief him before he addressed the assembled gold bugs.

A funny thing happened to Jerry Brown on his way to the presidency in 1980. But Hulbert and Davidson's trip still had mildly historic consequences. They were fascinated by the NCMR spectacle, as colorful as any medieval fair with its jugglers, hucksters and fortune-tellers. They decided there was a need for independent evaluations of the investment advisors' cacophonous and competing claims. The result was the $135-a-year *Hulbert Financial Digest*, financed by Davidson and his associate William Bonner, now head of his own list-broking and public relations firm, and created by Hulbert.

Within weeks, Hulbert's work had caught the attention of one of the industry's scholars, Dr. Martin Zweig of *The Zweig Forecast*. Zweig was deeply offended by Joe Granville's antics, and when Granville gave his famous sell signal in early 1981, Zweig in effect handed over Hulbert and his objective rating of Granville's record to Alan Abelson at *Barron's* in much the same spirit as a second handing a peculiarly sharp rapier to a duelist. Hulbert's numbers showed that Granville's record was not particularly remarkable compared to the Dow or for that matter to the top-rated letters, of which Zweig's happened to be one. Partly this was because Granville's midnight signals were flashed only to those paying extra for his Early Warning Service, whereas Hulbert as a matter of policy restricted himself to the basic *Granville Market Letter*, and was therefore among those long-suffering Granville subscribers who were still reading his bullish January 3, 1981, *Letter* while hearing about his January 6 sell signal on the TV news. Additionally, Granville pays little attention to stock selection, believing that if you get the market direction right, the individual stocks selected will look after themselves. This Market Timing versus Stock Selection debate is a famous Wall Street perennial. More will be heard about it later.

Reader response to Abelson's use of the Hulbert numbers in his "Heard on the Street" column was so enthusiastic that he ordered up a full-length *Barron's* story. After that, in rapid succession, Hulbert was featured in several other publications and on the CBS Evening News and Louis Rukeyser's *Wall Street Week.* "Just WHO IS Mark Hulbert??" inquired *The L. T. Patterson Strategy Letter,* which mixes investment advice with the latest news of the international conspiracy it believes is directed by the Rockefeller-funded Trilateral Commission. It noted darkly that "he appears to be the new fair-haired boy of the liberal media!" and sounded the alarm: *"THE HULBERT LETTER—MAY BE OUT TO 'GET' HARD MONEY PUBLISHERS!!"*

By mid-1981, the circulation of the *Hulbert Financial Digest* had soared past 3,000, making it one of the most successful letter launches in recent years. Hulbert had built a better investment advisor-trap, regardless of the consistency of their money, and the world was beating a path to his post office box. By 1985, *HFD*'s circulation was over 14,000.

Hulbert has achieved this impact by the simple expedient of listening to what the investment letter editors actually say. He aims to duplicate the experience of the ordinary reader by subscribing to the investment letters anonymously and noting their recommendations on the day they are received. (Many letters are also sent to him free, but Hulbert has noticed that these have the curious habit of showing up a day or so earlier.) The core of *HFD* is a table listing the performances of hypothetical "paper" portfolios constructed by Hulbert on the basis of each letter's recommendations, as they would be understood by the average reasonable reader. Unless the letter says specifically to the contrary, Hulbert fully invests each paper portfolio, giving equal weight to each recommendation, rebalancing when new buy and sell recommendations are made, or if stop-losses or other stated key points are reached. Where holding cash is the order of the month, Hulbert hypothetically invests in treasury bills, crediting the portfolio with interest. He also adds in dividend payments and commissions costs. Each portfolio performance is calculated from scratch every year, so that every letter's record can be inspected either year by year, or cumulatively by multiplying (NOT adding) each year's percentage increase—or decrease. A version of this table is reproduced on pages 68 to 75. But as a service to those readers of this book whose pocket calculators aren't within reach, cumulative results are supplied from the point when Hulbert began his service.

Some purists argue that Hulbert should invest real money and report the results. Putting a rating service's money where the advisors' mouths are would raise its costs, to put it mildly, and no one has yet been heroic enough to try. But Hulbert doesn't agree with the critics anyway. "They just don't understand the distinction between a real and a representative portfolio," he says. He aims to reproduce an average result that will be valuable to the average subscriber, whereas individual experiences may differ sharply. Rebalancing, for example, is necessary because some letters suggest that subscribers allocate their assets in various proportions without keeping track of price changes, with the result that readers whose subscriptions began at different times would buy different amounts of each stock as its price moves up or down.

Hulbert's contribution to the Market Timing versus Stock Selection debate is to construct a second parallel set of portfolios in exactly the same way as the first, except for replacing the recommended equity portion with an equivalent exposure to the New York Stock Exchange Composite Index. This enables him to separate the market timing performance of an investment letter from its prowess at stock selection. If the investment letter is a successful stock picker, its portfolio with picks will appreciate faster than the portfolio invested in NYSE Composite. Conversely, if the NYSE Composite portfolio does better, that means the letter has been better at predicting the market's overall direction than thinking of particular stocks in which to ride it.

In 1984, for example, the paper portfolio derived from Glen Cutler's *Market Mania* appreciated 6.4 percent,* one of the top performances in that flat year. This was especially remarkable because the small, thinly traded stocks Cutler favors were generally hit hard. His market timing portfolio, by contrast, gained only 3.5 percent. (Cutler made generally bearish noises about the market all year, although it basically did no worse than move sideways, but his specific actions were more positive, presenting anyone trying to assess investment letter records by eyeball with a typical quandary, and illustrating why Hulbert favors a ruthlessly quantitative approach.) By contrast, the market timing portfolio derived from Stan Weinstein's *The Professional Tape Reader* has generally tended to do better than the portfolio based on his stock selections.

The fact is that the expedient of listening to what the investment letters say isn't that simple at all. Advisors can be chronically vague, artfully ambiguous and deviously unsystematic, forgetting bad calls and remembering good ones rather too well. But even beyond the resulting problems of interpretation, there are knotty methodological questions that can only be cut through by the exercise of brute judgment on the part of the portfolio builder. For example, in choosing a suitable commission level for his paper portfolios, Hulbert is forced to strike a balance between large traders, who can get deep discounts, and small traders, who cannot. Both letters that recommend active trading (Stan Weinstein's *The Professional Tape Reader*) and those that tend to buy and hold (Glen Parker and Norman Fosback's *Market Logic*) have complained loudly that Hulbert's choice gives an unfair advantage to the other. And not even this sort of unsatisfactory compromise is available to approximate the effect of taxes on the individual subscriber. So Hulbert has felt unable to take account of taxes at all, although he lists the average holding period for each letter's investments in the hope that

---

*All such percentages in this book are taken from *The Hulbert Financial Digest*.

this will help the reader figure out whether they might qualify as capital gains.

Another nasty methodological knot: in order to achieve comparability between the different types of investments and to make as few assumptions as possible about the finances of the reader, Hulbert does not use leverage in his paper portfolios unless specifically instructed otherwise. That is, he does not buy stocks "on margin"—putting down only a fraction of their value —and for the few letters he follows that recommend the purchase of silver or gold, he buys bullion rather than the futures contracts that command far greater quantities of gold per dollar down payment. This was why, when Charles Stahl of *Green Commodity Market Comments* was informed by a journalist that his paper portfolio's 21.3 percent gain was one of the top performances in the six months ending in December 1980, he gurgled cheerfully and then promptly proceeded to look a gift Hulbert in the mouth: "In 1980 I made over 1,000 percent for each ounce of gold traded." The gains would have been that much greater if his advice had been used to trade futures contracts. So would the potential losses.

Hulbert worries about such complaints. He adds them to his long list of things to worry about. Periodically his worrying results in a refinement of his system, as when he began to adjust for commissions. This in turn provokes a fresh set of complaints.

But the worrying Hulbert did before he started stood him in good stead. Like cockroaches surprised by a light, the investment letters froze into intense awareness when Hulbert hoved on the scene, only to explode into frantic scurrying for the exit when they realized the horrid implications of what he was doing. But the usual exits were already blocked. For example, in 1981 both Tom Holt of the *Holt Investment Advisory* and Howard Ruff of *Ruff Times/Howard Ruff's Financial Survival/Success Report* argued that Hulbert had simply not been measuring long enough to establish the wisdom of their investment strategies, which would only emerge over the longer term. Two years? "Maybe three," said Holt. Time would obviously cure this problem. By the end of June 1985, Hulbert had been monitoring Holt's portfolio for five years. During that period it had usually been 40 percent to 50 percent short, and overall it had lost 28.8

percent of its initial value. Ruff's so-called "Phantom Investor" model portfolio simply dematerialized in September 1984. Hulbert was keeping vigil over its last reported sighting, but calculated that counting the positions it owned at that time as holds, it was down 0.03 percent over the five-year span.

Vern Myers of *Myers' Finance and Energy* maintained that his record was inherently unquantifiable because he did not recommend stocks in any precise way. "My subscribers have to read between the lines." This was a particularly bold argument, because recommendations too obscure to be quantified would presumably be equally difficult for would-be investors to follow. But Hulbert managed to glean enough between Myers' lines to feed his computer until the end of 1983, when Myers was down 3.3 percent. Then he gave up, on the grounds that Myers had indeed succeeded in becoming too vague to support a model portfolio. Diego Veitia of *World Market Perspectives* responded to Hulbert's monitoring of his performance by arguing in effect that there was no one here but us scholars and thinkers: "We don't make many recommendations. We're a philosophical publication, free-market, Austrian-school," he said. Of one specific investment move he protested, "We didn't recommend it, we *suggested evaluating it.*" Hulbert's method could not draw such fine distinctions. Neither could the ordinary investor.

The investment letter industry was quickly divided by the *Hulbert Financial Digest* into two camps: those who were not on Hulbert's rating roster but wanted to get on, hoping the resulting publicity would attract subscribers, and those who were on but wanted to get off, hoping to retain them. Hulbert's original list included most of the major letters, and he has added steadily until his haul began to approach one hundred. But this is only a fraction of the field. It raises the disturbing possibility that some obscure genius has been missed. Al Frank of *The Prudent Speculator* had a mere seventy-five subscribers when Hulbert added him in 1983, but on back-checking his five-year performance to July 1985 it turned out to be the best. Another little-known but long-established letter with what appears to be a superior record is J. Michael Reid's *Insider Indicator*, which Hulbert began following only in 1985.

And Hulbert's rigorous model-portfolio approach has had another important consequence, which should be stressed: he has not been able to rate most of the entire subspecies of letters that do not recommend (or suggest evaluating) specific invest-ments but instead make general comments on overall trends in the various financial markets. They simply don't provide enough grist for his computer. Yet many of them, like Ian McAvity's *Deliberations* and the Montreal-based *Bank Credit Analyst*, are very popular.

Indeed, by 1984 one overall-trend letter was showing all the symptoms of incipient superstar status: Robert R. Prechter's *Elliott Wave Theorist*. Prechter was then thirty-five, a Yale gradu-ate with a bachelor's degree in psychology who had spent some years playing guitar on the road with a rock band (its best-known song: "Some Guys Have All the Luck," later rerecorded by Rod Stewart). Then he worked in Merrill Lynch's technical department before starting his letter in 1978 and settling outside Atlanta with his wife and child. When describing Prechter, his peers in the advisory industry did not actually come up with the untranslatable Renaissance term for the fairly fierce qualities then considered the prerequisite of princehood: *virtù* (roughly, prowess). But it was what they meant. They usually described him as "the next Richard Russell," notwithstanding the alive-and-kickingness of the present Richard Russell. This was all the more impressive because Prechter's method was highly contro-versial: he undertook to interpret the "Elliott Wave," a pattern of wavelike movements in financial markets allegedly first dis-cerned by California accountant R. N. Elliott in the early 1930s. Prechter drew increasing attention with a remarkable run of successful calls in 1983–4. He also entered and won the United States Trading Championship competition organized by Dr. Norman Zadeh, running his real-money option account from $5,396 up to $29,269 in the four months ending in May 1984, during which he traded some 1,400 options contracts and paid $35,000 in commissions. Prechter said frankly that his motive was publicity and the strain was too great to be sustained. Hul-bert did begin following Prechter in his expanded Timing Scoreboard section in 1985. By this time his hot hand seemed to have cooled, but he was right about the late 1985 rally.

Prechter is unquestionably serious about Elliott. But the investment community's fascination is an example of the Hid-den Imam syndrome in action: the professional compulsion to believe that somewhere, sometime, some esoteric genius under-stood what's going on. Two other such Hidden Imams are the

Soviet economist N. D. Kondratieff, who was purged under Stalin but whose theory that economies move in a long forty-seven to sixty-year cycle is still advocated by letters like *Kondratyev Wave Theory* and Don Hoppe's *Donald J. Hoppe Analysis;* and W. D. Gann, a commodities trader whose increasingly popular numerological and astrological methods are employed in such letters as Phyllis Kahn's *Gann Angles* and Joseph Lederer's *W. D. Gann Technical Commodity Letter.*

Stalking the investment letters is not a new sport. Apart from various journalistic efforts, there are now letters entirely devoted to straight reporting of other letter views, like the *Dick Davis Digest* and the *Newsletter Digest,* published by Al Owen, a practicing physician in Huntsville, Alabama. Many letters, including the *Hulbert Financial Digest* and Bob Gross's *Professional Investor,* makes a point of regular commentary on the views of the rest of the industry. But the systematic evaluation of the investment letters' recommendations is such an appalling clerical task that it remained unthinkable until the advent of the computer. This was why, after signing up a number of subscribers, New York architect and private investor Sanford Hohauser eventually abandoned his plan for a Hulbert-like service in 1968.

Computerization, however, can mean merely a higher order of problems. Technical difficulties plagued *Focus on Wall Street,* a monitoring service put out from 1982 to 1985 by George Wein's Select Information Exchange subscription agency. *Focus on Wall Street* tracked nearly four hundred letters, cumulating their portfolios from July 1981 or from whenever it began following them. Since this exaggerated the performance of the letters it began measuring during bear market lows, it also reproduced the record for the last twelve months. But *Focus on Wall Street* followed the prudent but unrevealing course of printing only the few top performers. This was no doubt satisfying to its lawyers, concerned to avoid libel actions from low-rated advisors looking for a scapegoat, but it did not appeal to the bear-baiting and bull-boosting instincts of the public or the press. *Focus*'s main interest was reporting without comment lists of the advisors' most recommended stocks assorted into various intriguing categories—low-priced, potential takeovers and so on.

An equally forbearing attitude to the industry is found in the other performance-monitoring services that have sprung up recently. *Timer Digest*, edited by Bob James, a portfolio manager with investment advisors DeWees, Smith & Company, follows the market timing of some thirty letters, once again naming only the top ten, from which it constructs a consensus recommendation. Mannie Webb's *Rating the Stock Selectors* is an entertaining but discreet blend of digested market letters, regurgitated performance monitors and periodic editorial assertion, without any tabulation of results.

None of these services say much about their methodologies. Bruce Babcock's *Commodity Traders Consumer Report*, however, constructs paper portfolios rather like Hulbert's, albeit only for those advisors who have given their permission. Babcock concentrates on advisors specializing in the commodities markets, an exotic group even by the standards of the investment letter industry. He therefore rarely overlaps with the equity-oriented services followed by Hulbert. *Commodity Traders Consumer Report* verges on a magazine format, with intense, sophisticated interviews with advisors and the occasional hard-hitting feature, such as a derisive review of J. Welles Wilder's widely advertised Delta Society International, which for $3,500 plus $100 a year offered computer disks programmed to allow sixteen years' use of "the secret of perfect order behind the markets." (See?)

There is a mildly tragic quality about the relationship between Mark Hulbert and the investment letter editors who are his subjects/victims. Hulbert likes and admires these wandering prophets of the investment scene. He has passed through the valley of the shadow of academe with an unusual skepticism about the Random Walk and the Efficient Market Hypothesis, so that he is quite prepared to accept the possibility that some investors can consistently outperform the market. When, in the shambles of a journalist's office, he finds an investment letter he's never seen before, he beams at it happily, filled with an unmistakable love for the whole weird industry. He is continually bouncing forward like a friendly puppy, eager to discuss methodological perplexities and other matters of mutual concern. But he is rebuffed with oaths, blows (figuratively speaking —Hulbert is well over six feet tall) and threats of legal action. Qne advisor, Yale Hirsch of *Smart Money*, actually did sue for libel: the case was dismissed with costs in early 1985.

Hulbert has begun to suspect that some letter writers might not be interested in objective evaluation at all.

Hulbert is not a puppy, however. Despite his casual appearance, he is totally self-assured. Among the many complaints hurled at him when he began was his lack of "investment experience." And in fact he had taught himself all about the investment business in an astonishingly short time. But this allegation completely misunderstood what was required by a rating service, and a newsletter based upon it. It required a Hulbert. He had a powerful, highly trained mind; a firm grasp on the computer techniques necessary to monitor paper portfolios; and an iron capacity for work. He was prepared to spend New Year's Eves and July 4 weekends crunching numbers for his next issue, as well as the small hours of innumerable nights punting revised versions of the software required to computerize his entire operation back and forth like a football across the telephone system to his brother, a programming expert then completing his Ph.D. studies at the University of Illinois. Hulbert exemplified a Bob Gross adage about the investment letter industry: *a successful letter publisher must be capable of doing everything himself.*

Mark Hulbert regarded himself as a Marxist when he arrived at Pembroke College, Oxford. But he says that, perhaps unexpectedly, the Oxford tutorial system with its relentless insistence on logical justification and empirical verifiability dispelled the grand, deductive and theoretical Hegelianism that had entranced him at Haverford. (On the other hand, Haverford can probably claim some credit for Hulbert's equally heavily utilized quantitative side.) Now Hulbert inclines to an individualized version of the libertarianism common in the investment letter industry. Amid his other activities he has researched and written a closely reasoned book, *Interlock* (1982), arguing that the major New York banks were able to manipulate Carter Administration policy during the Iran crisis, from which they alone of all Iran's foreign creditors emerged mysteriously unscathed. Hulbert's unusual blend of implacable independence and gentleness may even be due as much to heredity as environment: his family are Quakers, but among his ancestors were Miles Standish and Aaron Burr.

Confronted with complaining investment letter editors, Hulbert applies the same test that his philosophy tutor applied to his Marxism—"give me an argument." But he reports that more often than not their argument turns out to be inchoate and emotional. Hulbert is scientifically curious about inchoate emotion. But he seems almost unaware that it is supposed to alter what he thinks.

Hulbert in fact is a rare example of a human being motivated to a considerable degree by pure rationality alone. His mind naturally works in a highly logical way. Questioned about his methods, he immediately begins to answer in numbered paragraphs, sometimes with verbal footnotes, always reaching a firm conclusion. Once his mind is made up, he will act, but not otherwise. Convinced by a philosophical argument about morality, he became a vegetarian, and now cooks a mean pasta primavera. His girl friend, Rebecca Ashe, is also a vegetarian. One of their friends recently slipped away from the faith. "Oh—I didn't think I had to have *reasons*," she responded when asked why. Hulbert was deeply impressed by this answer. He filed it away and will sometimes repeat it in wondering tones. Rebecca objects, but Hulbert's interest is not at all critical. He is more like an etymologist confronted with a strange new language that, he naturally assumes, must have its own rules, even if they are not quite obvious to him at this point.

At the end of June 1985, after five years of rating the letters, Hulbert's results looked like this (see pages 68 through 75).

It would be easy to say that these results are devastating. INVESTORS NEWSLETTERS ACCURATE AS A COIN FLIP, blared the New York *Daily News* in 1981. Dan Dorfman, in his round-by-round chronicling of Hulbert versus the investment letters, has preferred to say that their advice was no better than throwing a dart at the stock quotes page of the *Wall Street Journal* and buying whatever it hits. He could naturally be forgiven for noting quietly that Joe Granville, the chump who named a chimp after him and claimed to have cracked the market's code,

PERFORMANCE RATINGS FOR DECEMBER 31, 1985

NEWSLETTER (Composition of Portfolio)	Dec. Gain	1985 Gain	1984 Gain	1983 Gain	1982 Gain	1981 Gain	7/1 to 12/31/80 Gain	Risk Rating Note 1	See Note #2
Addison Report (Portfolios fully invested in "monitored" lists)*									
a. Conservative stocks (Fully invested)*	+4.1%	+15.3%	+4.4%	+28.9%	n/a	n/a	n/a	4.08	21-C
b. Speculative Stocks (Those rated "buys")*	+5.0%	+17.6%	-13.6%	+89.6%	n/a	n/a	n/a	6.63	29-C
Astute Investor (Portfolio fully invested in stocks rated "buy")	+7.4%	+44.3%	-5.9%	n/a	n/a	n/a	n/a	5.74	30-C
(Astute Investor—Timing Only)	+4.3%	+26.2%	+0.5%	n/a	n/a	n/a	n/a	n/a	n/a
BI Research (Portfolio fully invested in stocks rated "Buy")	-7.1%	+65.9%	+14.3%	n/a	n/a	n/a	n/a	11.13	5-C
Cabot Market Letter (Model Portfolio: Stocks and, at times, T-Bills)	+2.3%	+37.4%	-22.7%	+7.3%	+32.8%	+2.5%	n/a	6.95	12-A
(Cabot Market Letter—Timing Only)	+4.3%	-26.3%	+0.7%	+16.4%	+13.9%	-3.7%	n/a	n/a	n/a
Calif. Technology Stock Letter (Model Portfolio: Stocks & T-Bills)	+5.7%	-5.9%	-47.9%	+1.7%	n/a	n/a	n/a	9.70	11-A
(Calif. Technology Stock Letter—Timing Only)	+3.8%	+25.5%	+1.2%	+15.4%	n/a	n/a	n/a	n/a	n/a
Canadian Business Service Investment Report									
a. Very Conservative Stocks (Fully invested)	+2.1%	+20.7%	-4.9%	n/a	n/a	n/a	n/a	3.52	27-C
b. Conservative stocks (fully invested)	+3.7%	+17.2%	+.3%	n/a	n/a	n/a	n/a	3.67	27-C
c. Average risk stocks (fully invested)	+2.6%	+39.7%	-6.4%	n/a	n/a	n/a	n/a	4.53	11-C
d. Higher risk stocks (fully invested)	+4.7%	+21.4%	-10.7%	n/a	n/a	n/a	n/a	5.57	9-C
e. Speculative stocks (fully invested)	-1.4%	+13.8%	-10.8%	n/a	n/a	n/a	n/a	7.50	3-C
The Chartist									
a. Actual Cash Account (Stocks and, at times, T-Bills)	+8.2%	+23.3%	+1.0%	+25.1%	+32.7%	-9.7%	+23.4%	4.24	11-A
(Actual Cash Account—Timing Only)	+2.6%	+20.6%	+5.0%	+16.2%	+12.1%	n/a	n/a	n/a	n/a
b. Traders' Stocks (fully invested)	+2.9%	+52.2%	+6.4%	+30.5%	n/a	n/a	n/a	6.27	24-C
Dessauer's Journal (International Portfolio: Stocks,Bonds,Currencies)	+4.3%	+41.8%	-0.0%	+21.0%	+20.1%	n/a	n/a	3.04	48-B
The Dines Letter (Supervised Lists of Stocks, Bonds, Options, T-Bills)									
#1. Good-Grade for Moderate Gains	+3.0%	+12.5%	-41.1%	+43.5%	+15.1%	-20.4%	+10.2%	3.68	9-A
#2. Speculative	+11.3%	+18.1%	+37.0%	+8.6%	+9.1%	+15.5%	+5.8%	6.42	9-A
#3. Growth	+7.2%	+23.3%	+71.9%	+7.0%	+25.1%	+14.2%	+5.8%	6.31	10-A
#4. Short-Term Trading	-0.0%	-2.6%	+27.4%	+90.1%	-4.3%	-13.2%	+19.3%	15.23	8-A
(Short-Term Trading Portfolio—Timing Only)	+3.9%	+18.0%	+1.9%	+15.2%	+18.1%	+16.5%	+11.3%	n/a	n/a
Dow Theory Forecasts (Portfolios fully invested in each list's stocks)									
a. Income Stocks (Invested in those "especially recommended")	+4.7%	+35.1%	+12.9%	+20.5%	+20.2%	-8.2%	+14.9%	3.12	12-C

b. Investment Stocks (Invested in those "especially recommended")	+4.4%	+35.3%	+2.3%	+15.6%	+28.4%	-4.2%	+21.8%	3.29	21-C
c. Growth Stocks (Invested in those "especially recommended")	+5.2%	+28.8%	-6.8%	+11.7%	+14.9%	+5.2%	+22.5%	5.07	18-C
d. Speculative Stocks (Invested in those "especially recommended")	+6.0%	+35.3%	-4.7%	+11.7%	+13.4%	-5.9%	+27.5%	4.61	24-C
Dow Theory Letters (Recommendations in "Investment Position" Box)	+1.0%	-5.9%	+1.8%	-6.8%	+19.2%	+10.2%	n/a	2.78	5-D
Emerging & Special Situations (Fully invested in stocks rated "buy")	+7.8%	+44.2%	-4.6%	+6.6%	n/a	n/a	n/a	8.23	19-C
Financial World (Fully invested in A+-rated stocks)	+1.7%	+19.3%	n/a	n/a	n/a	n/a	n/a	4.37	55-C
Fund Exchange Report (Mutual Funds)									
a. Balanced Model Portfolio	+3.3%	+20.2%	n/a	n/a	n/a	n/a	n/a	3.59	7-A
b. Conservative Growth Model Portfolio	+3.8%	+28.6%	n/a	n/a	n/a	n/a	n/a	3.60	5-A
c. Conservative Growth Margined Portfolio	+5.9%	+45.5%	n/a	n/a	n/a	n/a	n/a	5.62	5-A
d. Aggressive Growth Model Portfolio	+3.7%	+29.7%	n/a	n/a	n/a	n/a	n/a	4.72	5-A
e. Aggressive Growth Margined Portfolio	+7.1%	+40.1%	n/a	n/a	n/a	n/a	n/a	7.37	5-A
f. Taxable Bond Model Portfolio	+2.8%	+18.9%	n/a	n/a	n/a	n/a	n/a	1.71	5-A
g. Gold Model Portfolio	+0.6%	-9.9%	n/a	n/a	n/a	n/a	n/a	4.56	0-A
Garside Forecast (Fully invested in recommended stocks)	+1.4%	+17.8%	+1.6%	n/a	n/a	n/a	n/a	2.83	7-C
Granville Market Letter (Not including phone service)									
a. Aggressive Traders' Stock Portfolio (Fully Invested)	-1.5%	-22.7%	+2.9%	-25.2%	-29.7%	-3.3%	+10.6%	4.32	24-C
(Granville Market Letter's Aggressive Traders' Portfolio—Timing Only)	+0.2%	-4.2%	+7.7%	-15.2%	-12.9%	+5.0%	+19.2%	n/a	n/a
b. Option Portfolio (Fully invested when in options))	-37.1%	-97.8%	n/a	n/a	n/a	n/a	n/a	38.19	34-C
Green's Commodity Market Comments (Advice for *traders*; non-margined)	+0.6%	+13.1%	+4.8%	+20.2%	+48.4%	+11.6%	+21.3%	4.08	0-A
Growth Fund Guide									
a. Aggressive Growth Funds (Fully invested in funds most highly rated)	+6.1%ᵣ	+33.8%	-18.3%	+22.4%	n/a	n/a	n/a	5.36	3-C
b. Growth Funds (Fully invested)	+4.2%	+31.2%	+0.8%	+24.2%	n/a	n/a	n/a	3.78	3-C
c. Quality Growth Funds (Fully invested)	+3.4%	+26.4%	+5.5%	+22.4%	n/a	n/a	n/a	2.45	4-C
d. Special Situations Funds (Fully invested)	+3.4%	-20.9%	-3.6%	+30.3%	n/a	n/a	n/a	3.70	3-C
Growth Stock Outlook (Supervised Portfolio: Stocks, T-Bills)	+1.8%	-24.7%	+3.5%	+33.1%	+24.0%	+11.8%	+34.0%	3.58	41-A
(Growth Stock Outlook—Timing Only)	+2.5%	+19.5%	+5.4%	+17.6%	+18.5%	-0.6%	+14.9%	n/a	n/a
Harry Browne's Special Reports (Variable [Speculative] Portfolio)	+2.5%	+14.8%	+4.1%	+8.1%	+17.2%	-6.9%	n/a	2.14	6-A
Heim Investment Letter (Usually stocks and/or T-Bills)	+0.7%	+4.8%	+1.6%	+2.6%	-8.4%	+10.5%	+2.6%	0.91	1-A
High Technology Growth Stocks (Model Portfolio: Stocks, T-Bills)	+2.8%	-4.8%	-36.3%	n/a	n/a	n/a	n/a	10.18	33-A
(High Technology Growth Stocks—Timing Only)	+4.3%	+25.5%	+1.5%	n/a	n/a	n/a	n/a	n/a	n/a
High Technology Investments									
a. Long-Term Portfolio I (Stocks and, at times, T-Bills)	+19.6%	+50.0%	-23.3%	+3.5%	n/a	n/a	n/a	10.63	8-A
b. Long-Term Portfolio II (Stocks and, at times, T-Bills)	+3.4%	+103.3%	-2.6%	-19.2%	n/a	n/a	n/a	11.84	8-A
(Long-Term Portfolio II—Timing Only)	+2.9%	+15.8%	+8.6%	+12.0%	n/a	n/a	n/a	n/a	n/a
Howard Ruff's Financial Success Report									
a. "Phantom Investor" (Stocks, commodities, coins, T-Bills)	-1.5%	+2.3%	-13.2%	-14.9%	+43.8%	-2.4%	-6.8%	2.73	24-D
b. "Optimum Switch Hitter" (Mutual Funds)	+1.0%	+12.6%	n/a	n/a	n/a	n/a	n/a	2.19	3-A

PERFORMANCE RATINGS FOR DECEMBER 31, 1985

NEWSLETTER (Composition of Portfolio)	Dec. Gain	1985 Gain	1984 Gain	1983 Gain	1982 Gain	1981 Gain	7/1 to 12/31/80 Gain	Risk Rating Note 1	See Note #2
Holt Investment Advisory (Recommended stocks, bonds, options, T-Bills)	-2.1%	-17.4%	-0.4%	-8.2%	-11.8%	+7.9%	-6.1%	3.82	6-B
(Holt Investment Advisory—Timing Only)	-1.1%	-5.4%	-1.2%	-6.6%	+4.0%	+11.4%	-6.7%	n/a	n/a
Indicator Digest ("Growth Portfolio": Stocks, T-Bills)	+5.2%	+6.9%	-10.3%	+11.8%	n/a	n/a	n/a	3.98	16-B
(Indicator Digest—Timing Only)	+2.9%	+18.7%	+1.1%	+17.0%	n/a	n/a	n/a	n/a	n/a
Insider Indicator (Portfolio fully invested in past year's 'buys')	+1.6%	+25.6%	n/a	n/a	n/a	n/a	n/a	4.73	150-C
Insiders (Insiders' Portfolio)	+0.8%	+20.2%	n/a	n/a	n/a	n/a	n/a	4.48	37-C
International Harry Schultz Letter**									
a. US Stocks portfolio (formerly "Investment Table")	+2.9%	+8.7%	+7.4%	+2.1%	-5.5%	-17.5%	+41.2%	2.79	22-B
b. Portfolio constructed out of gold/silver trading advice (non-margined)	-0.2%	-2.8%	+20.3%	n/a	n/a	n/a	n/a	2.50	1-C
Investech (Long-Term Portfolio: Stocks, Options, T-Bills)	+0.7%	+32.7%	-16.7%	n/a	n/a	n/a	n/a	8.11	2-B
(Investech Market Letter—Timing Only)	+0.8%	+15.8%	+1.8%	n/a	n/a	n/a	n/a	n/a	n/a
Investment Values (Fully invested in stocks rated 'Buy')	+5.7%	+18.6%	n/a	n/a	n/a	n/a	n/a	5.61	16-C
Kenneth Gerbino Investment Letter (Fully invested in stocks rated 'Buy')	+4.3%	+0.4%	n/a	n/a	n/a	n/a	n/a	5.08	10-C
Kinsman's Low-Risk Advisory (Model Portfolio: Stocks, Bonds, Metals)	+0.9%	+10.2%	+7.3%	+9.0%	+18.2%	+7.2%	+6.0%	1.53	13-A
LaLoggia's Special Situations Rprt (Fully invested in 'Master List' "Buys")	+4.3%	+31.3%	-6.3%	n/a	n/a	n/a	n/a	3.73	22-C
Lynn Elgert Report (Model Portfolio: Stocks and, at times, T-Bills)	+3.3%	+41.7%	n/a	n/a	n/a	n/a	n/a	6.87	20-A
(Lynn Elgert Report—Timing Only)	+3.6%	+22.5%	n/a	n/a	n/a	n/a	n/a	n/a	n/a
Margo's Market Monitor (Model Portfolio: Stocks, T-Bills)	+2.3%	+22.2%	-5.8%	n/a	n/a	n/a	n/a	2.98	16-A
(Margo's Market Monitor—Timing Only)	+4.2%	+22.9%	+4.0%	n/a	n/a	n/a	n/a	n/a	n/a
Market Logic									
a. Master Portfolio (Stocks and at times T-Bills)	+5.1%	+37.3%	-13.7%	+28.0%	+41.0%	+8.6%	+18.9%	6.35	40-B
(Market Logic—Timing Only)	+4.3%	+26.2%	+1.3%	+17.5%	+17.9%	+2.2%	+12.5%	n/a	n/a
b. Actual Options Portfolio (Options, T-Bills)	+3.1%	+22.4%	+5.8%	+13.5%	+25.9%	+14.2%	+5.8%	2.24	9-A
Market Mania ('Under Observation Portfolio: Stocks, Options, T-Bills)	+3.4%	+1.8%	+6.4%	n/a	n/a	n/a	n/a	7.40	39-A
(Market Mania—Timing Only)	+4.3%	+24.5%	+3.5%	n/a	n/a	n/a	n/a	n/a	n/a
McKeever Strategy Leter ($50,000 Model Portfolio: Commodities, T-Bills)	-2.8%	+99.3%	-13.3%	n/a	n/a	n/a	n/a	12.10	0-A
Medical Technology Stock Letter (Model Portfolio: Stocks, T-Bills)	+9.2%	+83.3%	n/a	n/a	n/a	n/a	n/a	7.20	10-A
(Medical Technology Stock Letter—Timing Only)	+4.3%	+26.2%	n/a	n/a	n/a	n/a	n/a	n/a	n/a
Mutual Fund Strategist									
a. Buy-and-Hold Portfolio	+2.7%	+23.9%	n/a	n/a	n/a	n/a	n/a	1.70	5-C
b. Compuvest Timing Portfolio	+3.6%	+30.9%	n/a	n/a	n/a	n/a	n/a	4.59	2-A
c. Cycle/Reversal Discriminator Portfolio	+5.6%	+34.1%	n/a	n/a	n/a	n/a	n/a	6.27	1-A
New Issues (Fully invested in all open recommendations)	+2.4%	+18.1%	-30.7%	+11.6%	n/a	n/a	n/a	7.61	158-C
Nicholson Report (Model Portfolio: Stocks and T-Bills)	+6.1%	+21.4%	-7.2%	-11.4%	n/a	n/a	n/a	6.21	20-C
No Load Fund-X ("Follow the Stars Strategy'")									

Description									
a. Class 1 Funds (Most Speculative Growth Funds)								3.00	5-C
b. Class 2 Funds (Speculative Growth Funds)	+3.5%	+25.2%	n/a	n/a	n/a	n/a	n/a	3.20	5-C
c. Class 3 Funds (Higher Quality Growth Funds)	+3.4%	+38.1%	n/a	n/a	n/a	n/a	n/a	2.21	5-C
Nourse Investor Report (Recommended Portfolio: Stocks, T-Bills)	+0.6%	+22.1%	n/a	n/a	n/a	n/a	n/a	2.85	0-B
(Nourse Investor Report—Timing Only)	+0.6%	+11.9%	n/a	n/a	n/a	n/a	n/a	n/a	n/a
Option Advisor									
a. Conservative Portfolio (Options and T-Bills)***	-2.9%	+0.6%	+153.3%	-83.5%	n/a	n/a	n/a	8.43	5-A
b. Aggressive Portfolio (Options and T-Bills)	-6.0%	-43.2%	+27.6%	-83.1%	n/a	n/a	n/a	22.29	12-A
OTC Insight (Model Portfolios: Stocks, T-Bills)									
a. $10,000 Conservative	+3.1%	+52.6%	n/a	n/a	n/a	n/a	n/a	5.32	7-A
b. $10,000 Moderately Aggressive	+4.2%	+70.0%	n/a	n/a	n/a	n/a	n/a	7.49	8-A
c. $10,000 Aggressive	+4.1%	+59.4%	n/a	n/a	n/a	n/a	n/a	9.21	6-A
d. $25,000 Conservative	+4.0%	+66.7%	n/a	n/a	n/a	n/a	n/a	4.31	8-A
e. $25,000 Moderately Aggressive	+3.8%	+66.0%	n/a	n/a	n/a	n/a	n/a	6.78	10-A
f. $25,000 Aggressive	+5.9%	+77.6%	n/a	n/a	n/a	n/a	n/a	8.85	7-A
g. $50,000 Conservative	+2.2%	+60.5%	n/a	n/a	n/a	n/a	n/a	4.47	11-A
h. $50,000 Moderately Aggressive	+2.9%	+77.5%	n/a	n/a	n/a	n/a	n/a	7.88	11-A
i. $50,000 Aggressive	+4.4%	+59.0%	n/a	n/a	n/a	n/a	n/a	8.88	8-A
Outlook (Standard & Poor's)									
a. Master Portfolio (Fully invested in recommended stocks)	+6.0%	+25.0%	n/a	n/a	n/a	n/a	n/a	4.53	10-C
b. Master Lists									
1. Foundation Stocks (Fully invested in those best situated for purchase)	+3.6%	+19.6%	-14.5%	+12.3%	+19.9%	+18.1%	+8.8%	4.32	4-C
2. Growth Stocks (Fully invested in those best situated for purchase)	+3.3%	+5.4%	+1.0%	+10.5%	+11.0%	+17.6%	+19.6%	5.83	3-C
3. Speculative Stocks (Fully invested in those best situated for purchase)	+6.0%	+50.7%	+1.0%	+21.4%	+31.0%	+19.6%	-1.6%	4.70	8-C
4. Income Stocks (Fully invested in those best situated for purchase)	+5.0%	+29.0%	+12.8%	+28.0%	+10.6%	+17.9%	+10.8%	3.90	4-C
Patient Investor (Current Year's Model Portfolio—Stocks and T-Bills)	+2.5%	+25.1%	n/a	n/a	n/a	n/a	n/a	3.89	11-A
Personal Finance									
a. Income Portfolio (Fully invested in those recommended as "buys")	+5.4%	+63.7%	+5.8%	n/a	n/a	n/a	n/a	4.61	11-C
b. Growth Portfolio (Fully invested in those recommended as "buys")	-3.3%	+34.8%	-26.8%	n/a	n/a	n/a	n/a	7.23	17-C
Peter Dag Investment Letter (Model Portfolio: Mutual Funds)	+1.9%	+14.5%	+5.5%	+6.0%	n/a	n/a	n/a	1.11	5-A
(Peter Dag Investment Letter—Timing Only)	+2.6%	+16.2%	+7.7%	+15.9%	n/a	n/a	n/a	n/a	n/a
Plain Talk Investor									
a. Personal Portfolio (Stocks and T-Bills)	+5.0%	+35.5%	n/a	n/a	n/a	n/a	n/a	4.37	22-A
b. High Risk Portfolio	+0.2%	+1.4%	n/a	n/a	n/a	n/a	n/a	2.78	7-A
(Plain Talk Investor High Risk Portfolio—Timing Only)	+1.9%	+12.4%	n/a	n/a	n/a	n/a	n/a	n/a	n/a
Professional Investor									
a. NYSE Scan (Fully invested)	+3.3%	+20.4%	-22.1%	+14.1%	+34.5%	+14.4%	-6.1%	2.76	51-C
b. AMEX Scan (Fully invested)	+2.3%	+21.0%	-9.8%	+48.2%	+39.1%	+34.0%	-6.9%	3.15	63-C
c. OTC Scan	+1.4%	+31.4%	-1.7%	+29.3%	+21.6%	+30.8%	-4.4%	2.58	57-C
d. Investment Grade Scan (Fully invested)	+5.0%	+50.2%	-10.5%	-18.5%	+23.7%	+12.5%	+3.0%	4.76	4-C

PERFORMANCE RATINGS FOR DECEMBER 31, 1985

NEWSLETTER (Composition of Portfolio)	Dec. Gain	1985 Gain	1984 Gain	1983 Gain	1982 Gain	1981 Gain	7/1 to 12/*1/80 Gain	Risk Rating Note 1	See Note #2
Professional Tape Reader (Model Portfolio: Stocks and, at times, T-Bills)	+2.1%	+6.4%	-23.6%	-9.8%	+30.0%	-6.7%	+22.9%	5.18	30-A
(Professional Tape Reader—Timing only)	+3.4%	+16.7%	-3.1%	+8.6%	+20.8%	+2.4%	+13.5%	n/a	n/a
Professional Timing Service									
a. Open Stock Positions (Fully Invested)	+3.0%	+27.6%	-19.0%	+22.4%	-2.5%	n/a	n/a	6.86	4-C
b. Gold futures trading (non-margined)	+0.6%	+11.4%	n/a	n/a	n/a	n/a	n/a	4.01	0-C
c. Stock index futures trading (non-margined)	+0.2%	+3.6%	n/a	n/a	n/a	n/a	n/a	0.64	1-C
Prudent Speculator (Actual TPS Portfolio****: Stocks and at times T-Bills)	+11.2%	+62.2%	-13.1%	+72.9%	+49.0%	+2.9%	+26.5%	9.34	120-A
(Prudent Speculator—Timing Only)	+7.2%	+42.7%	-8.5%	+24.4%	n/a	n/a	n/a	n/a	n/a
PSR Stockwatch (Model Portfolio)	+0.1%	+17.4%	n/a	n/a	n/a	n/a	n/a	6.55	33-A
(PSR Stockwatch—Timing Only)	+3.7%	+23.1%	n/a	n/a	n/a	n/a	n/a	n/a	n/a
RHM Survey of Warrants, Options & Low-Priced Stocks (Invested in 'Buys') Speculator	-0.2%	+6.6%	-42.2%	+8.6%	+23.2%	-50.1%	n/a	6.54	10-C
a. Selected Stocks (Fully invested in those best situated for purchase)	+3.4%	+21.9%	-38.6%	+8.8%	+45.3%	-10.8%	n/a	5.04	70-C
b. Trading Portfolio (Stocks and T-Bills)	-1.1%	-3.2%	+5.1%	n/a	n/a	n/a	n/a	3.63	9-A
(Speculator Trading Portfolio—Timing Only)	+4.3%	+19.4	+0.0%	n/a	n/a	n/a	n/a	n/a	n/a
Stockmarket Cycles									
a. Model Portfolio (Stocks, T-Bills)	+10.4%	+23.6%	n/a	n/a	n/a	n/a	n/a	6.08	5-A
(Stock Market Cycles Model Portfolio—Timing Only)	+4.3%	+25.1%	n/a	n/a	n/a	n/a	n/a	n/a	n/a
b. Mutual Fund Portfolio	+5.6%	+11.4%	n/a	n/a	n/a	n/a	n/a	6.62	1-A
Switch Fund Advisory (Model Portfolio: Mutual Funds)	+3.2%	+20.8%	+1.8%	+16.4%	n/a	n/a	n/a	1.76	8-A
(Switch Fund Advisory Model Portfolio—Timing Only)	+3.4%	+18.5%	+2.5%	+14.6%	n/a	n/a	n/a	n/a	n/a
Systems & Forecasts (Stocks, Bonds, Options, Mutual Funds)	+4.0%	+22.0%	+22.2%	-6.9%	n/a	n/a	n/a	2.33	9-B
(Systems & Forecasts—Timing Only)	+3.5%	+20.1%	+4.1%	+8.2%	n/a	n/a	n/a	n/a	n/a
Telephone Switch Newsletter									
a. Equity/Cash Switch Plan	+4.6%	+8.5%	-12.1%	+19.0%	+39.2%	+6.0%	+31.7%	5.07	5-A
(Telephone Switch Newsletter—Timing Only)	+4.3%	+23.6%	+4.7%	+17.5%	+30.3%	+0.7%	+19.2%	n/a	n/a
b. Gold/Cash Switch Plan	+0.6%	-1.1%	-5.9%	-7.8%	n/a	n/a	n/a	3.99	0-A
c. International Funds/Cash Switch Plan	+5.0%	+37.4%	-1.5%	+14.7%	n/a	n/a	n/a	3.01	4-A
Tony Henfrey's Gold Letter (Gold Share Portfolio for U.S.-dollar investors)	-10.0%	-28.3%	-28.1%	+6.9%	+93.3%	n/a	n/a	7.41	8-A
United Business & Investment Reports									
a. Growth Stocks (Fully invested in those best situated for purchase)	+3.6%	+21.6%	-5.5%	+1.7%	+6.7%	-14.1%	+15.8%	4.39	24-C
b. Cyclical Stocks (Fully invested in those best situated for purchase)	+5.9%	+15.2%	-16.9%	+7.0%	+15.6%	-12.9%	+28.2%	5.76	14-C
c. Income Stocks (Fully invested in those best situated for purchase)	+4.9%	+20.3%	+4.2%	+14.7%	+13.8%	-3.8%	+4.6%	3.77	7-C
Value Line Inv. Survey (Fully invested in "Group I" Timeliness Stocks)	+3.8%	+35.1%	-8.6%	+34.8%	n/a			5.14	100-C

	+2.4%	+23.7%	-24.0%	+24.1%	+50.2%	-17.6%	+72.3%	7.14	28-C
Value Line OTC Spec'l Sit. Survey (Fully invested in "esp.-recc." stocks									
Wall Street Digest (Fully invested in stocks rated "buy")	+3.1%	+13.1%	n/a	n/a	n/a	n/a	n/a	6.75	15-C
Weber's Fund Advisor (Real World Portfolio: Mutual Funds)	+4.9%	+22.1%	n/a	n/a	n/a	n/a	n/a	3.31	2-A
Wellington's Worry-Free Investing (Model Portfolio: Muutual Funds)	+3.5%	+29.5%	n/a	n/a	n/a	n/a	n/a	2.09	5-A
(Wellington's Worry Free Investing—Timing Only)	+4.3%	+24.1%	n/a	n/a	n/a	n/a	n/a	n/a	26-A
Zweig Forecast (Model Portfolio: Stocks, T-Bills)	+7.2%r	+41.8%	+2.7%	+1.5%	+24.6%	+24.0%	+23.2%	3.90	26-A
(Zweig Forecast—Timing Only)	+4.5%	+24.3%	+0.5%	+14.3%	+13.5%	+4.5%	+13.6%	n/a	n/a
Zweig Performance Ratings Report (Fully invested in 'buys' and 'shorts')	+3.2%	+29.8%	+5.9%	+17.5%	n/a	n/a	n/a	4.02	45-C
The Riskless rate of return: a T-Bill only portfolio	+0.6%	+7.6%	+9.8%	+9.0%	+10.9%	+14.2%	+5.8%	0.06	
STOCK AVERAGES									
a. DJIA (including dividends, reinvested monthly)	+5.4%	+33.6%	+1.0%	+25.9%	+27.2%	-3.7%	+14.3%	2.91	
b. Standard & Poor's 500 (including dividends, reinvested monthly)	+4.8%	+31.7%	+6.2%	+22.5%	+21.6%	-4.9%	+21.7%	3.32	
c. Wilshire 5000 Value-Weighted Index (dividends reinvested monthly)	+4.5%	+32.6%	+3.0%	+23.5%	+18.7%	-3.7%	+23.2%	3.50	
d. AMEX Market Value Index (without dividends)	+1.6%	+20.5%	-8.4%	+31.0%	+6.2%	-8.0%	+17.3%	3.52	
e. NASDAQ OTC Composite (without dividends)	+3.5%	+31.4%	-11.2%	+19.9%	+18.7%	-3.2%	+27.2%	4.46	

In general when constructing these model portfolios, the HFD adheres to each newsletter's actual recommendations, resorting to the following procedures only when the newsletter is silent or vague about what to do. If a newsletter says nothing to the contrary, the portfolio the HFD constructs will be fully invested (with no margin) in those recommendations most highly recommended at a given time, with each position carrying equal weight. With each transaction, furthermore, the portfolio is rebalanced to keep this equal weighting. Cash positions earn the T-Bill rate, dividends are credited, and a 2% round-trip commission is deducted (0.05% for commodities). Transactions are made at the closing price on the day the newsletter is received (or at the average of the high and low in trading after hotline recommendations); initial public offerings are purchased at the average of their high and low aftermarket prices (therefore the gains and losses for new issues newsletters *exclude* first day premiums). A more complete description is available upon request.

The Timing Portfolios (those in italics following some letters' listings) were constructed exactly as were their corresponding portfolios, except that the stock portions were replaced by the NYSE Composite Index. For example, if a newsletter recommends that 60% be in stocks and 40% in T-Bills, its corresponding Timing Portfolio will have 60% "invested" in the NYSE Composite and 40% earning the T-Bill rate. You thus can see whether a newsletter's stock picks did better or worse than the market as a whole.

(r) December gains were calculated from a revised figure for their 11/29/85 values.

(1) The risk ratio is the standard deviation of each newsletter's monthly performance since 1/1/85; the larger the number, the greater the risk.

(2) The figure to the left in this column is the number of securities in the portfolio at the end of the month (cash equivalents don't count). The figure to the right signifies how clear and complete are each newsletter's recommendations, with 'A' the most clear and complete to 'D' the least. An 'A' rating signifies that the letter recommends a model portfolio; a 'B' rating signifies that the letter gives overall portfolio allocations but not advice on what to buy or sell to get in line with that advice; a 'C' rating is for letters with just lists of recommended stocks. A 'D' rating is reserved for those letters for which advice sometimes is missing from issue to issue and for which recommendations sometimes come in the form of categories of investments rather than specific securities.

*For the first five months of 1985, the HFD constructed portfolios for the *The Addison Report* to include only the "buys," while since then the two portfolios have included both "buys" and "holds." Had the HFD constructed the portfolios to include both for the entire year, the gains would be: Conservative, +24.4%; Speculative: +22.0%.

** *The International Harry Schultz Letter* includes recommendations from many different markets around the world; two portfolios are followed here, but this is *not* a complete list of all Schultz's recommended portfolios.

*** *The Option Advisor*, like several other newsletters, has changed the riskiness of its portfolios overtime. We have included the 1983 performance of a riskier portfolio with the 1984 and 1985 performances of a less risky portfolio because both were given the name "Conservative" by the newsletter.

**** *The Prudent Speculator's* actual portfolio utilizes margin. As an on-going portfolio, its margin level need only be kept above the maintenance level of 30%; a new subscriber, however, would be unable to use anything less than 50% margin. The HFD's calculations assume that each year the portfolio starts out with 50% margin.

TIMING SCOREBOARD

The following tables compare the records of various newsletters in timing the stock, gold and bond markets. Chosen for the comparison have been the intermediate trading systems maintained by these newsletters. Within each category, each system earns the same rate of return when in the market and the same rate of return when in cash. The tables were designed to aid, in particular, the mutual fund switcher. Thus, in the event a newsletter recommends actually going short the market on a sell signal, we calculate two portfolios for it—one which does go short and the other which goes into cash as would a mutual fund investor. In addition, the transactions reflected below all were made at the closing price on the day subscribers would have been able to act on the advice. No commissions were debited. In addition we show the number of switches generated by each trading system. (The figure is in the parenthesis following that period's gain or loss). A switch into or out of the market is counted as one switch, so a roundtrip in and out of the market counts as two switches.

STOCK MARKET TIMING—Records trading the NYSE Composite

NEWSLETTER (Portfolio to compare to)	Dec. Gain	1985 Gain	1984 Gain	1983 Gain	1982 Gain	1981 Gain	7/1 to 12/31/80 Gain
Dines Letter							
a. Short-Term Trading Signals: 100% short on sells	+4.3%(0)	+11.1%(4)	-9.3%(7)	+6.9%(2)	-6.3%(3)	+19.4%(1)	-7.3%(1)
b. Short-Term Trading Signals: 100% cash on sells	+4.3%(0)	+21.2%(4)	-1.3%(7)	+12.6%(2)	+13.2%(3)	+17.2%(1)	+11.3%(1)
Dow Theory Letters (Primary Trend Index: 100% cash on sells)	+4.3%(0)	+14.8%(5)	-2.1%(3)	+17.5%(0)	+12.3%(1)	+1.6%(1)	+19.2%(0)
Elliott Wave Theorist							
a. Traders	+4.3%(0)	+26.2%(0)	n/a	n/a	n/a	n/a	n/a
b. Investors	+4.3%(0)	+26.2%(0)	+9.8%(3)	+24.4%(1)	+10.2%(8)	-8.7%(0)	+15.7%(1)
Fund Exchange Report (Equity Trading Model)	+4.3%(0)	+24.3%(2)	+7.6%(3)	n/a	n/a	n/a	n/a
Garside Forecast (Long-Term Stock "Bell Ringer")							
a. 100% short on sells	-6.6%(0)	-26.2%(0)	n/a	n/a	n/a	n/a	n/a
b. 100% cash on sells	+0.6%(0)	+7.6%(0)	n/a	n/a	n/a	n/a	n/a
Granville Market Letter							
a. 100% short on sell signals	+0.2%(11)	-4.2%(8)	+14.2%(2)	-17.5%(0)	-14.0%(2)	+5.0%(1)	+19.2%(0)
b. 100% cash on sell signals	+0.6%(0)	+11.7%(4)	+18.6%(2)	+8.7%(0)	+10.9%(0)	+11.8%(1)	+19.2%(0)
Indicator Digest (Trading Guide: All cash on sells and neutral readings)	+4.0%(1)	+20.4%(10)	-2.4%(10)	+8.3%(13)	+24.7%(6)	n/a	n/a
Investor's Intelligence (Mutual Fund Switching Advice)	+0.6%(½)	+7.7%(½)	n/a	n/a	n/a	n/a	n/a
Investech Market Letter (Mutual Fund Switching Advice)	+0.9%(0.2)	+16.0%(1.2)	n/a	n/a	n/a	n/a	n/a
Lynn Elgert Report (Advice For Mutual Fund Investors)	+4.3%(0)	+25.7%(2)	n/a	n/a	n/a	n/a	n/a
Market Logic (Mutual Fund Switching Advice)	+4.3%(0)	+26.2(0)	+1.3%(0)	+17.5%(0)	+17.9%(4)	+2.2%(¼)	+12.5%(0)
Mutual Fund Strategist							
a. Compuvest Timing Model	+4.3%(0)	+28.1%(2)	n/a	n/a	n/a	n/a	n/a
b. Cycle/Reversal Discriminator	+4.3%(0)	+28.6%(8)	n/a	n/a	n/a	n/a	n/a
Nicholson Report (Market Mood Indicator; 100% cash on sells)	+4.3%(1)	+14.3%(15)	-3.2%(26)	-4.0%(24)	n/a	n/a	n/a
Professional Tape Reader (Group Intensity: 100% Cash on Sells)	+2.1%(0)	+16.7%(2.3)	+1.3%(4½)	+16.3%(4½)	+9.5%(7½)	-2.7%(8)	+12.9%(1)

	1	2	3	4	5	6	7
a. Supply/Demand Formula Re: DJIA (100% short on sells)	+4.3%(0)	+11.2%(1)	+2.5%(3)	+17.5%(2)	-24.5%(2)	+20.0%(3)	+-3.2%(2)
b. Supply/Demand Formula Re: DJIA (100% cash on sells)	+4.3%(0)	+20.6%(1)	+11.4%(3)	+25.7%(2)	+1.2%(2)	+13.3%(3)	+14.2%(2)
c. Supply/Demand Formula Re: S&P 500 (100% Short on sells)	+4.3%(0)	+8.2%(2)	n/a	n/a	n/a	n/a	n/a
d. Supply/Demand Formula Re: S&P 500 (100% Cash on sells)	+4.3%(0)	+19.7%(1)	n/a	n/a	n/a	n/a	n/a
Stockmarket Cycles (Mutual Fund Switching Advice)	+4.3%(0)	+27.1%(4)	n/a	n/a	n/a	n/a	n/a
Switch Fund Advisory (Inactive Investors Switch Signals; no shorting)	+4.3%(0)	+26.2%(0)	+1.3%(0)	+17.5%(0)	+32.4%(1)	+14.7%(1)	+19.2%(0)
Systems & Forecasts							
a. Time Trend: No Shorting	+4.3%(0)	+22.5%(10)	+8.6%(15)	+18.7%(7)	n/a	n/a	n/a
b. Mutual Fund Trading Advice	+3.5%(0.2)	+20.1%(10.15)	n/a	n/a	n/a	n/a	n/a
Telephone Switch Newsletter (Equity/Cash Switching Advice)	+4.3%(0)	+23.6%(1)	+4.7%(3)	+17.5%(0)	+30.3%(1)	+0.7%(1)	+19.2%(0)
Value Line Investment Survey (Market timing advice: no shorting)	+4.3%(0)	+26.2%(0)	+1.3(0)%	+10.7%(1)	+10.9%(0)	+6.7%(1)	+19.2%(0)
Weber's Fund Advisor (No Shorting)	+4.3%(0)	+26.2%(0)	n/a	n/a	n/a	n/a	n/a
Zweig Forecast--Short Term Trading Index	+4.3%(0)	+24.6%(14)	n/a	n/a	n/a	n/a	n/a
NYSE Composite	+4.3%	+26.2%	+1.3%	+17.5%	+14.0%	-8.7%	+19.2%

GOLD MARKET TIMING—Records Trading Gold's London P.M. Fixing Price

	1	2	3	4	5	6	7
Elliott Wave Theorist							
a. Traders (Shorting allowed)	-0.5%(0)	-11.1%(7)	n/a	n/a	n/a	n/a	n/a
b. Investors (No shorting)	+0.6%(0)	+7.6%(0)	n/a	n/a	n/a	n/a	n/a
Fund Exchange Report (Gold Switching Model) (No shorting)	+0.6%(0)	-3.6%(6)	-1.3%(6)	n/a	n/a	n/a	n/a
Garside Forecast (Gold Bell Ringer)							
a. 100% short on sells	+0.5%(0)r	+4.1%(1)	n/a	n/a	n/a	n/a	n/a
b. 100% cash on sells	+0.5%(0)r	+8.0%(1)	n/a	n/a	n/a	n/a	n/a
Market Logic (Gold Model)(No shorting)	+0.3%(1)	+11.6%(3)	-4.0%(3)	n/a	n/a	n/a	n/a
Telephone Switch Newsletter (Gold/Cash Switch Advice)	+0.6%(0)	+2.0%(2)	n/a	n/a	n/a	n/a	n/a
Zweig Forecast (Gold Model)(No shorting)	+0.6%(0)	+3.3%(4)	n/a	n/a	n/a	n/a	n/a
Gold Bullion	+0.5%	+6.1%	-19.2%	+17.5%	+14.0%	n/a	n/a

BOND TIMING RECORDS—Records Trading the Dow Jones 20 Bond Average

	1	2	3	4	5	6	7
Elliott Wave Theorist							
a. Traders	+2.7%(0)	+1.4%(4.5)	n/a	n/a	n/a	n/a	n/a
b. Investors	+2.7%(0)	+10.8%(1½)	n/a	n/a	n/a	n/a	n/a
Fund Exchange Report (Bond Switch Advice; All Cash on Sells)	+2.7%(0)	+16.3%(6)	+11.7%(5)	n/a	n/a	n/a	n/a
Garside Forecast (Bond Bell Ringer)							
a. 100% short on sells	-3.4%(0)	-15.6%(0)	n/a	n/a	n/a	n/a	n/a
b. 100% cash on sells	+0.6%(0)	+7.6%(0)	n/a	n/a	n/a	n/a	n/a
Lynn Elgert Report (Monetary Model/Bond Switching Advice)	+0.6%(¼)	+8.5%(2¾)	n/a	n/a	n/a	n/a	n/a
Systems & Forecasts (Monetary Model)	+2.7%(0)	+15.1%(8)	n/a	n/a	n/a	n/a	n/a
Dow Jones 20 Bond Average	+2.7%	+15.6%	+4.3%	n/a	n/a	n/a	n/a

had by January 1985 lost nearly half the money of the unfortunate clients who followed his Aggressive Stock Traders' Portfolio. But writers like Dorfman also cruelly drew attention to the fact that figures like the highly promoted (particularly by himself) Howard Ruff had failed to match the Dow Jones Industrial Average—a return that could have been obtained by blind buying of the thirty big, bland, boring stocks that make it up. *In fact, Ruff and most of the advisors hadn't even matched the return on treasury bills*—the professional's equivalent of the savings account. Interest payments on those treasury bills, unlike the return on stocks, would have been absolutely guaranteed by the U.S. government. And during this period inflation was too low to nullify their value. This stellar performance by treasury bills (a.k.a. cash) is a measure of the power of disinflation and a highly significant feature on the investment scene in the early 1980s.

Mark Hulbert thinks it's all right to beat up on advisors—but only up to a point. After all, he says, it's not surprising to find that the average advisor has average results. His comments can perhaps be summarized as Hulbert's First Law.

Hulbert's First Law
IT IS *E-X-T-R-E-M-E-L-Y* HARD TO BEAT THE MARKET OVER TIME

The corollary of Hulbert's First Law is: *If anyone says he consistently makes spectacular profits, don't believe him.*

The SEC has traditionally spent a lot of time prowling around looking for attempts to mislead innocent investors with extravagant claims, to the point where advisors find it difficult to make any intelligible assertions about their records at all. But a few colorful specimens still slip through. Hulbert keeps a file of the more striking direct-mail solicitations, including a letter asserting that it earned "consistent profits of 922 percent during the last few years," and another kindly offering to show how to make 4,000 percent annual profits "regularly." While noting scrupulously that he hasn't tracked the letters making these particular claims, Hulbert doubts them. Although advisors may show dramatic gains in individual years, Hulbert's work shows that over a prolonged period average annual increments of even 20 percent to 30 percent are quite exceptionally rare.

Perhaps the most entertaining recent story about direct-mail claims involves the *Stock Market Performance Digest*, which derives its stock selections by scanning the hundreds of recommendations made by other investment letters. "Imagine how much *more* money you'd have right now if you had invested in the following ten stocks," publisher Joel S. Nadel chided prospective subscribers in a twelve-page mailing late in 1984, referring to a list showing stocks appreciating from 184 percent to 1,152 percent in the previous seven months. "Obviously, you'd now be *quite wealthy* if you'd have been holding even a small portfolio of stocks like these . . ." This was far from obvious to one of *Barron's* otherwise imaginative readers, who wrote in to point out that all of Nadel's ten "star-performing stocks" had lost value in the seven-month period and one of the companies had actually been in bankruptcy proceedings when the year began. A $10,000 portfolio equally apportioned among them in January would have been down to $3,067.17 by July, not counting commissions and dividends.

Stock Market Performance Digest's explanation reveals at the very least something about marketing methods and the larger newsletter publishers (Nadel's Newsletter Management Corporation puts out more than forty). Lawrence J. Tell of *Barron's* was told that an outside marketing organization, in preparing the mailing, had simply picked out stocks with large differences between their 1984 lows and highs and calculated the difference as "profit." Apparently the outside marketing organization did not realize that such differences were desirable only if the low came *before* the high. The editor of *Stock Market Performance Digest* had not actually seen the promotion before 425,000 copies were mailed out, and no one else spotted the error. Moreover, despite citing the stocks in its mailing, the *Digest* had not after all recommended them during the year. They seem to have been offered as a sort of helpful example.

Mark Hulbert is also careful to point out that there are far more things in an investment letter than are measured in his paper portfolios. Many letters, even apart from those that explicitly focus on general market trends and eschew specific stocks, are clearly read for their overall philosophizing and world view, such as *Howard Ruff's Financial Success Report*, which for some reason the SEC never compelled to register as an investment advisor. Some letters on Hulbert's list make many selections for which he has difficulty getting compatible data,

most notably the *International Harry Schultz Letter*, which features a cast of thousands of recommendations, leaving virtually
no investment vehicle unmounted anywhere in the world.
Other letters aim to provide thorough coverage in narrow areas,
like Michael Murphy's *California Technology Stock Letter*, Michael
Gianturco's *High Technology Investments* and *Market Logic*'s sister
publication *New Issues*. This renders them highly vulnerable if
the market decides to T-bone their areas as it did in 1984, but it
will continue to interest people who are interested in that sort
of thing.

Very few letters have their recommendations adopted right
across the board. People pick and choose. They have to. Even a
subscriber absolutely determined that the equity portion of his
portfolio should follow, for example, Bob Gross's recommendations in *The Professional Investor* is still faced with a choice of up
to a hundred and fifty stocks. Gross's is one of several letters
offering more than one model portfolio, leaving subscribers to
decide how to allocate between them. Competing advisors who
virtuously restrict themselves to one set of selections complain
that this is like leaving bear traps in the path of every conceivable market move: something is bound to be caught. Obviously,
time would tend to expose such a dependence on luck, but
Hulbert attempts to placate both sides by also including an
average performance for the multiportfolio letters.

And people interpret. Many readers of Joe Granville regularly adjust for his bearish predilection, and subscribers debate
the true meaning of Richard Russell's *Dow Theory Letter* like
classical Greeks arguing outside the temple at Delphi after the
oracle has spoken. Ian McAvity of *Deliberations* is irresistably
drawn to predict precise market turns, the triple somersault of
the advisory business. But his subscribers don't seem to mind,
because while he's climbing back up to his trapeze they can
follow the less daring course of listening to his running commentary and inspecting his beautiful charts (McAvity "draws
the best charts and comes to the damnedest conclusions"—H.
Schultz) to see if the various market trends are still intact. This
technique of trend following often means that a market move
may be half over before you've realized that the previous trend
has reversed and a new one is underway—but then, quite regularly McAvity calls a perfect turn for you. Much less aggressive
but even more like a chart service is Martin Pring's *Pring Market*

Review, which can track up to two hundred separate United States and international items in some forty pages, often with moving averages appended, all tastefully trimmed in blue and explained in careful prose. Pring's book *Technical Analysis Explained* (2nd edition, 1984) has become the bible for the latest generation of technicians.

Even the paper portfolio method reveals that every dog has his day. Howard Ruff was one of the top performers of 1982, catching a silver rally and soaring 43.8 percent in a year when the Dow plus reinvested dividends gained 27.3 percent.

The limitations of paper portfolios are well illustrated by the sad case of Harry Browne. His *Harry Browne's Special Reports* is a particularly clear and well-argued letter. Although Browne was one of the earliest of the hard-money advisors, he was remarkably swift to spot that inflation was stalling, bailed out of precious metals right at the high in January 1980, and devoted much space to perceptive pondering of the new era. It was a Browne study that could hardly have failed to be instructive to its readers in a time of profound investor uncertainty. During much of this period, Browne even took the radical step of favoring treasury bills, which, as it turned out, yielded one of the highest returns around. Unfortunately, Browne's translation of his thoughts into portfolio strategy was ruined by a number of unsuccessful forays into silver and foreign currency, quite possibly because his elbow was being jogged by bored subscribers. From June 1980 to June 1985, his "variable" portfolio was up only 34.6 percent, as opposed to a pure treasury bill portfolio's gain of 66.8 percent and the dividend-reinvested Dow's 100.8 percent. (Browne also offers a "permanent" portfolio, which Hulbert finds too general to follow.) It's probable that Browne's performance, like that of Robert Kinsman's equally low-risk *Kinsman's Low-Risk Advisory*, would have looked rather better after taxes, since he could deduct his losses, and interest from a treasury bill portfolio would be taxed at up to 50 percent.

This probably did less damage to Browne's circulation because of his sheer literary skill. In January 1984, for example, his subscribers found themselves reading witty parodies of six other letters, with prizes for guessing which was which. The investment industry, after all, is a branch of show business. Much the same could be said for Harry Schultz, a gold bug whose willingness to become a dollar bull and a bond booster when there was money to be made is not reflected in his U.S. stock portfolio's results.

Nevertheless, Hulbert still sticks to his paper portfolios. They offer at least some basis for comparison. As a loyal son of Oxford positivism, Hulbert freely concedes that all the above ineffable qualities of investment letters may well exist—but how, he asks, if they can't be measured, can they be discussed meaningfully? *"Whereof we cannot speak,"* he says with a smile, quoting Wittgenstein's Proposition 7, the last sentence of his *Tractatus logico-philosophicus, "thereof we must remain silent."*

It is entirely natural for the investment letter writers to resent Hulbert. They are generally remarkable in terms of intellect, if not necessarily of character, and their highly developed egos are right out there on the front line, doing their bit in the human race's long battle against metaphysical despair at the realization that nothing, not even tomorrow's sunrise, can really be known with certainty. They are far from being totally cynical. When their predictions are wrong, they grieve bitterly, and a feeling that Hulbert does not have to share their pain causes them to regard him, as a normally sensible member of their profession once hissed, as a "parasite."

But in fact Hulbert's merciless measuring machine does seem to be quietly grinding out glad tidings of great joy for the entire investment business. This development has gone generally unnoticed amid the public demonstrations of shock, horror and heated denial over Hulbert's First Law—that it's *extremely* hard to beat the market over time. It can be expressed as Hulbert's Second Law.

Hulbert's Second Law
IT MAY BE HARD. BUT IT CAN BE DONE

And the corollary is: *We know who does it.*

In order to appreciate the radical implications of Hulbert's Second Law, it is necessary to review the Efficient Market Hypothesis, a.k.a. the Random Walk, which was circumnavigated cautiously in chapter 1. (Special incentive! The names of the market-beating letters will be listed at the end of the chapter! Or!!, as L. T. Patterson would say.)

Academe has cooked up a choice of three varieties of EMH. As presented by Yale's Professor Burton G. Malkiel in his lucid and influential *A Random Walk Down Wall Street*, the "narrow" or "weak" form of the Efficient Market Hypothesis runs as follows:

> The history of stock price movements contains no useful information that will enable an investor consistently to outperform a buy-and-hold strategy [assuming adequate diversification] in managing a portfolio.

This is obviously the specter of death itself for the technical analysts, whose entire profession consists of perusing the history of stock price movements. Technicians have never been short of enemies on Wall Street. Even the supremely tolerant Fred *(Where Are the Customers' Yachts?)* Schwed treated them with gentle derision back in 1940. But the fundamentalists cannot be complacent, because next on the menu is the "semistrong" form of EMH:

> No publicly announced news event can be exploited by investors to obtain above-average returns.

In other words, there is no point in analyzing financial statements and estimating earnings because the market has already discounted the future in its current price. There are no returns to investment research, fundamental or technical, and any portfolio managed with the help of research will not perform better than the averages. And since stock prices tend to stagger randomly around what is actually a pretty fair valuation by the market, any stock selected at random—even by the proverbial dart thrown at the *Wall Street Journal*'s quotation pages—will do at least as well as one unearthed by any amount of laborious digging.

And then there is the "strong" form of EMH:

> Not only all the news that is public but also all information that it is possible to know about a company has already been reflected in the price of the stock.

Obviously, this poisonous concoction leaves everybody in the investment business lying on the floor kicking their feet in the air. Even a corporate insider who learned that some major contract had been canceled would find, according to the "strong" form of EMH, that the market had already anticipated any attempts to unload his stock. Academics are accustomed to forcing EMH down throats gagging at its counterintuitive taste. But accepting the strong form literally seems to be more than they themselves really want to swallow.

There can be no question that the Efficient Market Hypothesis embodies a great truth. The price system is an amazing phenomenon, able to reconcile an infinity of information. And today it does so faster than ever before. The returns to research, or at least to professional expertise, were quite obvious in 1898 when Roger Babson asked his employer, the Boston brokerage house E. H. Gay & Company, why he was required to sell bonds to family friends in Gloucester, Massachusetts, at 98 1/4 when the firm was buying them in New York at 80. He was invited to the New York office (which, it is no doubt irrelevant to note, was run by George D. Baker, later the great benefactor of Harvard Business School) and fired. Babson immediately started his own bond business, undercutting his former employer among its New England clientele. Over time, however, and with improved communications, these kinds of flagrant inefficiencies in the marketplace have all but vanished.

By the 1970s, after Wall Street professionals had been demoralized by the excesses of the go-go years and the collapse of the two-tier market, the finance professors who espoused the Efficient Market Hypothesis had become completely confident of their position—just as confident as the economics professors who in the 1960s had urged the Keynesian "New Economics" on the Kennedy and Johnson Administrations. Both theories were deeply scientistic, and both coincidentally had the effect of making practicing businessmen look foolish, or at least deluded, and professors look smart. This element of cultural conflict between Wall Street and academe should not be overlooked. In a telling comic vignette in his modern stock-market classic *Supermoney*, 'Adam Smith' reports that when he asked the instructor of an EMH seminar what he thought of the market, "he looked at me like I was crazy." After the question was repeated, he replied "I have all my money in a savings account." The conflict might even be detected in Professor Malkiel's own classes, although Malkiel himself has extensive Wall Street connections. Dan Seligman of *Fortune* recently reported a Malkiel lecture in which he

> . . . had the students in stitches describing a study whose principal finding was an utter lack of correlation between mutual fund rankings from one year to the next. In this context he mentioned the Mates Investment Fund, which was ranked No. 1 among mutual funds in 1968 but never got above No. 300 in subsequent years. Malkiel's throwaway line was that Fred Mates eventually got out of the mutual fund business and took to running a singles bar in New York called, appropriately, Mates. Evidently assuming this was a made-up detail, the Yalies groaned and hissed at the line; however, it happens to be true.

So why do Wall Street's stock pickers stay in business? Easy, say Efficient Market Hypothesis proponents: luck. As Malkiel puts it:

> Let's engage in a coin-tossing contest. Those who can consistently flip heads will be declared the winners. The contest begins and 1,000 contestants flip coins. Just as would be expected by chance, 500 of them flip heads and these winners are allowed to advance to the second stage of the contest and flip again. As might be expected, 250 flip heads. Operating under the laws of chance, there will be 125 winners in the third round, 63 in the fourth, 31 in the fifth, 16 in the sixth, and 8 in the seventh.
>
> By this time, crowds start to gather to watch the surprising ability of these expert coin-tossers. The winners are overwhelmed with adulation. They are celebrated as geniuses in the art of coin-tossing—their biographies are written and people urgently seek their advice. After all, there were 1,000 contestants and only 8 could consistently flip heads. The game continues and there are even those who flip heads nine and ten times in a row. The point of this analogy is not to indicate that investment fund managers can or should make their decisions by flipping coins, but that the laws of chance do operate and they can explain some amazing success stories.

A powerful parable. But heads can be turned (!) amid all this coin flipping. The probability of tossing heads in any one throw is 0.5—it must come down heads or tails—and the probability of ten heads in a row is $(0.5)^{10}$ or about 2,000 to 1, which is why Malkiel began with a thousand contestants and gets vague at the ninth and tenth rounds. However, from a statistical point of view, one thousand coin flippers are not a big enough set to produce with absolute certainty one series of ten or even nine heads. And in the stock market, there are more than two possible outcomes. At the very least, the stock (1) could go up, (2) go down, or (3) do nothing. The odds of tossing ten heads in a row with a three-sided penny are sharply worse: $(0.33)^{10}$ or 200,000 to 1. But the range of possible outcomes in the stock market is actually much greater. The investment could go up infinitely or down to zero (or turn into an infinite loss, if it happens to be a short sale).

Moreover, EMH proponents have a suspicious tendency to vagueness when it comes to specifying to what exactly their coin flip is analogous. Is it the odds of a successful stock pick, as they sometimes assert, or the chance that a whole portfolio will appreciate? If the odds of the former are 0.5, the odds of the latter, assuming equal allocation between the stocks, must be 0.5 *(raised to the power of however many stocks are in the portfolio)*. This makes an appreciating portfolio much more of a feat. Similarly, it makes a vast difference to the probability calculation whether the coin flip represents price action over a day or various combinations of days, such as a year or five years. All have been used by EMH proponents. They unite only in their conclusion that Wall Streeters deserve no respect.

The point here is that the universe of investment advisors is not infinitely large—certainly nothing like big enough to accommodate the odds implied by the coin-flip analogy. Mark Hulbert follows nearly one hundred investment letters. Several appear to have beaten the market over a prolonged period. Although Hulbert is the first to say that a few years may not be long enough to prove anything absolutely, this is more than can be shrugged off easily as just dumb luck.

Particularly because statisticians have pretty stiff standards of proof. Human beings habitually rely on forecasts, such as medical diagnoses and weather predictions, that might well fail to look good against the coin-flip test.

. . .

By the 1980s there were clear signs that the finance professors' castle was crumbling, exactly as their economist colleagues' Camelot fell in the 1970s after enjoying one of those brief shining moments of glory. "Anomalies" were being discovered, where returns seemed clearly superior to those of the overall market. Some of these anomalies are actually money managers with long records of beating the market: Warren Buffett of the Buffett Partnership, which ran from 1956 to 1969, now chairman of Berkshire Hathaway, Inc.; Charles Munger of Wheeler Munger & Company, which ran from 1962 to 75; Walter Schloss of Walter J. Schloss & Associates; William Ruane of the Sequoia Fund; John Templeton of Templeton Growth Fund. And one widely recognized anomaly is an investment advisory: Arnold J. Bernhard's *Value Line Investment Survey*.

Value Line is virtually a reference service, providing a fact-packed statistics-stuffed page on every one of 1,700 public companies, plus quantities of analysis and advice. But since 1965 it has also rated its stocks into five categories in order of safety and timeliness. Not only did these stocks obediently perform in the order laid down by *Value Line*, both cumulatively and in all but a few of the succeeding twenty years, but the Group I stocks substantially outperformed the overall market. This phenomenon naturally attracted scholarly attention, including at least seven serious academic papers. But *Value Line*'s results have not been explained away, and one prominent EMH theorist, former Massachussetts Institute of Technology professor Fischer Black, conceded as early as 1971 that it represented an exception to the rule. "I continue to be amazed," said Black in 1985, by which time he himself had entered Wall Street as a vice president of Goldman, Sachs. He still believes in the Random Walk, he says, but now thinks that institutional investors should merely fire all their analysts but one—and then buy him a subscription to *Value Line*.

Other anomalies just seemed to crop up all on their own. Studying them has become a major occupation for the rising generation of academics now snapping at the heels of the original Random Walkers. Their checklist includes:

- *The Small Firm Effect*, the tendency of shares of low-capitalized firms, ones with relatively small dollar amounts of stock outstanding, to outperform shares of the higher-capitalized firms.

Many of these small companies may not have enough stock to enable an institutional investor to take a position. But individual investors can.

* *The Low Price-Earnings Multiple Effect*, the tendency of the stocks of firms whose share price is low relative to their earnings to outperform stocks of firms whose P/E Multiple (the number you get when you divide the price by the earnings) is high.

* *The "January" Effect*, the tendency of stocks to perform well in January compared to the rest of the year. Sometimes thought to be a market rebound from tax-loss selling in December, but also present in European countries without any comparable tax law.

* *The Weekend Effect*, the tendency of stocks to perform badly on Monday, regardless of prevailing conditions. These "calendar effects" were particularly irritating for EMH proponents, since they had spent a lot of time stomping on Wall Street's innumerable superstitions about seasonal rallies and demonstrating that any such predictable move would be anticipated away.

* *The Insider Effect*, the tendency of a stock's price to rise after purchases have been reported to the SEC by the company's officers and other insiders.

* *Earnings Surprise Effect*, the tendency of stocks to rise if a consensus of analysts upgrades or alters their earnings estimates substantially.

* *The Net Current Asset Value Effect.* This confirms a classical rule of fundamental analysis: that a stock should be bought when its share price is two-thirds or less of its net asset value per share —calculated by taking its current assets, subtracting its liabilities and preferred stock, and dividing by the number of shares outstanding. Many of these stocks are already small-firm, low P/E situations. But a portfolio of low P/E small firms selected at random seems to be outperformed by one using the Net Current Asset Values rule, suggesting that the latter is a significant independent factor.

* *The Closed-End Fund Discount Effect.* Closed-End Mutual Funds —those with a fixed number of shares—generally trade at a lower price than the underlying value of the shares they own. Nobody really knows why, but academics assumed under the Efficient Market Hypothesis that the market knew what it was doing. Apparently it didn't, however, because a policy of buy-

ing deeply discounted closed-end funds would have yielded above-average results ever since World War II.

Like plants growing in a wall, several of the investment letters on Hulbert's list turn out to have their roots in one or other of these anomalies, including some that appear to have achieved consistently superior performance.

The founding fathers of EMH are not unaware of these "anomalies," and from time to time several others besides Fischer have indicated revisionist thoughts. Contemplation of the spectacle of closed-end fund discounts caused Burton Malkiel to restrain his faith in EMH, and indeed he recommended the purchase of closed-end funds in the first edition of *A Random Walk Down Wall Street* in 1973, after which they did duly appreciate. At the end of the 1970s, Professor Franco Modigliani actually said straight out that the market was just plain undervaluing corporate America's assets, a point of view that appears to have been vindicated by its gains in the 1980s.

Essentially, however, the academic response to anomalies has been to complicate the issue by introducing the concept of risk. The anomalous superior returns, it was said, arose because people were simply taking more risks. Adjusted for risk, the returns would be equal. (Except of course for profits made by exploiting the "calendar effect" anomalies, since riskiness is the same on Tuesday as Monday—another reason why their appearance caused such dismay.)

For the purposes of calculation, "risk" was defined as volatility—the extent to which a stock tended to fluctuate from year to year. This had the great advantage of being easily measured. A portfolio consisting entirely of treasury bills, which obviously do not fluctuate in price, was said to be "riskless." (Unless there's inflation, of course. But let's forget about inflation.) By subtracting the return on the treasury bill portfolio from the return on an actual portfolio, a "risk-adjusted" return was obtained. Unfortunately, however, this still did not wash out the anomalies mentioned above. So the more determined academics have begun to argue that "risk" is being "misspecified."

Mark Hulbert, needless to say, is intrigued by the concept of "risk." He has calculated the "risk rating" of the investment letters he follows by recording the fluctuations in each one's monthly performance and finding its "standard deviation"—the statistical procedure for measuring variance. This does serve the useful purpose of indicating that in 1984, for example, the investments favored by the top-performing *Option Advisor* were several orders of magnitude more volatile than those of its competitors—twenty or thirty times in the case of another 1984 high-performer, *The International Harry Schultz Letter*. Hulbert has a horrible feeling that many of his subscribers haven't really understood this lethal point. (For more on the question of risk, see Appendix I.)

But the investment business already knows that options are volatile. The concept of "risk" impresses it even less than the Efficient Market Hypothesis. Partly this is because it is even more counterintuitive than EMH. Investors worry about losing money, not about an investment's volatility. They are quite happy if a stock moves upward in irregular leaps, although that irregularity would boost its "risk" in the academic sense. Nor are investors convinced that *Value Line*'s Group 1 stocks' 6,627 percent gain from 1965 through 1983 should be adjusted downward for an alleged "risk" that somehow failed to make its presence felt throughout that period. They might also be influenced, if they knew, by the news that the attempt to revolutionize money management in line with the Efficient Market Hypothesis (the celebrated "Modern Portfolio Theory," which sought to maximize reward and minimize risk according to the "Capital-Asset Pricing Model," utilizing the individual volatility, or "beta," of each stock) has run into serious problems in principle and in practice. They might even conclude, if it occurred to them, that any scientific hypothesis that can only be defended by intensifying its complexity is a classic candidate for a throat-slashing by Occam's razor—the rule, first propounded by a medieval scholar, that entities should not be multiplied needlessly and that simple explanations are best.

The deadly struggle between academics and Wall Street professionals continues, tempered only by the fact that both sides totally ignore one another. It would be a work of charity to leave it on a harmonizing note. From 1925 to 1981 the average annual rate of return compounded annually on common stocks was 9.1 percent. This is a phenomenal achievement. It means that $1 invested in common stocks in 1925 would have grown to $133.62 by the end of 1981. It is precisely because of the efforts of the thousands of men and women engaged in the financial markets that a strategy of buy-and-hold is such formidable competition to active portfolio management, and capital continues to be allocated throughout the vast American economy in such a way that it grows rather than grinds to an arteriosclerotic halt.

After inflation, of course, that $133.62 would be only $25.13. Almost all the intervening inflation has occurred since 1970. Since that time, returns to common stocks have been so poor as to knock their inflation-adjusted annual return over the past fifty-six years down to some 5.9 percent. Why common stocks did not adjust to inflation to compensate for their greater risk is a matter of controversy among academics. Modigliani thought they should have. And the idea that common stocks represent the last undervalued asset, and have not gone through an inflation-era price jump like real estate or commodities, continues to beguile the investment letter community.

And now, as promised (and remembering that many investment letters have escaped Hulbert's net), here are those that according to his figures have cumulatively outperformed the market:

FIVE-YEAR PERFORMANCE*

(6/30/80–6/28/85)

NEWSLETTER	GAIN/ LOSS	NEWSLETTER	GAIN/ LOSS
Prudent Speculator	+272.9%	Outlook—Speculative Stocks	+132.4%
Dines Letter (Growth Portfolio)	+241.3%	Value Line OTC Spec. Sit Svc.	+131.2%
Value Line Group 1**	+214.3%	Prof. Investor—OTC Scan	+130.3%
Growth Stock Outlook	+206.5%	The Chartist	+127.8%
Green's Commod Mkt Comments	+177.6%	Market Logic—Average of 2 Portf.	+119.2%
Prof. Investor—Amex Scan	+172.2%	S & P 500 (Total Return)	+114.6%
Zweig Forecast	+146.2%	Dines Letter (Speculative Port.)	+113.8%
Outlook—Income Stocks	+142.6%		
Market Logic—Master Portfolio	+139.3%	Wilshire Value Weighted (+ Div)	+112.3%

FIVE-YEAR PERFORMANCE* *(Continued)*

(6/30/80–6/28/85)

NEWSLETTER	GAIN/ LOSS	NEWSLETTER	GAIN/ LOSS
Dow T. Forecasts—Income Stocks	+112.0%	T-Bill Only Portfolio	+66.8%
Outlook—Average of 4 Portfolios	+108.2%	Outlook—Foundation Stocks	+61.5%
Dines Letter (Trading Portfolio)	+105.3%	United Business—Income Stocks	+60.0%
Dow Forecasts— Investment Stocks	+104.9%	Prof. Investor—NYSE Scan	+47.2%
Telephone Switch— Equities	+101.8%	Prof. Investor—Inv. Grade	+35.5%
DJIA (Total Return)	+100.8%	Harry Browne's Special Reports	+34.6%
Market Logic—Option Portfolio	+96.7%	United Business Service— Average of 3	+34.6%
Dow Theory Forecasts— Average of 4	+94.8%	United Business Service— Cyclical Stocks	+24.6%
Switch Fund Advisory Model Portfolio**	+92.6%	Int'l Harry Schultz L.— U.S. Stocks	+23.7%
Professional Investor— Average of 4	+92.4%	Dow Theory Letters	+20.4%
Outlook—Growth Stocks	+90.5%	United Business Service— Growth Stocks	+16.0%
Dow T. Forecasts— Growth Stocks	+82.5%	Professional Tape Reader	+12.9%
Dow T. Forecasts— Speculative Stocks	+70.1%	Heim Investment Letter	+11.9%
Kinsman's Low-Risk Advisory	+67.8%	H. Ruff's Finc'l Success Rprt	−0.3%
Dines Letter—Average of 6 Portf.	+67.3%	Dines Letter (Moderate Risk Port.)	−12.5%
		Holt Investment Advisory	−28.8%
		Granville Market Letter	−45.3%

*As calculated by *Hulbert Financial Digest*
**These figures are based in part on data supplied by the newsletters themselves (making adjustments for commissions and dividends), data which Hulbert has no reason to believe is false.

CHAPTER FIVE

The Winners:
Fundamentalists

The habit of relating what is paid to what is being offered is an invaluable trait in investment. In an article in a women's magazine many years ago we advised the readers to buy their stocks as they bought their groceries, not as they bought their perfume . . . In the old legend the wise men finally boiled down the history of mortal affairs into the single phrase "This too will pass" [hoc etiam transibit]. Confronted with a like challenge to distill the secret of sound investment into three words, we venture the motto: MARGIN OF SAFETY.

—BENJAMIN GRAHAM, *The Intelligent Investor*

We are number-crunchers.

—CHARLES ALLMON, *Growth Stock Outlook*

Warren E. Buffett, chairman of Berkshire Hathaway and a leading anomaly in the Efficient Market Hypothesis, recently presented his own twist on the Great Coin-Tossing Controversy. Okay, he said in effect, it's true that if 225 million Americans called the flip of a coin twenty times, the 215 or so who by the end had guessed right each time might be quite indignant to be told by some academic that 225 million coin-flipping orangutans would have achieved the same result. *But what if forty of the orangutans came from a particular zoo in Omaha, Nebraska?* (Buffett lives in Omaha, Nebraska, although not of course in a zoo.) A wholly disproportionate number of the investment business's successful coin flippers, he argued, trace their origins to "a very small intellectual village that could be called Graham-and-Doddsville." And this must mean something. The phenomenon was particularly significant, he added, since these successful flippers—they included himself; Walter J. Schloss Associates' Walter J. Schloss; Tweedy, Browne, Inc.'s Tom Knapp; and Sequoia Fund's Bill Ruane—all operated quite independently, despite their similar investment philosophies, and had very little overlap between their portfolios.

The investment philosophy in question is that of the late Benjamin Graham, a classics scholar and litterateur who was also co-author with Professor David L. Dodd of the standard text, *Security Analysis* (1934), author of *The Intelligent Investor* (1949), for nearly thirty years a teacher at Columbia University's Graduate School of Business and a principal in the Graham-Newman Corporation investment management firm, where Buffett and his fellow anomalies served their apprenticeships. 'Adam Smith' in his book *The Money Game* described Graham as "the dean of all security analysts." This was a perceptive observation, particularly given the times. Graham had been badly burned in the Great Crash, and as a result his methods were so conservative that by 1967, when *The Money Game* appeared, they were widely regarded as antiquated, not just by the gunslinging money managers but even more so by the Efficient Market Hypothesis tribe of academics slithering through the rocks toward them. Indeed, Graham-style financial analysis, pejoratively known as "descriptive finance," had been almost completely evicted from the curricula of many business schools and replaced by "quantitative finance"—Beta, Capital Asset Pricing Models, risk-adjusted return and so on.

Graham himself was highly numerate. But he practically never went beyond simple if strenuous arithmetic. He assessed the financial health, strength and earning power of a corporation by applying a variety of standardized calipers to its publicly available financial statements—"ratio analysis." Indeed, in *The Intelligent Investor* he had specifically warned against the very higher mathematics in which the "new investment technology" gloried:

In forty-four years of Wall Street experience and study I have never seen dependable calculations made about common-stock values that went beyond simple arithmetic, or the most elementary algebra. Whenever calculus is brought in, or higher algebra, you could take it as a warning that the operator was trying to substitute theory for experience . . .

In 1972, after the gunslingers had been scalped and the academics appeared triumphant, 'Smith' 's second book, *Supermoney*, went into some detail about the survival of Graham's methods in remote fastnesses like Buffett's Omaha. And throughout this period, similar techniques also formed the basis of the "credit schools," through which commercial banks were putting their newly graduated MBA recruits in the hope of teaching them something useful.

Graham looked for value—hard. Most fundamental analysts focus on corporate earnings, reasoning that changes in earnings will swamp any fluctuation in the multiple placed on them by the market. Graham was interested in earnings too, although he tended to work with what had already been reported for the last twelve months ("historic" or "trailing" earnings) rather than estimates of future earnings, which he distrusted. But he went further. He looked at assets. This is why his methods appealed to bankers, who are compelled by their fiduciary responsibilities toward the humble depositors who have entrusted them with their life savings to take the ultracautious view that a company must have tangible assets to act as collateral for any loans in case its business should unexpectedly collapse. (Well, that's what the bankers used to say. Somehow, it didn't stop them from lending all that unrecoverable money to Iron Curtain countries and to the Third World. But that's another story.)

Graham and Dodd developed this technique in great detail, adapting it to a variety of industries and revising it through their book's numerous editions. And the concept of establishing a stock's intrinsic value is still central to most Wall Street research, although estimates of future earnings have generally come to overshadow any concern with underlying assets.

The investment record of Graham-Newman Corporation was indeed superior. One estimate is that $10,000 placed with the firm in 1936 would have yielded an average of about $2,100 for each of the next twenty years, and the return of the $10,000 principal thereafter. But skeptics have complained that this result was largely due to the performance of one stock: the Government Employees Insurance Company (GEICO). In 1948, Graham-Newman, in a private transaction, had put $720,000, perhaps a quarter of its assets, into a 50 percent interest in GEICO. By 1975 the value received by Graham's group from this investment had surpassed half a billion dollars.

Right off the bat, GEICO had contravened Graham's usual policy of diversification, another defense mechanism encouraged by his experiences in the Great Crash. And almost immediately its stock price rose past the level where it exceeded all his usual standards of prudent investment. But he had held on, regarding it as "a sort of family business." His reflections on this episode in a postscript to the 1973 edition of *The Intelligent Investor* could serve as an epigraph for all investment endeavors and should be considered carefully:

> Are there morals to this story of value to the intelligent investor? An obvious one is that there are several different ways to make and keep money in Wall Street. Another, not so obvious, is that one lucky break, or one supremely shrewd decision—can we tell them apart?—may count for more than a lifetime of journeyman efforts.

(In a footnote at this point, Graham revealed that Graham-Newman had insisted on the purchase price being completely covered by asset value and that only "dumb luck" prevented the deal foundering "on, say, $50,000 of accounting items.")

> But behind the luck, or the crucial decision, there must usually exist a background of preparation and disciplined capacity. One needs to be sufficiently established and recognized so that these opportunities will knock at his particular door. One must have the means, the judgment, and the courage to take advantage of them.

In 1975, GEICO suddenly announced that because inflation had sharply accelerated the cost of insurance claims, it had begun to make serious losses and was actually on the verge of bankruptcy. Apparently this had been completely unsuspected by its fundamentalist followers—including Graham, who still held large positions and had been a member of the board of directors. There was panic, institutional investors stampeded for the exit, and the stock, which a year or so earlier had traded at more than $60, collapsed all the way to $2.10. Graham's critics have not hesitated to cite this debacle as evidence of the limitations of fundamental analysis, especially when confined to published financial statements. But others argued at the time that Wall Street's reaction had once again just plain overlooked GEICO's true value. One of Graham's disciples, Warren Buffett, seized the opportunity to buy GEICO stock. By the mid-1980s, he owned a third of the company and its stock price was over $70.

Ben Graham died in 1976 at the age of eighty-two. By the end of his life, according to John Train's penetrating essay on him in *The Money Masters,* he had settled on two simple rules for stock selection. His recommended investment strategy was equally simple: the standard reference manuals like *Moody's* and *Standard & Poor's* should be combed carefully, and all stocks meeting these criteria should be bought. This would result in a portfolio sufficiently diversified to withstand unforeseeable accidents that might afflict any one of them:

1. *A stock should be bought when it trades at less than two-thirds of its net current asset value per share.* Net current (or "quick") assets are total current assets minus current liabilities, long-term debt and the aggregate redemption value of preferred stock, if any. This is tantamount to buying a company for the cash in its treasury—"buying a dollar bill for forty cents," as Buffett has frequently said. *AND:*

2. *The company's debt-to-net-worth ratio should be less than one.* This means that its long-term debt, including preferred stock, is less than 40 percent of its total capitalization. *Its current earnings divided by its stock price (its "earnings yield") should be twice the prevailing yield on AAA bonds.* A stock's earnings-price yield is of course—of course!—the reverse of price-earnings yield, so that a stock selling at ten times earnings has an earnings yield of 1/10 or 10 percent. *OR:*

3. *The company's debt-to-net-worth ratio should be less than one; and its dividend yield should be at least two-thirds of the AAA bond yield.* Dividend yield is the dividend paid on each share di-

vided by the share price, and is naturally lower than the earnings yield.

At the same time, Graham offered simplified rules for selling:

1. *Sell a stock after it has gone up 50 percent; or*

2. *Sell after two years, whichever comes first.*

3. *Sell if the dividend is omitted.*

4. *Sell if earnings decline so far that the stock's current market price is 50 percent over the price at which the buying rules suggest it should be bought.*

In other words, Graham would approve of a stock selling at $8, with current assets of $12, and previous twelve months' earnings (in early 1985, when AAA yields were 11.77 percent) of nearly $2 a share. Well, wouldn't everybody? Such a stock would have a P/E ratio of about 4, at a time when the S & P 500's P/E ratio on the prior twelve months' earnings was around 10.

This is what Graham called, with considerable understatement, "a margin of safety." It would be hard to imagine a safer investment than a stock selling for less than the cash it owns, with earnings capitalized at less than the prevailing market rate. Nevertheless, such situations do occur, although they are more common at the bottom of catastrophic bear markets. In between, Graham's disciples have to compromise.

Graham discussed his simplified rules in a famous seminar he conducted just before his death. At that time, he said that because of the sheer numbers of market researchers now beavering away, he didn't think the returns to "elaborate techniques of security analysis" were as great as they had been in the 1930s. "*To that limited extent,* I'm on the side of the efficient market school of thought now generally accepted by the professors." [emphasis added.]

Some of the professors have seized upon this comment as a sign that Graham was handing on the keys of Saint Peter to them. Professor Malkiel in his *Random Walk Down Wall Street* even rather naughtily reprints Graham's last sentence without his qualifying clause. Graham's disciples, who have continued to refine his doctrines, hotly disagree. And of course they have been sufficiently successful to constitute anomalies in the "efficient market." Ben Graham's own nephew was apparently indifferent to this doctrinal dispute. According to Joe Granville, by 1979 he had renounced fundamental analysis altogether, and became a convinced technician.

CHARLES ALLMON AND *GROWTH STOCK OUTLOOK*

Charles Allmon has no inhibitions about making his own claim to the Grahamite apostolic succession. He tells the tale with the forceful efficiency of a man who, having found a form of words he likes, sees absolutely no reason why he should not repeat it exactly the same way whenever he feels inclined to do so:

"Graham called me on the phone, as I recall in 1969, maybe 1970. He said, 'I've got a copy of your *Growth Stock Outlook* and I've been very intrigued by what you're doing here. How are you spotting these values?' I said, 'Mr. Graham, I'm taking a lot of your own criteria and trying to crank in my own for value relative to growth potential.' And he said, 'Well, it's a very intriguing idea. I think if I were young again, that might be the course I would take. It sort of speeds things up a little bit.'"

By 1985, Charles Allmon was sixty-four and at the height of his powers. His $175-a-year twice-monthly *Growth Stock Outlook* had a circulation of over 10,000. His net worth by his own estimation was over $4 million, not counting his interest in the letter. Allmon had twenty-one people working for him in a rabbit warren of offices inside a shabby former apartment building in Bethesda, Maryland. They included three certified public accountants and one actual and two incipient chartered financial analysts, although Allmon himself was entirely self-taught. He had over $150 million under management (minimum account: $150,000) and had refused offers of more than $5 million for his letter and portfolio management operation. *And of all the investment letters followed by the* Hulbert Financial Digest *between June 1980 and June 1985,* Growth Stock Outlook *was the only one that bad in every period both made money and outperformed all six major market indices*—the Dow Jones Industrial Average, the New York Stock Exchange Composite, the American Stock Exchange Market Value Index, the S & P 500, the NASDAQ OTC Composite and the Wilshire 5000 Equity Index. This was so even when they were adjusted to reflect both capital appreciation and dividends. Interestingly, Allmon had achieved this feat without ever coming top in any individual year.

Allmon's brilliant record extends even further back. Once a month, *Growth Stock Outlook* reports on its "$50,000 Supervised Portfolio," which reflects the fortunes of a hypothetical $50,000 invested in June 27, 1973, when the Dow Jones Industrial Average stood at 884.63. As of June 15, 1985, with the Dow at 1,300.96, this portfolio consisted of forty-one stock positions and cash worth a total of $394,716, an increase of 689 percent. This is the portfolio the *Hulbert Financial Digest* has followed since 1980, and the two tallies have agreed closely.

Additionally, *Growth Stock Outlook* rates and provides continuous detailed coverage of some 100 selected stocks, and every quarter it includes a similar survey of a further 400 or so newly issued stocks and companies that are promising but as yet too unseasoned to be given full coverage. From these lists, subscribers can construct their own individualized portfolios. Allmon's own measurement of the result indicates that he recommended 93 stocks between January 1, 1976 and February 1, 1984, of which 40 doubled or better, a total of 78 increased in price and only eight declined more than 25 percent. This of course was in a period when the NASDAQ OTC Composite Index, a broad-based average reflecting the smaller "secondary" stocks in which Allmon specializes, more than tripled. Even so, he beat it—and he was indisputably in the right place at the right time.

Allmon is a stocky terrier of a man. He has rapidly graying red hair, blue eyes and a fierce but friendly manner. He grew up in Ohio and Pennsylvania. After studying agricultural engineering and graduating youngest in his class from Purdue (1941), he worked for United Fruit and Firestone on their plantations in Honduras and Liberia. Allmon's hobby was photography. His Kodachrome shots of Africa were printed in *National Geographic,* and ultimately they led to a long career as a photographer and writer for the magazine, culminating in his becoming assistant illustrations editor and a member of its executive edito-

rial council. Allmon says he has visited more than sixty countries on five continents, and blown-up color photographs of
some of his most recent travels dominate *Growth Stock Outlook*'s
offices.

On a *National Geographic* assignment in Barbados in 1960,
Allmon met his future wife, a member of the little-known but
historic community of white West Indians. Gwen Allmon now
works part time for *Growth Stock Outlook* and presides with quiet
wisdom over the couple's magnificent home in Maryland's hunt
country, listening to her husband with calm attentiveness. (Despite his domestic opulence, however, Allmon drives to work in
a modest Datsun.) The Allmons are devout Presbyterians. The
elder of their two daughters is married to a Presbyterian minis-
ter and is herself ordained, working for a conservative Presbyterian group; their youngest attended the L'Abri study center in
Switzerland founded by Dr. Francis Schaeffer, one of the key
intellectual forces in the recent revival of conservative Protes-
tantism in America. All the Allmon women have formidable
academic records, of which their husband and father is touch-
ingly proud.

While at *National Geographic*, Allmon developed another
hobby: the stock market. In 1965, after several years of active
trading for his own account, he began publishing *Growth Stock
Outlook* in his spare time from his basement. He met its deadlines even when on a two-month *National Geographic* assignment
in Darwin, Australia. He resigned from the magazine in 1969.
"My hobby was making me fourteen times my salary," he
chuckles gleefully. "I figured it was time I quit."

Noting this twenty-year Allmon cycle, uneasy subscribers
might naturally be asking: what is his current hobby? There
seems to be little cause for alarm. Allmon's house is fitted with
neat wallfuls of filing cabinets, and he reads investment materials far into the night. He says he gets his best ideas away from
office distractions. Allmon does have extensive private investment interests, including land in Florida and in Hawaii, where
he's building a second home, and various venture capital deals.
In 1968 he and some friends grubstaked Hughes Computer Systems, a software company, making a profit of some $5 million
when they sold out in 1975 (too soon, Allmon says now—"a $100
million mistake"). He owns some 59 percent of Potomac Applied
Mechanics, which holds twenty-seven patents, including such

interesting devices as a fold-up lazy Susan for which Allmon has identified seventy-five uses. In the early 1980s he spent a lot of time and money trying to organize a $50 million to $100 million venture capital partnership, which would have been rather similar in conception to a British merchant bank. Eventually he shelved the idea, growling darkly about the damage done to the confidence of potential investors by irresponsible Wall Street investment houses. But he continued to brood about creating a major financial institution out of *Growth Stock Outlook,* possibly a closed-end investment company dabbling in leveraged buy-outs.

Charles Allmon appears to be almost pathologically competitive. He practically salivates at the mention of his major rivals and relentlessly derides the pretensions of the investment letter industry in general at the very investment conferences where their editors gather for a little tax-deductible Rest and Recreation. He tells audiences to refuse to consider an investment letter unless it's had a ten-year track record, thus eliminating 90 percent of the field and placing his younger competitors in an impossible position. He has even developed the antisocial habit of publicly offering to bet fellow speakers $10,000 that their more imaginative predictions, most recently an explosion in the gold price and/or precipitous deflation, will not occur. He has never had a taker, as he always points out. He says loudly and frequently that there are only five investment letters he respects —and that they aren't followed by the *Hulbert Financial Digest.* But he won't name them, and greets guesses with a shake of the head and a sly smile. A frustrated Mark Hulbert is about ready to conclude the five letters are a figure of speech.

Allmon is particularly scathing about technical analysis. In 1984 he reacted with extreme violence when Stan Weinstein of *Professional Tape Reader* suggested as a short sale Ames Department Stores, a discounter specializing in small-town markets that Allmon first recommended in 1966 at 1 1/16. No doubt partly due to Allmon's cries of outrage, a classic short squeeze developed, Ames shot up some 20 points to over 50, and poor Weinstein was stopped out. "We enjoy nothing more than to squeeze a short seller who receives vibes from charts," Allmon wrote in *Growth Stock Outlook.* There can be little doubt that he meant it.

Politically, Allmon can fairly be described as an unreconstructed conservative. But one notable consequence of his attitude to the investment letter industry is his outspoken support for the SEC. This is unusual at a time when most American conservatives have accepted the libertarian critique of government regulation, and when investment advisors in particular have been hopeful that ways might be found to alleviate its impact upon them. Allmon makes no real distinction between policing the advisors for honesty and punishing them for making sincere, or at any rate sincerely self-deluded, mistakes. He also adamantly refuses to credit the argument that, since it would be in the interest of companies to disclose the kind of financial information he needs to recommend their stock, they might possibly be inclined to do so without the SEC's mandatory reporting requirements. Indeed, in 1984 when fears of a Democratic victory in that year's presidential election could be felt on the investment-conference circuit like an occasional chill breeze on a spring day, Allmon would say with relish that at least a Democratic-controlled SEC would put Howard Ruff, who never registered with the SEC on the grounds that he was a newspaper and who was prominently identified with the conservative Republican cause, out of business. He himself, he used to add, would simply ride out what he believed would be the inevitable ensuing inflation with gold shares. Under such circumstances, of course, he could also rely on a sin-seeking SEC to excommunicate most of his competition.

Allmon's moralistic streak is also evident in his attitude to the options and commodities markets. "We do not play around with options," he barks in his portfolio management brochure. Speculating in options is undeniably dangerous, and many money managers eschew them, but Allmon uses the opportunity to preach a brief sermon: "They serve no useful purpose, create neither capital nor jobs." Options, of course, have a perfectly clear if somewhat marginal economic purpose: they allow the holders of a stock to ensure against the possibility that it might decline by placing a small bet to that effect with a speculator, so that their losses and gains will cancel out. Allmon's righteous wrath, however, is not completely implacable. An earlier version of his brochure damned commodities as "the ultimate crap game." Now, although they are still described as a "risky proposition," clients who insist on getting involved are referred to a commodities management firm run by a "longtime personal friend."

Despite his vociferous skepticism, Allmon attends investment conferences assiduously. His strong convictions have
made him an effective and popular speaker with a penchant for
the caustic phrase. Blue-chip stocks are "blue gyps." High-tech
stocks are "high-wreck." Computer stocks are "like Roman can-
dles; they burn brightly for a while and then snuff out." As for
"concept stocks," which trade on the strength of a plausible
story about the underlying business, "whenever I hear about
one, I feel like someone's putting his hand in my pocket." And
establishing a fellow-advisor's record is "like trying to get an eel
by the ears."

Nevertheless, at these conferences Allmon listens to all the
other advisors' presentations with great care. And he says he
reads almost everything available on investments, including
rival letters, excepting only Wall Street research ("the lazy
man's path to the poorhouse"). To some extent, Allmon is employing Contrary Opinion. He says he sold his gold stocks after
attending a famous conference put on by California letter editor
and money manager Ken *(Ken Gerbino Investment Letter)* Gerbino
in Palm Springs in January 1980. Gold enthusiasm was un-
confined, and Allmon noticed with disapproval that an unusually large number of participants had come equipped with
private jets. But conferences also provide him with the opportunity to meet his readers and particularly to listen to their stock
ideas. "I always jot those things down," he says. "I've never once
failed to check one of them out, no matter how obscure they are.
You never know what you're going to find." For example,
suggestions from subscribers triggered the research that first got
him into Sykes Datatronics, a telephone equipment manufacturer that went from $1.75 in 1979 to $34 in 1982, and then out
again before the trouble that subsequently brought it back to $4.

The fact is that Allmon is much more flexible than he might
appear. After some years of repeatedly citing IBM as typical of
the big, boring stocks favored by institutional investors, Allmon
bought it for some managed accounts because its price had
slipped below the $100 he considered justified. He denounced
Cetus as part of Wall Street's biotechnology craze, but in 1980
he put it on his list at $13.75 because with $5.50 per share in cash
and equivalents it was "basically an asset play." (It didn't work
out anyway, and Allmon reluctantly retreated.) Allmon offi-

cially espouses Benjamin Graham's position that the broad market can't really be timed and that investors should make buy and sell decisions based on the financial health of each individual stock. But in July 1984, when Allmon was nominally on holiday in Switzerland with his wife and was suddenly inspired to spend $2,000 on telephone calls giving orders to shift his portfolios from cash into stocks—the right move, as it turned out—one of his calls was to seek the opinion of Bob Prechter of the seven-year-old *Elliott Wave Theorist*, who writes only about the general market and gets not merely vibes but sequential waves of vibes from charts.

Experience may have taught Allmon this unobtrusive humility. "I've been round the track," he says. Many of his mistakes were made on his own account in the speculative markets of the 1950s. But he was disastrously wrong in the bear markets of 1973-4, a period not covered in the record he sent Mark Hulbert, when he kept his clients fully invested and suffered portfolio losses of up to 50 percent. "I got away from my Ben Graham," he says now. "I bought General Automotive Parts at twenty-nine times earnings. It was a good company—it was eventually bought by Genuine Parts—but not that good." Allmon's total circulation has never fully returned to his pre–bear market peak of 17,000. (But the situations are not strictly parallel because in those days he had two other letters and was charging as little as a mere $35 a year.) Again in the early 1980s, Allmon bought oil stocks because he shared the general opinion that the energy crisis could not be resolved as quickly as it apparently was. This time, however, his portfolios escaped without serious damage because his commitment was not as great and his selections were financially strong. "I still think I'll be vindicated eventually," he says, noting that some oil stocks in the mid-1980s were trading below book value.

Whatever the reason, Allmon is always watchful. "You can't feed too much information into the old human computer," he maintains. In an interview with *Barron's* Kate Welling in February 1984, when the stock market was looking so sick that many were beginning to talk about a new bear market, Allmon, then 40 percent to 45 percent in cash but already "itching to buy," compared the situation to that of nearly ten years before and recalled a memorable experience:

I was speaking in Detroit that October [1974.] There were about 700 people at that meeting. And I said that I felt this was just about the best buying opportunity that they'd seen since the Great Depression. And would they please hold up their hands, those investors who planned to buy. I only saw five hands go up. They were absolutely terrified. Well, those five, I asked, "Would you please see me after my talk here, because I'd like to get your opinion." Do you know that every one of those people were over 75 years of age?

Allmon's investment strategy is similar to Graham's in its use of diversification. With his managed accounts, he normally will not put more than 4 percent to 5 percent of a client's assets into one stock. And typically a fifth of each account's assets will be in larger issues that can be sold quickly if the client needs funds in a hurry. Beyond that, the major difference with Graham is Allmon's quest for stocks with rapidly growing earnings. And when he finds them, he plans to hold them for several years. "Value will out," he says. But it can take time.

"Growth stocks" have been fashionable on Wall Street too. However, these were major corporations that had already been fully recognized and were trading at high prices, like IBM or Avon—the Nifty Fifty. Allmon focuses on "secondary" companies with market capitalization of between $10 million and $100 million, many of them not listed on any exchange but traded over the counter (OTC). He says that these companies, not the large corporations, comprise the growth point of the American economy, where most of the new jobs, technologies and ideas are generated.

Allmon asserts flatly that this dynamic secondary sector is a permanent feature of the economy. Periodically, he agrees, other areas will attract more speculative interest, as the Nifty Fifty did in 1971–2. Indeed, in the bull market year of 1982, eleven of the investment letters followed by the *Hulbert Financial Digest* outperformed Allmon, some by a factor of two or three, although he was up a solid 24 percent. That year's leader, *Tony Henfry's Gold Letter*, rode the precious metals rally skillfully and was up 93.3 percent. But Allmon insists that over the longer run, three to five years, his chosen area will win out. Two years later, in a flat year, Allmon was thirteenth, with a 3.5 percent gain. Henfry was down 28.1 percent.

"We don't try to hit home runs," says Allmon. A company compounding its earnings at a 15 percent annual rate will double its stock price every five years, assuming its price-earnings multiple remains the same. (In fact, it would probably trend upward.) Doubling capital every five years is Allmon's stated aim. What's wrong with that? he demands. Significantly, this goal is just about what Hulbert's work has independently suggested is a practicable maximum.

Allmon's definition of a growth company involves a number of basic tests. Among them:

1. The company's current assets at least double current liabilities. "I've never seen a company with a strong balance sheet blow away. The stock may gyrate all over the place, but there's always a floor." Allmon pauses. Well, he adds, except in the 1973-4 bear market. Then stocks went through the floor—another indication of the epochal devastation wrought in those years. Allmon wants to know what a company could be sold for if it went out of business—its "break-up value"—and he does not accept the auditors' estimate of book value without a fight. He makes his own evaluation of a company's assets, checking for such things as understated real estate (good) or obsolete plant that hasn't been properly depreciated and is therefore shown at more than its true value (bad).

2. The company should have earnings increases of at least 15 percent going back three or four years. Going back earlier could distort the results by factoring in the high growth rates that much smaller company can obtain.

3. The company's sales should also have increased 15 percent a year. Otherwise earnings could be coming from expanding profit margins, which must stop eventually.

4. Its return on equity should be 20 percent to 25 percent—or, if lower, have increased sharply in the last year or two.

5. It should have little leverage and, ideally, no long-term debt. Leverage stimulates return on equity, but can mask continuous borrowing and a deteriorating balance sheet.

6. Its price must be right. Allmon usually won't pay more than 15 times earnings for a growth stock, although he recognizes that some industries like pharmaceuticals and computers are generally higher.

But these tests are only the beginning. To satisfy Allmon, a stock has to jump through an apparently endless series of hoops. Some are peculiar to particular industries. Retailers have to show that their inventory buildup is not outpacing sales and that they turn over their inventory quickly. Others are universal. Allmon does not like stocks that are already held in great quantity by institutional investors, whom he feels are prone to panics and selling stampedes in which individual investors can get trampled underfoot; in contrast, buying an unknown stock that is then discovered by the institutions can give you "quite a ride." Where a company pays a dividend, the payout ratio and the rate of dividend growth is scrutinized carefully. Allmon believes that dividend growth rate is in some ways a better indication of a business's health than earnings growth because it can more precisely reflect a competent management's assessment of future prospects. When Ken Fisher's book *Super Stocks* appeared in 1984, Allmon devoted a page in *Growth Stock Outlook* to proving that he had been using Fisher's key method, the comparison of total sales to revenues, for years. Generally, an Allmon stock has to have a price/sales ratio (price per share multiplied by the number of shares outstanding, divided by total revenues) of lower than 1.75. Some of his favorite stocks are below 0.75, like Ames in 1984. Allmon says that the price/sales ratio is particularly valuable in figuring out which stocks to sell short. In mid-1983 he printed a list of twenty-one short sale candidates chosen according to their price/sales ratios, which went as high as 298.8. One year later they were down an average of 48 percent.

Whereas some neo-Grahamites work solely from published financial statements, Allmon and his staff undertake very detailed research into each company's business, its prospects and its management. He spends much time talking to suppliers and customers. It can get quite personal. "I don't think we've ever been [invested] in a retailer that I haven't been in one of their stores," he told John Boland, the author of *Wall Street's Insiders* (1985) and editor of *Value Investing*. "When I'm traveling around and I see a chain I know is public, I'll go in and look around. I don't know how many restaurant chains I've been in—fifty at least. I want to see how the food is, whether the restaurant's dirty, whether the parking lot is full of rubbish."

Allmon's interest in Sykes Datatronics, for example, was

confirmed when a customer told him that he had found at least fifty uses for Sykes' product of which the company seemed unaware ("I said, '*What* did you say?' "). What Allmon hopes to find is a company that has quietly occupied a niche in its market, supplying some peculiar product for which there is little competition. He prefers solid, steady gains to speculative fireworks. He dislikes companies that make a high proportion of their sales to the military or the federal government because he has found they tend to perform poorly over the long term. He generally rejects high-technology companies with their unverifiable and often incomprehensible specialties in favor of what he calls "low-tech" companies. One of his earliest buys was Masco Corporation, which makes faucets. Between January 1965 and January 1985, it appreciated 2,322 percent. Allmon often says he would rather buy the stock of a firm making printout paper for computers than a computer manufacturer. And in fact he has been recommending a company that makes printout paper, Wallace Computer Services, since January 1975. In January 1985 it was up 617 percent.

Allmon is a severe judge of managements. He has been known to count the number of martinis an executive packs away at lunch (Allmon says he's not a teetotaler, but he serves nothing stronger than grape juice in his home). Once he sold a stock when he discovered that the company was building an executive gym. Although his method of operation requires extensive contact with company officials, he makes a point of noting in his brochure that "we strenuously avoid oversolicitous executives and fast-talking promoters." He dislikes companies owned by doctors and academics, whom he regards as out of touch with the real world, and he is particularly hostile to the presence of stockbrokers on a company's board of directors. As many as a third of all company managements, Allmon says in his usual swingeing way, are "downright dishonest"; another third are dubious. He is happiest with managements he's known for a considerable period and whom he trusts. He will often follow a company for many years before putting it on his recommended list. He keeps files on 18,000 companies. He is deeply interested in managements' attitudes to their own companies as reflected in their sales or purchases of its stock, and he regularly monitors and reports on insider trading as reported to the SEC.

To anyone with a computer programmer's cast of mind,

Allmon's system just naturally presents itself as a rather luxuriant decision tree, with nice crisp quantitative rules at each juncture that a computer can easily apply. And in fact other neo-Grahamites do rely heavily on computers, using their chosen filter rules to sift through all available stocks. Allmon disagrees emphatically with this technique. The difficulty of assessing an intangible such as management quality is one reason he gives. He often decries his 1965 Special Sell Recommendation on Teledyne, triggered by an earnings hiccough. The stock subsequently multiplied several thousand percent, becoming something of a Wall Street legend. "I just didn't give [Teledyne chief executive] Henry Singleton as much as I should have done," Allmon says now. Much of his research is designed to avoid the same mistake. He read Lee Iacocca's autobiography, a best seller in 1985, with scrupulous attention. On finishing it, he announced that he thought he'd buy some Chrysler.

It is possible that Allmon may just not like giving up control, to computers or anyone else. "I'm an investment committee of one," he says. Even his staff hasn't been told all the methods he uses to find likely new growth stocks. He still writes *Growth Stock Outlook*, in longhand, entirely by himself, claiming no one else can do it. He had delegated the writing of his second, smaller publication, *Junior Growth Stocks*, but in 1985 he folded it into the senior letter, partly to keep a closer eye on it. (Allmon once had a third letter, *Senior Growth Stocks*, concentrating on companies bigger than $100 million capitalization, but it was a victim of the 1973–4 market.) Allmon has dismissed several possible diversifications of his operations because of their potential demands on his own time. "I have to go where the returns are best." He has even been talking of not accepting any more money management clients, although to some extent that's also because it's difficult to pilot increasingly larger sums through the shallowly traded stocks he favors.

This investment committee of one seems to be working out just fine. Its energy is awe-inspiring, its individuality and independence unimpeachable, and if it occasionally repeats itself in conversation, this could be due to a lifetime of making things perfectly clear. It can even, despite its protestations to the contrary, be induced to reveal strong views about the overall market direction. These are sometimes highly intuitive, but nevertheless can be remarkably accurate. In February 1984, Allmon told a surprised *Barron's* that the Dow had been up in every year ending in a "5" since 1905:

> I suggest, based on this record, perhaps 1984 and 1985 will be the years of the big double cross. Everybody's looking for the presidential cycle to repeat, with an up year in 1984 and a down one in '85. Looks to me like you might be seeing the opposite.

Again, despite widespread Wall Street moaning as the 1980s began, Allmon was repeatedly quoted as saying that the decade would be a boom one in the stock market. By 1985 he was saying that it wasn't over yet. He has a long-standing prediction that by the year 2000 the Dow Jones Industrial Average will be "somewhere in the 3,000-to-5,000 range." But he also thinks that there will be a repeat of the 1973–4 wipeout sometime in the next eight or ten years, when just enough young people have entered the investment business with no memory of a real bear market. He suspects it may be heralded by a bursting of the real estate boom that possibly will begin where it is most speculative: New York City, which in Allmon's Middle American view will deserve everything it gets.

"We are number crunchers," Allmon says, proudly recounting his refusal to hire a student from Harvard Business School, which from his standpoint crunches insufficient numbers, or the wrong ones. However, as a professional photographer he was also involved in a highly technical craft, but one that ultimately and inescapably moved into the realm of value judgment. Showing a guest two photographs of his home, Allmon will pronounce with total authority on which is the better composition, brushing aside any aesthetic quibbles with supreme confidence. Stock selection too, perhaps, has its aspect of ineffable judgment. From fine art to finance has, after all, been but a step.

AL FRANK AND *THE PRUDENT SPECULATOR*

If Charles Allmon is like a terrier, Al Frank appears to be a large, affable Saint Bernard. The editor of the Santa Monica–based *Prudent Speculator* is six feet four inches and 270 pounds, a big, blond easygoing product of Southern California, who is soft-spoken, informal and warm in manner. His letter is written in what Mark Hulbert, who ought to know, has described as a "refreshingly low-key, forthright, humble, easy-to-read, under-standable style." The *Hulbert Financial Digest* in fact played a vital role in Al Frank's career: when it began to monitor him in 1983, his circulation was a mere seventy-five, but in that year he headed Hulbert's hit parade with a startling 72.8 percent gain, attracted a ton of publicity and acquired over 2,000 more subscri-bers. Frank was an instant power in the investment letter indus-try, and further testimony to Hulbert's impact upon it.

The next year, 1984, was rather embarrassing for Frank. He finished down 13.1 percent. This might seem to bear out Charles Allmon's initial growlings, as his hackles rose at the sight of this new rival, that a result like Frank's in 1983 could only be due to luck. But in the interim, Allmon had met Frank and had revised his opinion, partly because their investment philosophies are so similar. "I tell Al Frank he'll be fine in ten years' time," Allmon now says helpfully. Frank, who is almost ten years younger than Allmon, receives this encouragement evenly.

Despite 1984, *The Prudent Speculator* is one of the handful of investment letters that have cumulatively outperformed the market averages. When Mark Hulbert calculated its record back to June 1980, he discovered it had gained 272.9 percent in the five-year period, making it the top performer of all the letters he follows. And it seems to have done well right back to 1977, when it was founded. This is a matter of record because every three weeks in each issue of his letter, Al Frank reports on the prog-ress of his actual portfolio, complete with confirmation slips that are available on request. Frank began this portfolio with $8,006.59 on March 11, 1977. On July 5, 1985, Frank reported it was worth $251,745, an appreciation of 3,180 percent. This figure represents Frank's equity in the portfolio: he almost always buys stock on margin, borrowing most of the purchase price from his broker, so that his total holdings of cash and securities in the portfolio amounted to some $723,667. In comparing Frank's record to that of Charles Allmon, it should be noted that Frank's portfolio was smaller, making faster growth statistics easier, and was also more volatile, so that Allmon is ahead on a "risk-adjusted" basis.

Since Frank explicitly recommends margin, Hulbert allows for it in his calculations of the portfolio's performance. But he assumes the 50 percent rate that would be the maximum available to any new investor who wanted to duplicate the portfolio, rather than the 30 percent rate that Frank can command because of his paper profits. This means that Frank's actual portfolio always moves farther, in both directions, than the version that appears in the *Hulbert Financial Digest*. In 1983 the actual portfolio was up 122.8 percent; in 1984, it was down 22.67 percent. Another difference is that the portfolio really is Frank's own nest egg. Periodically, he has to sell a stock he still favors because he needs to withdraw cash for personal expenditures, such as buying a house in 1984. This is an example of the distinction Hulbert draws between a real portfolio and one that is representative of the average subscriber's experience.

Besides reporting on his actual portfolio, Frank also monitors a larger list of recommendations, sometimes as many as seventy, a habit he got into when he could not afford to buy all the stocks he liked for his own account. He comments on market conditions and gives advice on portfolio strategy adjusted according to subscribers' risk preferences—BOLD SPECULATOR, MODERATE SPECULATOR or CONSERVATIVE INVESTOR. In 1982, Frank began to accept discretionary managed accounts. He now has about $20 million under his care.

Despite Al Frank's outward calm, his life has been turbulent. He was born in 1930 in Des Moines, Iowa, and brought to California when he was five. He grew up in a family of poor tailors, far removed from any thought of the stock market. When Frank was forty-two, he had the interesting experience of learning in a casual conversation with his second wife that he had been adopted—she had been told by his adoptive mother and said she didn't know that he didn't know. His natural father had been a Swedish baker; his unmarried natural mother a young Jewish girl whose rabbi had placed the child in an observant home.

Frank says he did poorly in high school. However, he

learned enough about printing to be able to support himself as a journeyman Linotype operator during the regular nomadic episodes that have punctuated his life, when, he says, he "got unhappy" and took to the road. Frank went to Los Angeles City College to learn bookkeeping, but gravitated into psychology and the University of California at Los Angeles, only to flunk out twice and go off traveling. He ultimately graduated from Berkeley, where he built up a printing business, married and had two children. But complicated personal crises saw him on the move again. Among other activities, he had a spell in Las Vegas as a shill—a casino employee who plays at the gambling tables to attract real customers—and lived for an extended period in a girl friend's authentic peasant hovel in Majorca before running out of money and working his passage home on a Norwegian tanker.

Back in California, Frank remarried, had another daughter, and divorced again. Gradually, he was working his way into academic life, getting master's degrees in American Studies and Rehabilitation Counseling from California State University at Los Angeles while teaching high school, and eventually entering the doctoral program in Educational Philosophy at UCLA. Frank supported the Progressive school in educational theory, an intellectual tradition often linked with political liberalism. He still refers to himself as a "Henry George socialist," for example disapproving of the option market for vague reasons of social utility, a position paradoxically close to that of the arch-conservative Charles Allmon. But Frank never finished his doctoral dissertation, which was to be on the concept of consciousness in education. As a graduate student, he was able to teach college-level courses, and until 1981 he remained basically a journeyman adjunct professor, sometimes lecturing at four Los Angeles colleges in a day, commuting between them on his Honda motorcycle. Now, he says, he has wiped educational theory out of his mind so completely that, upon agreeing to check an unfamiliar point for a friend, he has opened his old textbook to find voluminous marginal annotations on the matter in his own handwriting that he no longer has the slightest recollection of making.

What appears to be Al Frank's destiny caught up with him in 1969. As a doctoral candidate at UCLA, he met Professor George Kneller, the prominent educationist, who was renowned on the campus not least for his substantial success in the stock market. Frank was inspired by Kneller's example. He went out and bought a few hundred dollars' worth of the Enterprise Fund mutual fund. It halved. He put a little money into Whittaker Corporation at $27. It fell to $15, where he sold it, on its way down to about $1. All this annoyed Frank intensely. He began to study the market. He read everything he could, and when he finally reached Ben Graham's *The Intelligent Investor* he saw the light. "It made sense to me," he says. "I never had much money and I always looked at bargains."

As time went on, Frank flourished, and people began to ask him for advice. In the mid-1970s someone showed Frank some investment letters, revealing a whole world whose existence he had not previously suspected. He decided to produce one as a hobby, and sent a mailing to a hundred friends and acquaintances. ("The acquaintances subscribed.") Frank began his letter in 1977. At first he called it *The Pinchpenny Speculator*, but he later changed to *The Prudent Speculator* after deciding that the younger generation, unfamiliar with the concept of penny-pinching, thought it meant he was following only speculative penny stocks.

Frank has his own personal definition of "speculator." All investing, he believes, is uncertain and therefore speculative. Although he feels the stock market is in a rising trend dating back to 1974, he says he can only really feel comfortable about its direction for around three weeks forward. This corresponds with Ben Graham's reluctance to predict the general market. Two other Grahamite principles to which Frank adheres are diversification and patience. Frank will not commit more than 5 percent of any managed account to any one stock. His actual portfolio consisted of eighty-nine stocks in early 1985. And once he has bought a stock, Frank expects to hold it for at least four years. From 1977 to early 1984, he recommended selling only two stocks (although several were bought out profitably in takeovers). Frank expects that about one out of every six of his stock selections won't work out—for example, he bought White Motor shortly before it went bankrupt—but he thinks the others will compensate for it. Like Charles Allmon, Frank explic-

itly eschews the spectacular in favor of the steady and sustained.
He says he hopes for 20 percent to 25 percent portfolio appreciation each year—and every year.

Unlike Allmon, Frank is not looking for growth as such,
but for bargains. He is quite happy if they're bland blue chips,
and indeed restricts himself almost completely to stocks listed
on the New York Stock Exchange, which are mostly senior
corporations. That's quite enough to be going on with, he says.
"You could make a lot of money just trading IBM around its
fundamental value." Again unlike Allmon, but like Graham,
Frank relies exclusively on published sources of information.
His companies are usually better known anyway, and he argues
that, given a sufficiently diversified portfolio, the chances of
hidden surprises like severe over- or undervaluation of companies' assets will cancel out.

Frank says he has some twenty-five or thirty key measures
of a stock's acceptability, of which half a dozen are crucial.
Which means that a potential purchase can display these characteristics in an almost infinite number of combinations, he adds,
not liking the idea of yielding control to a computer either.

1. The stock should preferably be around 70 percent of its book
   value per share, although Frank will relax this criterion if
   others are met.

2. Its price/earnings ratio should be low, perhaps 70 percent of
   its historic levels or of the P/E ratio of some comparable industry or market average.

3. Its cash flow (earnings with depreciation and other write-offs
   added back in) should have been consistently strong. "And the
   price/cash-flow ratio is more important than price/earnings,"
   says Frank. "Companies can manipulate their earnings by altering their depreciation schedules, and in terrible years they
   often write off *all* their problems at once. It's a game. A stock
   selling for two or three times cash flow per share is wonderful
   —it may have all kinds of write-offs and no earnings, but it's
   wonderful."

4. Its price/sales ratio should be around 0.75 for a growing company, or 0.4 for a large stable one.

5. Its return on equity or book value should be 10 percent to 15
   percent. "As a rule of thumb, a stock's return on equity should

be the same as its price/earnings ratio to be fairly valued," says Frank. However, he emphasizes that a stock trading at half its per-share book value in effect offers an opportunity to buy double the company's nominal return on equity.

6. Its return on sales, or total revenues, should be at least 3 percent, if it's an industrial company. In combination with a low price/sales ratio, says Frank, this is a strong indication of an undervalued stock.

7. Its earnings should preferably be in an uptrend, although Frank believes this should not be overemphasized.

Frank takes a generally less rigorous view of his criteria than Allmon. This is particularly true in the case of earnings trends and of liquidity, as measured by current assets versus current liabilities (the "acid test ratio"). Larger companies simply don't meet or need Allmon's 2-to-1 standard, says Frank. "Our method allowed us to buy Royal Dutch Petroleum"—a solid performer since 1981. Frank also bought Chrysler as early as 1983. Two other sharp differences are their attitudes to dividends, which Frank dislikes, preferring to see the money reinvested in the company, where he hopes it will mutate into an eventual capital gain; and to debt, which Frank positively favors, believing it enables companies to build up earnings faster.

Frank also has his differences with Benjamin Graham, apart from attempting to fine-tune his technique for use between bear-market bottoms. A major Frank deviation is when to sell—although he is quick to add that he hasn't really figured it out himself yet, either. "Graham's background was in the 1920s bond market," he says, "and selling after a 50 percent increase made sense there. But some stocks go up a 1,000 percent. When I bought Western Pacific Industries at 6 and it went to 9, I thought Oh boy!, and sold. Then I bought it back at 11 1/2 and since then it's been up to 115, as well as making a $23 cash payout." Furthermore, says Frank, some of his eventual big winners have deteriorated sharply after he bought them, spending months and even years under water. For example, he bought Stop & Shop, the Boston supermarket chain, at around 16 in 1978; it sank to 12 in 1980, but then it rallied to above 60—despite splitting twice and bringing his effective cost to 4. Whenever he buys a stock, Frank has calculated a "goal price" by techniques like extrapolating earnings, multiples and per-share book value. He is reluctant to leave until it's reached.

Frank also admits to using a few technical indicators of overall market direction to get some idea of the climate for his bargain hunting. He is careful, however, to make frequent reaffirmations of his fundamentalist faith and, especially, to deny that he's fallen as low as using charts. He prefers numbers. He watches moving averages of the major market indices like the Dow and the New York Composite Index, and in particular takes any crossing by an index of its two-hundred-day moving average as evidence that a trend is developing in that direction. He assesses the broad market with the "Advance/Decline line," a standard technical tool computed by subtracting each day's declining issues from the advances, with moving averages used to smooth out volatility. Historical records are available to indicate the point at which the market is allegedly "overbought" or "oversold." He checks the momentum of these broad market moves by looking at "On-Balance Volume," the daily total quantity of stock traded whose price finished up at the close less the quantity whose price finished down. This too is often expressed as a moving average. Both measures can be combined into another Frank favorite: the TRIN or "Arms" index, designed to reflect buying and selling pressures and computed by dividing the ratio of advancing issues to declining issues by the ratio of up volume to down volume. Once again, historical yardsticks are available to gauge the results. He also compares the number of new highs daily with the number of new lows: a solid majority of highs means a bull market; an overwhelming majority means a top.

Frank's idea is to use his technical conclusions about market direction in combination with his fundamental conclusions about each stock. For example, he thought that both the stocks he sold in his first seven years were fully valued. He chose to sell them when the overall market was looking weak. He can also reduce his exposure to margin. "You can't make money timing the market," Frank says, "but you can protect a well-selected stock portfolio." One of the best indicators of an overbought market, he adds, is the paucity of stocks that fit his fundamental criteria. At the August 1983 top, he was recommending only eight stocks besides those he held in his portfolio. Protection does not always work out, however. In early 1984 he simply guessed wrong and stayed fully invested—and margined—as the market subsided.

Neo-Grahamite purists object to Frank's market timing, just as they object to his use of margin. He is quietly unrepentant. "I'm not trying to hit a home run," he says, "but I'm trying to stretch a two-bagger out of a single."

CHAPTER SIX

The Winners: Chartists

You can observe a lot by watching.

—YOGI BERRA

There are no atheists in foxholes, and very few thoroughgoing rationalists in the financial markets. The reason is the same in both cases. War and the markets reveal too plainly the terrifying unpredictability of life, a truth that much human action is designed to obscure. One pleasing consequence of this situation is that many stock market aficionados are humbly willing to consider any idea no matter how eccentric, asking only that it work —or give some hope of working. By contrast, an academic idea has to prove its pedigree but not necessarily its practicability.

Which is by way of an introduction to the bitterly contested subject of technical analysis. Whereas the fundamental analyst focuses on the assets and earnings of the company whose stock he is trying to evaluate, the technical analyst attempts to predict the stock's future price from the way it is already trading in the market, as measured by various yardsticks, or "indicators." The fundamentalist tries to assess overall market direction by looking at general economic conditions; the technician by looking at the action of the market itself. "When the market speaks," proclaims Joe Granville, a particularly pugnacious technician, "I go down on my knees and say 'Yes, Master.' "

Among technicians, "chartists" are a radical subset. They maintain that when the actions of prices and/or various indicators are traced on a chart, certain visually identifiable and colorfully named patterns recur regularly and can be used to predict future movements. "They speak knowingly of broken tops at Coca-Cola, cradles at Gerber's Baby Foods, inverted bowls at National Biscuit, and descending channels at Columbia Broadcasting," wrote a skeptic, John L. Springer, in 1971. Chartists attract skeptics. For example, John Magee, coauthor with Robert D. Edwards of a key chartist text *Technical Analysis of Stock Trends* (1948), published his weekly *Technical Stock Advisory Service* out of an office in Massachusetts with its windows boarded up and its walls painted off-white to ensure "neutrality." Beyond extracting stock quotes from the daily papers, Magee did not read business news for at least two weeks—"until the newsprint was yellowing," says his longtime aide Susan MacFarlane—on the grounds that it might distort his judgment. Magee seems to have taken special delight in scandalizing visiting journalists by saying that he had no idea what the companies that he recommended on the basis of their charts actually produced.

If pressed, chartists will offer rationales for their favorite formations in terms of investor psychology. For example, they say that a "resistance level"—the tendency of a stock to stall repeatedly as it approaches a particular price—happens partly because people who bought the stock at that price earlier and have been suffering with it ever since dump it as soon as they can get out without taking a loss and thereby losing face. If the stock eventually gets through the resistance level (an "upside breakout"), the people who sold there are chagrined and will buy if it ever comes back down, so that the resistance level becomes a "support level." Thus in the following chart, which was first presented by Joe Granville in a lecture at New York's New School for Social Research in 1961, the "upside breakout" and "downside breakout" occur with the surpassing of the immediately previous high and low, which were potential sticking points. And the "parabolic peak" (also known as a "spike" or a "blow-off") has reached the same altitude as the other major high, suggesting that a resistance level is developing there.

Echoing Roger Babson, Granville concluded that stocks move in accordance with basic physical laws: (1) a body at rest tends to remain at rest; (2) a body in motion tends to remain in motion; (3) what goes up must come down; (4) it takes more energy to go up than to come down (hence "bull markets are generally longer than bear markets").

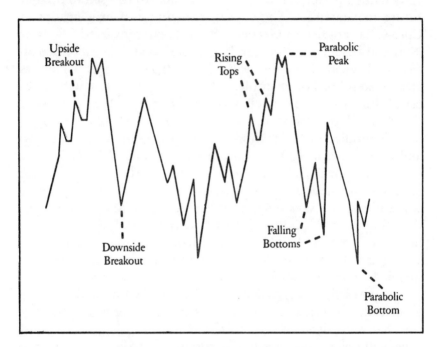

Ultimately, however, the chartists' answer to queries about why their formations work is: "because they do." This can be viewed either as an admirable adhesion to the scientific method, which since the days of Sir Isaac Newton has emphasized that the observation of facts must precede the formulation of theory; or, alternatively, as an outrageous lapse into mysticism. For example, the chart reproduced above actually traces not a stock but the first seven bars of Bach's "Jesu, Joy of Man's Desiring." Joe Granville, an enthusiastic amateur pianist, assigned the number 1 to the lowest note in the theme and so on through the melody as follows:

4,5,6,8,7,7,9,8,8,11,10,11,8,6,4,5,6,7,8,9,8,7,6,5,6,4,3,4,5,
1,3,5,7,6,5,6,4,5,6,8,7,7,9,8,8,11,10,11,8,6,4,5,6,2,8,7,6,5,4,1,4,3,4.

To Granville, who likes to be tantalizingly coy about his religious beliefs but says he's "about as far from being an atheist as it's possible to get," Bach conforms to the principles of charting for a simple reason: there is order in the universe; the human ear demands each successive note in Bach's score to fulfill "its innate sense of natural harmony." To others, this sort of thing proves, equally simply, that chartists are crazy. (A note of caution before you take sides: just to complicate matters, recent musical scholarship has established that Bach was indeed interested in numerology—the cabalistic significance of numeric relationships—and quietly built number patterns into his compositions . . .)

In a sense, technical analysis shares one vital assumption with the academics' Efficient Market Hypothesis: both assert that all information about a stock is reflected in its price. But the difference is that EMH maintains that prices have no memory, that their future movements are random, that notwithstanding Shakespeare, what's past is emphatically not prologue. The academic assault upon charting has been particularly ferocious. Professor Burton Malkiel even claims to have shown "a chartist friend of mine" a chart with "a beautiful upside breakout from an inverted head-and-shoulders pattern (a very bullish pattern)." The chartist "practically jumped out of his skin" and got all excited about the stock in question. Then Malkiel cruelly revealed that the chart had been derived by flipping the ubiquitous coin, marking a step up for heads and down for tails.

This is actually more of a debating point than a decisive argument. The coin flips could have produced a curve that reminded a mathematician of a particular quadratic equation or reminded a doctor of the peculiar temperature chart that indicates a patient is suffering from Pel-Ebstein's syndrome; Malkiel would hardly conclude that mathematics or medicine were thereby discredited. (In fact, Howard Ruff used to explain his pessimism in the early 1980s by quoting a physician subscriber who had written in to point out that the United States inflation chart looked like the temperature chart of a malaria victim, with its alternating, ever-more-acute highs/fevers and recessions/chills.) But other aspects of the academic attack have been apparently devastating: *no computer programmed to look for any of the classic chart formations has ever found that they can be correlated with the subsequent major price trends they are supposed to predict.* All the refinements suggested by chartists in an attempt to defend their profession have also failed. Of course, as a matter of logic, it is always possible to find in retrospect some rule that would best have predicted price trends in any given period. But there is no guarantee that in the next period it will continue to hold up. And it may be completely absurd: a computer reviewing the market of the late 1960s is supposed to have told its handlers after due cogitation that the best policy would have been to buy stocks with names ending in "x"—it was the era of Xerox and Syntex.

Nevertheless, charting continues. In Wall Street firms, it is an established part of most research departments, having long since graduated from what a prominent Wall Street technician, Alan R. Shaw of Smith Barney Harris Upham, has called its "sore-knuckle days," when its practitioners had to keep their charts hidden in desk drawers that could be slammed shut whenever a superior patrolled past. It has proved unexpectedly attractive to engineers, who are used to thinking in terms of waves and frequencies. It is even spreading internationally, and has been particularly well received in Japan, where merchants had quite spontaneously developed their own methods of charting for use in the rice market as far back as the seventeenth century.

This paradox is a serious problem for the academic critics of charting. As economists, they are professionally obliged to believe that the free market will place an appropriate value on everything in the long run, and that people will eventually refuse to pay more than a product is worth to them. Even insinuating unpleasantly that brokers like charting only because it stimulates customers and generates commissions does not really refute the point that ultimately the customers have to like it too. So the academic critics have fallen back on the defense that this just happens to be, well, rather a *long* long run. "Until the public catches on to this bit of trickery, technicians will continue to flourish," wrote Professor Malkiel in the first edition of *A Random Walk Down Wall Street* in 1973. In his 1985 Fourth Edition, he was still saying exactly the same thing. In the interim, however, the long run had not merely extended itself but appeared to have taken off in the wrong direction. The membership of the professional technicians' affinity group, the Market Technicians' Association, has risen from 13 in 1973 to over 160 in

1985. By contrast, institutional membership of the *Journal of Finance*, which one quantitatively inclined Wall Streeter, Eugene H. Hawkins of Investment Analytics, suggests is a proxy for interest in the Efficient Market Hypothesis and Modern Portfolio Theory, fell from 145 in 1979 to 18 in 1983 alone. Even John Magee's *Technical Stock Advisory Service*, now run by Dr. David Funk, is still going strong in Boston and charging $720 a year. The least that can be said is that the market for investment advice, at any rate, does not appear to be particularly efficient.

The bitterness of the controversy between technicians and academics makes it easy to overlook that both sides show some small sign of recognizing the same facts. Thus chartists' explanations of their formations quite often center on the presumed actions of insiders, for example in the well-established phenomenon of a stock showing sudden strength in advance of the announcement of an impending takeover because people in the know are buying. Insider activity, of course, has turned out to be associated with one of the better-known anomalies in the Efficient Market Hypothesis. Similarly, many technicians accept that their indicators can deteriorate over time, implicitly acknowledging the academics' argument that any successful system would immediately be swamped by investors rushing in, and become "fully discounted." Garfield Drew's odd-lot indicators were merely one example.

Perhaps too much and simultaneously too little is expected of charting—too much in that it certainly does not appear to provide a simple answer to the market, at least independent of the interpreting chartist; and too little in that it may say something important about the way the human mind assimilates information. For example, a portfolio manager for a large institutional investor confesses anonymously that in the early 1970s he took two years off and spent them "lotus-eating" in the Aegean. When he got back, his method of recouping was to spend many hours going through chart books, in effect re-creating the stock market's experience while he was away. "I can thank [the] Mansfield [Stock Chart Service] for getting me back on track," he says. In this situation, he found that a picture was indisputably worth the proverbial thousand words.

Fortunately, ajudicating the dispute between chartists and their critics can be left to more determined diplomats. Thanks to Mark Hulbert's work, it is possible to slither past the issue entirely and go directly to the chartists who, regardless of the theoretical merits of their systems, appear to have beaten the market. The Ancient Greeks, after all, were able to navigate quite happily with the Ptolemaic system, even though it assumed the world was flat.

CHARLES STAHL AND *GREEN'S COMMODITY MARKET COMMENTS*

Some of the investment letters in Mark Hulbert's flock denounce Charles Stahl's *Green's Commodity Market Comments* as a black sheep in their midst. In fact they claim it's a goat—a letter specializing in commodities rather than in stocks, bonds and other financial instruments. It's unfair, they say, to compare them with it. Of course, from the point of view of the investor, it is quite reasonable to assess commodities and stocks together because they are, after all, competing investment opportunities. But *Green's* was the one pure commodity letter on Hulbert's initial list, and he admits that its inclusion was a rough judgment. He follows Stahl's recommendations only in the gold and silver markets, which when the *Hulbert Financial Digest* got underway in 1980 were sizzling and had attracted the attention of many of the other advisors. Moreover, Hulbert decided which investment letters to follow partly by conducting an informal survey of District of Columbia libraries. *Green's* was unmistakably among the most popular services. The copies in the Federal Reserve Library were particularly heavily thumbed.

Stahl's record in the past five years has been formidable. The *Green's* Portfolio for Traders has never lost money in any of the periods monitored by Hulbert. From June 30, 1980 to June 1985, it had gained a total of 177.6 percent, against a dividend-reinvested S & P 500 score of 114.6 percent—and a decline in the price of gold bullion amounting to more than 50 percent. And, as Stahl points out, this does not recognize the fact that most of his clients would be buying on margin (commodity futures contracts typically requiring a deposit of 10 percent or less) so that their gains could be ten times greater. Hulbert wants to minimize margin considerations, which vary according to the capacity of individuals to persuade their brokers that they can afford the risk. So he treats Stahl's recommendations as if it were possible to buy fractional unmargined contracts. He argues that this gives a result roughly equivalent to purchasing the underlying bullion, from which the leveraged experience of each investor can be extrapolated.

Glimpsed in his Princeton, New Jersey, office in the fall of 1984, Charles Stahl was a substantial, avuncular figure in shirtsleeves and suspenders. He puffed a big cigar while talking with a heavy East European accent and watching the monitor screen on his desk with increasing attention. Gold had closed higher two days running, but it had not been able to make it three days in a row for over three months. Stahl thought that a third up day would be a bullish sign. He hoped that would happen. He had been having some trouble with his market calls recently—he was eventually to say that 1984 had been his worst year for two decades—and his optimistic comments about gold had begun to take on a wary tone. But the rally stalled, and gold finished down. Stahl shrugged philosophically. He had seen worse.

"In 1945 I saw a man exchange a kilo of gold for a flask of water—" Stahl begins with a cheerful wave of his cigar, carried away in the middle of a friendly disputation. But then he stops abruptly. His mouth is trembling. He cannot continue. It was when he was a prisoner on a six-day train journey from Auschwitz to Mauthausen; half his fellow inmates died. For years he avoided talking about it precisely because the memory was too overwhelming. Charles Stahl does not have the gold bug's genuine love for gold. He regards it as an inverse stock market for the free world, bullish when things go wrong. "You should have 5 percent to 8 percent of your assets in gold as insurance," he says, "and hope it goes down."

The story Stahl tells, with some prompting because he does not always reveal what he has not been directly asked, is involved and harrowing. He was born in 1921 in Lvov, a city that had been part of the Austro-Hungarian Empire, was then in Poland, and is now in the Soviet Union. He was trained as an architect, but married into a family that was prominent in jewelry and metal-trading throughout Eastern Europe. When Hitler and Stalin partitioned Poland in 1939, Stahl and his wife fled to Hungary. The buttons on their clothes were made of solid platinum and covered with a thin layer of cloth. In Budapest, fortified by this unorthodox method of capital transfer, Stahl studied economics and continued in the family business: eventually he was able to tell how much gold was in a coin simply by weighing it in his hand. In 1944 he was arrested for funneling money to OSS agents and sent to Auschwitz. As a Roman Catholic, he was classified as an Aryan, although he was actually of Jewish descent. He survived partly because his linguistic abilities made him useful to the camp authorities. Back in Budapest, he discovered that Russian troops were billeted in his house. He had to sneak in one day to recover the gold and diamonds he had secreted in the window frames. By 1947, Stahl was trading metals and stocks in Geneva and writing for Polish newspapers. In 1953 he arrived with his family in the United States.

Stahl's troubles were not over. In 1956 he figured in a drama the New York papers eagerly dubbed "The Case of the Disappearing Broker." The broker was Stahl. He had been chairman of De Pontet & Company, a New York Stock Exchange member firm, but resigned by mail from Amsterdam and vanished after a Canadian mining stock he was promoting, Green Bay Mining and Exploration Ltd., had described a perfect parabolic peak, from fifty cents to $12.50 and back to $1 in a few months, reportedly costing investors some $6 million. Stahl was eventually discovered in Rio de Janeiro. In March 1957, New York Attorney General Louis K. Lefkowitz announced that as a result of investigations into an alleged manipulation of Green Bay stock, Stahl had voluntarily signed a consent injuction before the U.S. vice consul in Rio, permanently barring him from the securities business. Stahl subsequently returned to the United States and attempted to have the injunction vacated. He argued that he had been shattered by his failure to find additional financing in Europe, that his family had lost its own fortune of $4–5 million in the Green Bay collapse, and that he had learned of the attorney general's action only when he was in Brazil and had been given to understand that he could return to present exculpatory evidence. Lefkowitz opposed him, issuing a colorful press release accusing Stahl of being part of "a plot by firms and individuals behind the Iron Curtain to seize control of American, British, Dutch and Canadian corporations producing vital defense materials . . ." Stahl's plea was denied.

Stahl is anguished at the mention of these events that took place nearly thirty years ago. One point that seems to emerge clearly is that he was frightened by far more than litigation—ostensibly by the political pressures he thought he saw behind the authorities' actions, but perhaps also by the prospect of any further experiences at all with a hostile state. In papers filed in his attempt to reopen the case, Stahl explained his retreat to Rio graphically: "I was broken, desolate and slept not at all. I lived on coffee and cigarettes. A nervous breakdown was imminent. My wife's urgings that I take a rest, so that my health and thinking processes might be restored, made sense." Now he says simply: "I was ashamed."

It all seems a long time ago. Stahl has lived on the outskirts of the elegant college town of Princeton, New Jersey, since 1954, and almost never goes to New York anymore; in fact, he doesn't even go out for lunch. In 1966, after some years of commuting to Montreal, where he was associated with a manufacturing concern, he began the biweekly *Green's* for a commodities broker. In 1968 he became *Green's* sole proprietor. He now publishes it with the help of a staff of five out of a large house next door to his home, an arrangement that has allowed him to preserve the surrounding rolling acres of lawns. He keeps in touch with the markets by means of the wire services and frequent international telephone calls. ("You could run this business from the North Pole if you have the communications. It's *better* if you're far away.") An associate maintains an office in London; the recent death of another deprived him of a Zurich base. And unlike many market letter proprietors, Stahl openly admits to reading not only other letters ("about two or three dozen") but even financial magazines ("two dozen").

Stahl's operation today has the efficiency and almost domestic comfort of long-established routine. He has a computer but doesn't use it much, updating his principal charts by hand and using card files to help keep track of his approximately 2,000 subscribers. Framed letters from public officials look down supportively from the walls, a memento of the period when he engaged actively in public debate on behalf of the Johnson and Nixon Administrations' efforts to finesse inflation and prop up the dollar. Stahl's women assistants don't like the cigar smoke, and the official compromise is that he meticulously shuts the door of his office, although while he is in the kitchen eating a luncheon sandwich they sneak in with an air freshener. Two sleeping cats keep him company, but decline to wake up for an interview.

Stahl does not advertise aggressively. He had major surgery in 1983 and rarely goes on the lecture circuit anymore. His subscribers ($240 a year) and consultation clients ($5,000 annual retainer, $200 each phone call) are mostly professionally involved in the gold and silver market, and have been with him for years. "It's a dying business," he says calmly about his letter. His two daughters have other interests, and he has no successor.

But it won't lie down. "Stahl has had some amazing calls," says Hulbert, citing a neatly nailed slump in the gold price early in 1984 and in silver a year earlier. On March 15, 1985, Stahl appeared on Louis Rukeyser's *Wall Street Week* and proclaimed the end, at last, of the two-year bear market in precious metals: the next week, gold and silver shot up by record amounts—as did Stahl's Trading Portfolio, which gained an unmargined 13.9 percent in that one month. His success in keeping *Green's* Trading Portfolio above water was all the more remarkable because, like some of the gold bugs he deplores, he had been probing for a reversal in the major trend for over a year. Somehow, he had avoided paying too high a price.

Stahl independently tracks his own portfolio, scrupulously sending out two test letters to different points in the country to duplicate his subscribers' experience with the U.S. mail. His results broadly parallel Hulbert's. But not so those of Bruce Babcock's *Commodity Traders Consumer Report. CTCR* showed Stahl sharply down for both 1983 and 1984. The apparent explanation is a sharp reminder of how important methodology can be. Both Hulbert and Babcock agreed on the number of calls Stahl made in 1983, and judged the same proportion to have been successful. But unlike Hulbert, Babcock aims to simulate an investor's experience by hypothetically "buying" a futures contract, using the minimum margin stipulated by the New York Commodity Futures Exchange, which is rapidly eaten up by any losses. During this period the margin required for silver contracts has been twice as high as the margin for gold. Consequently, by buying one contract per recommendation, Babcock was leveraging gold calls twice as much as silver calls. This is too bad for Stahl, because for those two years he did distinctly better in the white metal than in the yellow, which on Babcock's reckoning has brought him down.

There may be no solution to this dispute. Babcock says that, after all, the only way you can trade futures is to buy futures contracts. Hulbert says that to do so without regard for margin requirements in effect lets Exchange regulations make crucial decisions about how much leverage you want. He points out that when Harry Browne of *Harry Browne's Special Reports* recommends futures contracts, he weights his purchases for the different margin requirements specifically to adjust for this problem.

Another controversy about Stahl's results has arisen because of his habit of recommending different courses of action for traders and investors. Stahl mentions his Investors Portfolio so sketchily, once every several issues, that Hulbert decided it was insufficiently clear and stopped following it. This may have been a mistake. In response to the complaints of a wounded subscriber, Hulbert attempted to reconstruct the Investor Portfolio results for 1984, and found that it appeared to be down some 30 percent. Stahl says that his Investors Portfolio is meant to be long-term, with fundamentals determining his recommendations. By contrast, decisions affecting his Trading Portfolio are made on technical grounds.

Green's Commodity Market Comments consists of four green pages stiff with facts and figures about the supply and demand for gold and silver. This fundamental component probably reflects the commercial interests of much of Stahl's clientele. But although Stahl never prints a chart, he discusses his recommendations almost entirely in chartese: moving averages, support and resistance levels and so on. He tends to assume a certain sophistication on the part of the reader. In early 1981, for example, Stahl recommended his traders try to play a rebound after gold and silver reached his specified targets on the downside, taking a small profit if the rally was "swift" but holding on for a greater profit if it was initially "belabored." Gold did rally as he forecast, but some subscribers must have called Stahl to inquire about its adjectival status, because in his next letter he scolded that "any trader worth his salt could see the rally was belabored."

Stahl's recommendations are relatively few, even for his

Trading Portfolio. Although commodity futures are incompara-
bly more volatile than the stock market, he refuses to provide a
telephone hotline with his service. "I want to discourage traders," he says. "Because if you trade too often, you have to lose,
there is no way . . . One rule in life: *undertrade*. Another rule"
—he adds helpfully—*"buy on weakness, sell on strength."*

Beyond this, Stahl has no rigid system. "I look for a pattern," he says. "You can only do it if you did it for a long time."
In forty years of trading precious metals, he believes he has
developed a "feel" for the market. It has become so familiar to
him that he says he no longer keeps up all his charts daily, since
he can visualize the changing situation in his head. Among the
key measures he watches are Open Interest and On-Balance
Volume. Open Interest (the sum of contracts outstanding at the
end of the day) serves as a measure of momentum. Stahl believes
that if it is rising as the price moves decisively up or down, the
price trend should continue in that direction. He regards a
decline by the open interest when the price is rising as neutral,
but a decline when the price is weakening suggests a buying
opportunity. On-Balance Volume is a running total of the total
daily volume of a given commodity, adding the volume on days
the price rose and subtracting it when the price fell, so that it
can be either positive or negative. If the points representing
these totals are moving in an upward or a downward zigzag,
they are said to be in a rising field trend or a falling field trend.
These are respectively bullish and bearish.

Stahl has also invented his own measure of "internal momentum" for picking market bottoms. He has named it the
Coefficient of Relative Strength. It is computed for each commodity by establishing a running total of the amount by which
its closing price each day was above or below the midpoint
between the day's high and low prices, and can also be positive
or negative. Stahl notes that his Coefficient tends to turn positive if a new bottom is being made. In bull markets, he says, the
closing price is typically closer to the day's high than to the low.

Despite his charting predilections, Stahl's thinking is obviously suffused with the fundamentalist conviction that inflation
will recur. It was masked by the strength of the dollar, he argued
in 1984, which was partly a vote of confidence by the rest of the
world in America in general and the Reagan Administration in
particular. But eventually, he believed, the dollar would decline

to adjust for the chronic American balance of payment deficit. In addition, he believed that inflation was the only way to liquidate the burden of unpayable debt assumed by the Third World and Eastern Europe. The world's financial structure, he felt, was so precarious that any determined attempt to wring out inflation would precipitate a catastrophe: "We had as much deflation as we could stand two or three years ago," he said, referring to the collapse of banks like Continental Illinois and Mexico's threatened default. "Only a depression can eliminate inflation. And a depression would be worse than inflation, so in the final analysis we have to have inflation."

All of which, he thought, meant another prolonged boom in the precious metals—eventually. Stahl says that silver normally swings more wildly than gold, but in this cycle he thinks gold may move faster. Silver consumption is no longer outstripping production, as it was in the 1970s, and much more is being hoarded by investors. The idea that there is some economically correct ratio between the silver and gold prices—it used to be 30 to 1 and more recently has been 50 to 1—provokes a gutteral scoffing.

Stahl's view on what causes inflation is eclectic to the point where an academic might reasonably accuse it of lacking intellectual rigor. It embraces "bottlenecks, Acts of God, the creation of money and government deficits." This pragmatism reflects the fact that Stahl has not succumbed to the occupational disease of precious metals specialists and become a conservative ideologue. He opposes any return to the gold standard as impractical, and has quietly declined to visit South Africa on moral grounds. He believes that completely free markets are politically impossible, despite the coincidence of sharing birthplaces with Ludwig von Mises, who as a leader of the "Austrian School" was a central figure in the revival of free-market economics in the United States and who has become virtually a patron saint to many investment letter editors. Stahl's public stands in the 1960s were invariably in favor of schemes aimed (vainly) at retaining government control over the currency; and as a dedicated attendee of the International Monetary Fund's annual conferences in Washington, he echoes the conventional wisdom of central bankers that the United States should have helped to bail out the Fund in 1983, a proposal that was nearly derailed by spirited gold bug opposition.

Nevertheless, as the 1984 presidential election approached, Stahl seemed quite content with Reagan's apparent economic success. "For a refugee," he said, "the U.S. is the end of the line. There's nowhere else to go."*

DAN SULLIVAN AND *THE CHARTIST*

It's Sunday midnight in New York City's Madison Square, but the roar of the traffic is continuous as Dan Sullivan stands gazing up past the grimy trees at the soaring, floodlit buildings. Sullivan, who was born in 1934, has spent virtually his entire life in Southern California. His home and the office where he writes *The Chartist* investment letter are both just across the road from the Pacific Ocean, in the small town of Seal Beach, near Los Angeles. He hasn't been in Manhattan for more than twenty years.

Finally, a familiar object hoves into view in the shape of a nocturnal jogger. Sullivan, who runs an hour on the beach each morning and competes in marathons and triatholons, hails it with a delighted wave. "There's a community among runners," he explains enthusiastically. The jogger reacts with New York suspicion and gives Sullivan a wide berth, which fortunately he is too nearsighted to notice.

In the gossipy world of investment letters, Sullivan was long regarded as a recluse. He never spoke at investment conferences, did not publish his telephone number and had never given an interview until he talked to *Barron's* in early 1985. When confronted with this charge, Sullivan protested mildly. He was *quite* well known in Seal Beach where his home number was openly listed, he said, rather unrealistically since (apart from anything else) the only address appearing in *The Chartist* is its post office box in neighboring Long Beach. However, he did admit, "I'm the antithesis of Joe Granville. I don't seek public-

*Tragically, while this book was in preparation for publication, Charles Stahl died of a heart attack. His letter has been purchased by the Powell Monetary Analyst Service.

ity." (Subsequently, Sullivan did have an office number for *The Chartist* listed with Long Beach Directory Inquiries. Apparently it just hadn't occurred to him before.)

Despite his shyness, Sullivan has obviously been doing something right. *The Chartist*, biweekly and $115 a year, has survived since 1969 in a notoriously difficult business. Hint: it is one of the handful of letters that can claim to have outperformed the market. *The Chartist*'s Actual Cash Account and its Trading Portfolio have consistently matched or beaten the broad market Dow since the *Hulbert Financial Digest* began to follow them in 1980 and 1983 respectively. Moreover, according to figures regularly carried in *The Chartist*, Sullivan's Actual Cash Account, which is indeed his actual cash account with confirmation slips available on request, has an even longer record of success. Begun in 1969 with $64,458, it had increased some sixfold to over $360,000 by mid-1985, at a time when the Dow made it all the way from 950 to 1,350. An exact compound growth rate is difficult to calculate because Sullivan has added some further capital and extracted rather more for personal use. Mark Hulbert, while noting that his own results for the Actual Cash Account recommendations differ from Sullivan's because of these personal withdrawals, says he has no reason to doubt *The Chartist*'s count. When in June 1985 Hulbert calculated the Actual Cash Account back for the previous five years according to his methods, it turned out to have appreciated 127.8 percent against the dividend-reinvested Dow's 100.8 percent.

Now entering his fifties, Dan Sullivan is at the age when he is delicately poised between appearing boyish and looking like a leprechaun. He is a slim, diffident, medium-sized man with blue eyes, graying hair, an impacted suntan and a rapid, nervous blink. The son of an Irish-American doctor and a WASP mother, he is a lapsed Catholic who still finds himself saying the Act of Contrition on turbulent airplane flights and seems astonished at the idea of considering any other faith. He briefly studied business at Loyola College in Los Angeles before managing his own liquor store in Whittier, which he continued to do until 1975. Superficially a casual Californian, Sullivan says softly that there are other things in his life besides the stock market. He obviously derives great comfort from the sense of community in Seal Beach. He has worked with the same secretary for years; friends drop by when needed to help put the letter out. But he is equally obviously deeply competitive: drawn from handball to running by his former wife, he reports that he can now beat her times despite being seventeen years older. The couple divorced in 1982, but remain very friendly.

Whatever some of its victims may think, the stock market is emphatically not a horse race, according to Sullivan. As a young man, he went to the races for years trying to figure out a successful gambling system. It gave him early experience with a fairly efficient market. Betting odds are calculated by monitoring and adjusting for the public's willingness to put money on one horse rather than on another, and Sullivan found that the popular perception about form as reflected in the odds was usually sufficiently accurate to make it very difficult for the individual gambler to beat. And he was distressed to realize that in addition the track was taking 15 percent off the top of every bet. By contrast, he says, the stock market has returned on average some 9 percent a year in dividends and capital gains over many years. Sullivan prefers these odds. They shape his investment strategy: preserve capital, cut losses, look for the isolated superprofit—"three, four, five hundred percent." He has achieved this repeatedly, in stocks like Resorts International, Tandy Corporation and Toys R Us.

Sullivan's introduction to the stock market was oddly parallel to that of Al Frank, his fellow Californian who lives just up the coast in Santa Monica and who also publishes his personal holdings in his letter, *The Prudent Speculator*. They just happened to reach completely different conclusions. Sullivan bet on his first stock in the early 1960s: Korvette. He lost. The experience drove him to read every book about the stock market that he could get his hands on. He got the idea for publishing his Actual Cash Account from *How I Helped More Than 10,000 Investors to Profit in Stocks* by E. George Schaefer ("one of the Hall-of-Famers"). His attitude to strategy was deeply influenced by Gerald Loeb's *Battle for Investment Survival*, which advocated an "Ever-Liquid Account" focusing on a few stocks, following up gains with further purchases and possibly eventual margining, but retreating quickly into cash at the prospect of losses. And Nicholas Darvas's *How I Made $2 Million in the Stock Market* was a key source of his basic technique: Relative Strength.

In every market cycle, Sullivan points out, some stocks fight the declines and outperform the rallies. They have powerful sponsorship that makes them consistently strong relative to the broad market as measured by the Dow or some other index, and they will probably continue to do well. The Relative Strength method does not call turns: it follows trends. "Buy high, sell higher," says Sullivan. "But if you're wrong, relative strength can kill you because it gets you in at the top."

In the late 1960s the Relative Strength concept was the subject of a fierce academic debate as one of the first possible anomalies in the Efficient Market Hypothesis to be rigorously tested. Reviewing the evidence in his seminal book *Stock Market Logic* (1976), Norman Fosback concluded that the most the critics of Relative Strength were able to establish was that it worked better in stronger markets than in weak ones. Dan Sullivan is indeed widely regarded as being more effective in bull markets —he demurs, citing his record in the 1973–4 bear market—and he does aim to integrate his stock selection with market timing. Asked about Efficient Market Hypothesis criticisms of the relative strength method, Sullivan says earnestly that it wouldn't work if everyone realized how good it was.

The mathematics of calculating Relative Strength can be complicated. The most straightforward method is to compare the stock against the market over an arbitrary period. If the stock has gone up 50 percent and the index is up 25 percent, the stock's relative strength could be said to be 1.5 minus 1.25 = 0.25. Or the stock price could be divided by the index, giving 1.5/1.25 = 1.2. But this method can lead to distortions if at the beginning of the period the stock was performing some major gyration, such as a correction. More elegant techniques attempt to determine the true trend by considering all the prices for the period under consideration, and also to adjust for each stock's volatility and make other refinements. But the amount of calculation involved is distressing. Only institutional investors could afford the computer hardware that made it thinkable—until the advent of the personal computer.

A simple alternative is to use a chart. Each day's stock price can be divided by that day's Dow or S & P, and the result scaled so that it too can be traced on the stock's daily price chart. Then the two lines can be compared by eye. Standard charting techniques apply: thus if the stock price moved to a new high, the relative strength line had to move to a new high to confirm it. Sullivan says this method is quite feasible, although because comparisons between stocks are difficult it can sometimes be a little subjective.

Sullivan himself prefers to rank stocks in order of their Relative Strength according to a secret process of calculation he has developed himself. He also has proprietary methods of determining precisely when to buy and sell, which he is reluctant to discuss. He will say, however, that he looks for stocks whose short-term relative strength is holding up well in order to screen out stocks with good long-term relative strength that are actually topping. But he adds that this is tricky because too much short-term relative strength can mean that the stock is temporarily overbought.

Like Al Frank, Sullivan began circulating his market opinions in letter form to friends. At first he mentioned only one or two stocks. But in the mid-1970s he chose as his major recommendation a stock called U.S. Shoe, which immediately "gapped" upward—jumping several points without trading, giving no one a chance to buy. Then it languished for several years, during which Sullivan's recommendation ignominiously marked the high. Badly burned, he realized that the following he had developed was now large enough to distort the market in any individual stock. So he began to offer a diversity of selections.

In 1980, Sullivan decided on another change. Until then, he had tended to sell his stocks when they showed weakness, in a variation of a formula he had derived from Gerald Loeb, who maintained that stocks should be sold whenever they retracted 10 percent. But now, looking back over his record, Sullivan concluded that this method was causing him to be shaken out too quickly during transient market disturbances, such as that year's panic when the Hunt brothers attempted to corner the silver market. Now Sullivan treats all the stocks he selects for his Actual Cash Account at the beginning of each market cycle as a unit. He charts their composite progress as if they were one stock and sells them together. The idea is to allow individual stocks to go further into negative territory without being "stopped out"—hitting the points at which Sullivan has placed either an actual or a mental "stop-loss" order, triggering automatic sale. This gives the stocks "room to play," as Sullivan says. Only occasionally will he take a stock out from under this umbrella and shoot it, as he did in March 1985 when United Guardian ran into unprecedented selling. Disciplined portfolio management, he insists, is quite as important as stock picking.

When Sullivan decides the market has reached the end of a cycle—a "juncture period"—he will keep those individual stocks that have proved successful, place stop-losses under them, and "go for broke" with their paper profits. He disagrees completely with the old Wall Street adage that "bears make money, bulls make money, but hogs go broke." The biggest winners need two or three cycles, he thinks. But he will never let them go below his buying point and lose him "hard money."

Sullivan's new policy applies only to his Actual Cash Account. He recommends exactly the same stocks for his Trading Portfolio (plus extra batches of others from time to time), but here he retains close stops. Sullivan likes to take profits in increments, first recovering his original investment and then taking a more speculative attitude to the balance. In both portfolios, in sharp contrast to many technicians, Sullivan makes relatively few recommendations, and he tends to hold them for more than six months. "As you get older, you get more long-term oriented."

Sullivan says he's satisfied with his new Actual Cash Account technique, although it has its problems. Several times he has given up almost all his gains in various stocks before being stopped out. In the December 6, 1984, issue of *The Chartist*, for example, Sullivan could be observed doggedly defending his not selling John Blair and Verbatim out of his Actual Cash Account until absolutely compelled to by looming losses, thus relinquishing paper profits that had once amounted to 158 percent and 289 percent respectively—or a total of $44,562. (And, as Sullivan pointed out in pained tones, "We're not talking hypothetical; that's real money.") Basically, Sullivan argues that his Actual Cash Account method is safer and will produce greater profits in the long run, although he adds that not everyone will have the patience to follow it. Mark Hulbert's calculations do show the Actual Cash Account as markedly less volatile than the Trading Portfolio. But up to now it hasn't done as well.

At least every four weeks, Sullivan says, he looks through chart books covering all possible stock purchases. He concentrates entirely on equities, regarding commodities and options as mere gambling. Nevertheless, it is ironic that, despite his letter's name, he prefers to express his favorite relative strength technique as an algorithm rather than graphically. In fact, he pays little attention to the celebrated chart formations like double tops or head-and-shoulders, and responds blankly to questions about Dow Theory ("an old method they used to use"). But he is interested in support and resistance levels. Until recently, a favorite buying point was if a stock topped out, made a high and a low in the next six weeks, and then broke through the low. Sullivan found that after the selling flurry subsided, the stock often recovered completely, so he began to wait, selling only if there was a second breakdown. "Just as if someone was charting the chartists," he observes. However, nowadays this doesn't work as well, which is another example of the continuous erosion to which all technical indicators are subject.

If he's not a pure chartist, however, Sullivan is a pure technician. "I really don't care what the companies do," he says of his stocks, almost apologetically. "I just follow the smart money."

Sullivan picks stocks within the context of the overall market "weather." But no market-timing indicator is perfect, he cautions. His own are mostly aimed at breadth, such as the Advance/Decline line and moving averages of advances and declines. One Sullivan market-timing measure is adapted from the "Sentimeter" invented by Edson Gould and employed in his *Findings and Forecasts* letter in the 1970s. It turns on the amount investors seem willing to pay for a dollar of dividends from the stocks comprising the Dow Jones Industrial Average. Gould thought that a ratio above 30 to 1 indicated speculative excess. In March 1985 the Dow was about 1,270 and its component stocks were paying over $57 in dividends, so that the ratio was only some 22 to 1. Sullivan took this as a sign that the bull market had some way to go, despite the nervousness he felt because so many advisors seem to agree with him.

Another measure Sullivan watches closely is his "90+" test of momentum. This states that if 90 percent of NYSE stocks exceed their ten-week moving averages, a long-term buy signal has been given. Since 1969 there have been eight 90+ readings, the last in September 1982. On February 5, 1985, 89.5 percent was achieved, but after that there was some slippage. This wasn't quite good enough, because in the fall of 1973 the ten-week series had moved above 89 percent, only to be followed by a 400 Dow point drop.

About the rest of the 1980s, Sullivan is basically bullish. His study of market breadth is one reason. The slaughter among the broad market of non-Dow stocks in 1973-4 when the average American Stock Exchange stock was down 90 percent, has inspired a central theme in his investment philosophy: that 1973-4 was a "once-in-a-generation experience," the direct equivalent of the 1929 Crash. What would it take to change his mind? Sullivan responds like a good trend follower: "The market would have to go down," he says.

Sullivan says he prefers picking stocks to writing his letter —which, however, he does with a certain harassed eloquence. Presumably this strain will grow worse now that he has begun to manage money for clients ($50,000 minimum). But all that jogging and sun seems to have been good for Sullivan's stamina, if not for his contact with the rest of the world. "I never want to retire," he says.

BOB GROSS AND *THE PROFESSIONAL INVESTOR*

His peers in the investment letter business are eager to prepare you: Robert T. Gross, proprietor of *The Professional Investor*, is aptly named. Yet here it is, hours before his legendary early afternoon reveille, and Gross is not in his bedroom, where he is said to lurk all day, but is instead bounding brightly around the spacious waterside home in Pompano Beach, Florida, out of which he works. He is neither unshaven nor in his usual pajama bottoms but is neatly dressed and groomed. It is true he is joking about how one noted investment letter writer has a glass eye and another, a Dr. Strangelove–type arm spasm as a result of a stroke, so that they couldn't be seated next to each other at the recent Market Technicians Association conference. But that's perhaps more Truly Tasteless, as he points out himself, than genuinely gross.

Gross in fact points out a great deal himself. A more appropriate name for him might almost be that of Al *(Prudent Speculator)* Frank. He announces immediately, for example, that his

spruce appearance is specially for the benefit of a visiting journalist (me). He would indeed normally be in bed, unshaven, etc.
His Rolls-Royce, in which he had insisted on having his visitor
chauffeured, is a publicity gimmick inspired by a long-ago picture on the jacket of Richard Ney's best-selling *Wall Street Gang*
showing the triumphant author debouching from one. Gross
has even had the house cleaned and the lawn trimmed because
he has checked around and discovered that his interviewer's
attention is easily distracted by such details.

Gross says he believes that honesty, about mistakes in the
market and the like, is the best policy; and the consensus is that
he means it. This did not prevent him from answering my
unwary query about his circulation by giving his total mailing
of 9,100 instead of the number of long-term subscribers, which
he later says is 8,000. But he felt guilty for months afterward—
and a *Barron's* article citing the higher figure did duly bring
retribution in the form of industry peers who wish to make
known their own considerably smaller off-the-record estimates.
The reality is that much of Gross's self-revelation is clearly
uncalculated, motivated by sheer nervous energy. It can extend
to several levels, as when, amid exuberant and detailed discus-
sion of the advantages of renewing bachelor life in his early
fifties, it emerges that he knows the exact date his wife left him
(August 3, 1982) and how many days away is the anniversary.

Bob Gross's record during the five years that the *Hulbert
Financial Digest* has followed *Professional Investor* qualifies him as
at least a partial anomaly in the Efficient Market Hypothesis.
Whatever his personal reputation, Gross is disciplined and systematic in his letter. In each issue, he lists four different groups
of stock selections, which he calls "Scans," complete with the
price when originally recommended, gains or losses, and recommended stops. The Scans consist, in order of conservatism, of
"Investment Grade," New York Stock Exchange, American
Stock Exchange (Amex) and over-the-counter stocks respectively. Gross's Amex and OTC Scans have cumulatively outperformed the market fairly consistently while Hulbert has been
monitoring them, scoring gains of 172.2 percent and 130.3 percent
against the dividend-reinvested Dow's 100.8 percent. For both,
however, 1981 and 1984 were down years. Gross's NYSE and
Investment Grade Scans have done rather worse, gaining only

47.2 percent and 35.5 percent. Thus an average for Gross's port-folios is 92.4 percent.

Gross has achieved this record in spite of a self-inflicted handicap. He offers no advice on how readers should allocate their assets between his Scans or what proportions they should be holding in cash at any given time. There are sometimes over fifty stocks in each Scan, which makes it probable that subscribers regard them more as shortlists, exercising independent judgment on which stocks actually to buy. But in the absence of advice to the contrary, Mark Hulbert is obliged to construct the *Hulbert Financial Digest*'s model portfolios for *Professional Investor* by investing equally in each Scan, including all the stocks, and staying fully invested at all times. This method puts a heavy demand on an investment advisor's stock-picking ability. It means that he can never go into cash during a bear market unless he actually sells all his selections. Just lightening up by selling a few stocks won't do, because the *Hulbert Financial Digest* simply rebalances the portfolio to keep equal dollar amounts in the remainder. It has to do this in order to duplicate the experience of new subscribers and to get any kind of consistent record at all. Of course, the advisor can avoid this problem either by giving subscribers general direction on cash proportions, as Stan Weinstein does in *Professional Tape Reader*, or by running a full-blown model portfolio with specific positions in cash and securities, like Charles Allmon in *Growth Stock Outlook*. But some advisors, perhaps unconsciously influenced by youthful experiences on the racetrack, prefer to hand out tips without instructions on their use, which Hulbert then has to supply. Even Dan Sullivan, despite insisting on the importance of disciplined portfolio management, does not specify cash proportions in his Traders Portfolio.

One reason for the relatively poorer performance of the Investment Grade Scan is a further illustration of the importance of rating service methodology. Until August 1983 the Investment Grade Scan had gained every year, according to the *Hulbert Financial Digest* count. But then, seeking to hedge a short position, Gross accidentally recommended the purchase of too large a number of put options on the Amex Major Market Index. This was a disaster. In two months the Investment Grade Scan lost 25 percent of its value. Gross instantly admitted his error when a puzzled Hulbert called to check if he was reading his copy of *Professional Investor* right, merely adding wistfully that it seemed that no subscribers had been hurt. "Frankly, I don't know what was going on in the head of the author," Gross wrote in *Professional Investor* the next month. Hulbert felt he had to follow the letter rather than the spirit of the advice, although none of Gross's subscribers seemed to have fallen into the pit. (Harry Schultz was involved in a similar freak accident in 1982, when he had gone "short against the box"—which entails both a long and a short position—to lock in a profit in Columbia Pictures: on successive days he was stopped out of his long position and then trapped short when trading was suspended in Columbia after Coca-Cola made a bid for it. The moviemaker eventually reopened sharply higher, wiping out 10 percent of Schultz's U.S. Stocks portfolio.

Nevertheless, Hulbert remains impressed by Gross's record, particularly by the performance of his Amex Scan. He points out that it only slightly underperformed the Dow in 1981, one of its two down years, and in 1982 it posted a substantial gain despite a weak showing for American Stock Exchange stocks generally, especially in the first half of the year.

"I'm Irish full face and Jewish in profile," Gross wisecracks cheerfully. He is short and stocky, with thinning dark hair and blue eyes. He was born in New York in 1932. His father was a Jewish cost accountant who had been working on Wall Street during the 1929 Crash; his mother was an Irish ex-secretary, and Gross was brought up Catholic. High school did not agree with Gross, and after graduating, he worked as a laborer and a carpenter. But when the Korean war broke out, he served as a paratrooper, and subsequently, after selling automobiles for six months, he studied at George Washington University on the GI Bill. Then he was successfully an industrial chemist with Colgate-Palmolive, where he patented a method of gelling alcohol for use in hairdressing; a journalist writing for chemical industry magazines; and an advertising and public relations executive.

In 1968, Gross's interest in the stock market led him to join *Indicator Digest*, leaving two years later after the usual disagreements. Almost immediately, in January 1971, Gross began *Professional Investor*. At first it leaned heavily on digesting other services, and Gross published a series of witty and informative pamphlets surveying the investment letter industry and detailing how to start a letter yourself. He also experimented with other investment products, and for a time linked up with Don Worden, which brought him to southern Florida where the influx of investment letters was paralleling that of the kudzu vine and the fire ant. In recent years, Gross has increasingly relied upon his own opinions of the market, employing a small support staff and doing the writing and research himself.

There's not much that's obviously unique about Gross's investment methods, but apparently he makes them work. He says he's 80 percent a pure technician, although he is modestly reluctant to be called a chartist on the rather strict grounds that he doesn't draw charts himself. Every week, however, he flips through two thousand or more Mansfield charts looking for interesting stocks on the basis of the formations revealed. "There are about four or five chart formations I look for, but they're hard to describe in a few words. They're not simple patterns that you would recognize from Edwards & Magee; it's sort of a gestalt thing. And it's all contingent on being right on the market trend. Otherwise the best-looking formations can abort." Two favorites are saucer bottoms and sudden upside breakouts. Gross points out that he is also simultaneously assimilating the supplementary technical and fundamental information that the Mansfield service kindly prints right on its charts, such as volume, relative strength, insider activity and earnings trends.

Gross then corroborates his technical findings with a little fundamental fact-finding, partly to avoid situations like rumored takeovers, which he regards as too unreliable to be worth the risk. His research is restrained. He no longer calls company managements, saying he finds them too optimistic, but instead he studies public sources of information like *Value Line.* In his heart, Gross remains a technician. He is still reproaching himself for getting fascinated by fundamentals and recommending oil stocks in early 1983.

Gross is a moderately active trader. His Scans often have more than 100 transactions a year, with only a minority of the holdings exceeding six months. He says he enjoys trading ("it's like going to the track"), and was once even more active, slowing down largely for personal reasons. But very few traders, he says, make money in the long run. Included in *Professional Investor's*

$200 annual subscription price is a telephone hotline, but Gross almost never uses it other than to comment on general market conditions, to pose puzzles and to tell blue jokes. He has also begun to offer Scans, which Hulbert doesn't monitor, for options, telephone switch funds and gold stocks. The latter has not made a trade since 1980, although by Gross's reckoning it nevertheless has shown a substantial profit since its inception in the 1970s.

The difference between the performances of his various Scans does not seem to have made much of an impression on Gross. Pressed for an explanation, he suggests that maybe his technical approach works better with the speculative stocks found on the Amex and OTC—and that trading patterns on the New York Stock Exchange may have been distorted by the growth of options, index futures and institutional business. Some Gross-watchers think the difference lies in his policy on stop-loss orders. They say the stops he recommends in his NYSE and Investment Grade Scans are significantly closer than those in his Amex and OTC Scans, with the result that they are hit more often and the portfolios trade more. Gross says he's not conscious of any difference. Another theory is that he just has better contacts among Amex and OTC professionals.

Gross ponders a lot about market timing, despite not building his conclusions into his portfolios, except indirectly by selecting fewer stocks and by sometimes selling short. Each issue of *The Professional Investor* systematically lists the status of some forty-nine market indicators—the "Indicator Scan." These range from the two-hundred-day Moving Average of the Dow to "Merrill's Second Hour Index"—a cumulative measure of activity in the second hour of each trading day, which according to Arthur Merrill of the respected *Technical Trends* service is positively correlated with the market's overall trend several months out, possibly because professional traders wait to take their positions until dust has settled after the opening. Gross comments tersely on each indicator, and combines them to give three composite readings, reflecting simple arithmetical formulas and his own weighting of the indicators.

Late in 1983, Gross unveiled what he called his Trinity Index. This was a merger of three classic indicators, which technicians glean avidly each week from *Barron's* Market Laboratory page: the Specialists Short Sales Ratio, the number of shares New York Stock Exchange specialists sell short weekly divided by the total number of shares sold short by all investors that week; the Members' Short Ratio, weekly short sales made by NYSE member firms for their own account divided by total weekly short sales; and the Public Short Ratio, the weekly total public short sales divided by total NYSE volume. Traditionally, the first two indicators are supposed to reflect informed opinion; the third reflects the public and is therefore presumed to operate inversely. Gross hoped in combining them to smooth out their individual volatilities, which he also attempted to do by using moving averages. He reported that the Trinity Index had a record in predicting rallies five to twenty-six weeks in the future that had stood up when tested for the previous eighteen years. In a pragmatic vein, he conceded that the Members' Shorts figure included Specialist Shorts and that the index was "not mathematically clean, but for whatever reason it works." To his great disgust, Trinity proceeded to signal an imminent rally throughout 1984's sideways drift. Eventually the market did clamber higher, and as Trinity's second birthday approached, Gross was still hopeful about it.

Throughout 1984, a difficult year for him, Gross was making baffled bullish noises. He persistently maintained that, as he said in his August 24 letter, "if a one-third to two-thirds retracement of the biggest, fastest, largest upmove in history is not simply a normal secondary in one of the two greatest bull markets in a century [the move beginning in August 1982], we don't know what is." In the fall, although generally skeptical that charting techniques can be applied to the averages, he thought a "flag" formation in the Dow Jones Industrial Average suggested it would rise another 125 points or so before any retraction, and said he was looking for another upward explosion. The market sagged, but an upward explosion did come in January 1985, carrying to within striking range of Gross's objective. So he continued to maintain that the primary trend was up, although commenting sourly on the unusual profile of this bull market. He shrugs off attempts to elicit longer-term prognostication. "I could turn around in two or three weeks, depending on the indicators. It's enough to stick my neck out week to week."

Of all the investment letter editors, Bob Gross may be the most compleat small entrepreneur. His operation is totally vertically integrated—he does all his own printing and collating on massive machines that lurk in his home behind discreetly closed drapes. He is a master of direct-mail techniques, writing his own solicitation letters which are regarded as classics in the genre. He is acutely aware of trends, and engages in periodic special promotions including rather intense-looking one-day miniconferences, for example, on trading techniques for switch funds and options, at which his scabrous monologues reinforce his reputation.

The flip side of this self-sufficiency is that Gross is obviously lonely. He lives by himself, apart from occasional visits from his two daughters, and is a compulsive maker of late-night telephone calls to other investment letter editors, who are often suffering from the same occupational disease. Gross takes an almost familial view of the industry: he was one of the financial backers of the 1985 *Lowe* v. *SEC* Supreme Court challenge to registration requirements. *Professional Investor* requires a lot of work, and it may be that Gross now simply lacks the emotional energy to make further refinements to an already successful format. He himself says that his circulation has suffered because he doesn't work as hard at making speeches and showing the flag at investment conferences as his neighbor and fellow Rolls-Royce flaunter Stan Weinstein, proprietor of *The Professional Tape Reader*.

There is a nonquantifiable charm to Gross's service. He describes it on the masthead as a "financial magazine," partly for the benefit of any securities regulators who might be snooping around, and he is a vivid writer who offers a lot of entertainment value. His published comments on other letters are restrained on the downside but often droll. Faced with the *Crawford Perspectives'* call for a 1929-style Crash right before the August 1982 upward explosion, he remarked deadpan, "You win some; you lose some." (And he was careful to congratulate Arch Crawford when he called the January 1985 rally.) However, Gross, who reads widely and is actually something of a closet intellectual, is merciless in his attitude to prose. He once hit Robert Nicholson's *The Nicholson Report* with a censorious "sic" when it referred to an "enervating, 10 percent rally," even though he agreed that an energizing one was imminent. It's another hint of the punctilious heart beneath the bohemian exterior. Deep in there somewhere is a persona more suited to a name derived from something clerklike. Scrivener? Levy? O'Cost Accountant?

JAMES DINES AND *THE DINES LETTER*

In a profession noted for unusual personality types, James Dines is by common consent an outstanding specimen. "Ah! Jimmy Dines, we could write a book about him alone," said Bob Gross in one of his industry surveys, adding that Dines had been "at various times . . . pleasant, waspish, humble, arrogant, wildly bullish, morbidly bearish, humorous, pedantic, metaphysical, very, very right, dead wrong, appeasing, and pugnacious." And that was before Dines' tergiversations in the early 1980s, which seem, however, to have earned him a place on Mark Hulbert's list of winners.

For over twenty years Dines was very close to *Barron's*, in whose pages he appeared many times and which sternly defended him against regulatory harassment. But now he refuses to talk to anyone associated with the magazine and has even demanded that it not report his public speeches. He characterizes editor Alan Abelson as a "mad dog" and "a wet, slippery asshole" and publisher Bob Bleiberg, once a personal friend, as a "back-stabbing bastard." It appears that Dines is still distressed by *Barron's* coverage of his celebrated telegram to subscribers on June 15, 1982, announcing the end of the bull market in gold—his long-awaited "Much Vaunted All Out One And Only Gold and Silver Sell Signal," or MVAOOAOGASSS in acronymic Dines language. The metal was then at $315, exactly nine times higher than when Dines first recommended it in 1961, but down $550 from its 1980 peak. After MVAOOAOGASSS, gold promptly began a major rally back up to above $500. Dines' telegram, however, had simultaneously flashed a stock market buy signal at 796 on the Dow, and since the stock market's subsequent rally was considerably bigger and better than that of gold, Dines insists that he be given credit for what he describes as "a brilliant call." Reporting his version of events in *Barron's* has not appeased him. Nor did it appease one of his ex-subscribers, who wrote in to point out that the stock market surge had in turn been surpassed by the appreciation of the very gold-mining stocks Dines had said to dump.

Irwin James Dines, who suppressed his first name at an early age, was born in 1931. He is a slim, dark-haired man of medium height. His ascetic face with its hollow cheeks and high forehead looks disturbingly like a skull, or an eighteenth-century death mask. His eyes are hostile and alert, but when he chooses to charm he can wrap on a wide rubber-lipped smile. He is divorced, with two daughters.

Dines was educated at Oberlin College and the University of Chicago and Columbia University Law Schools, where he was a National Honor Scholar. He served in military intelligence in Korea, and then was recruited as a security analyst by the New York brokerage house Auerbach, Pollak and Richardson, reportedly because of the precocious stock-picking chart-reading prowess he had displayed as a customer. In 1960, Dines moved to A. M. Kidder & Company, where he began to write his own market letter. But, as with Joe Granville at E. H. Hutton, Dines' iconoclastic views disturbed the management, and in October 1962 he was forced out, taking *The Dines Letter* (*TDL*) with him.

Dines had quarreled with A. M. Kidder over technical analysis in general and gold in particular. He had become convinced of the classical conservative argument that government expansion of the money supply would lead to inflation and an international financial crisis, from which the individual investor's only refuge would be gold. But Americans had been prohibited from owning gold during the New Deal. So as a substitute Dines wanted to recommend American–South African Investment Company, a goldmine play. This was directly contrary to conventional Wall Street wisdom, and he was eventually allowed to print only one sentence on the subject, on March 24, 1961. From this stems Dines' claim, now prominently displayed in each issue of *TDL*, to be "The Original Goldbug." (Some dissenters think the honor belongs to James H. Sibbet of *Let's Talk . . . Silver and Gold*, who says he began to recommend gold stocks in the winter of 1957–8.)

The Great Debate over gold and inflation has continued for more than twenty years. In the long term, and sometimes in the short term, Dines certainly scored some resounding triumphs. He foresaw the devaluation of the dollar, the depreciation of paper currencies relative to physical assets, and the gold boom. Ultimately, however, it would seem that events justified Bob Gross's caveat years before: "When Dines is wrong, he stays that way too long (meaning six months to a year). He gets bellicose about his 'wrongness' and begins protesting too much ever more loudly."

Much the same happened in the stock market. Dines was at least partially right in the long run: the market did not do well after 1966, either in nominal or in inflation-adjusted terms. But in 1973, when the bear market climax began, Dines was temporarily "unbelievably bullish," as Ronald Nevans later recorded his position in a gripping survey of the advisors' performances in *Financial World* magazine. He reversed himself only very belatedly, and then returned to being so negative that he refused to recognize that any rebound had occurred until months after the December 1974 low. Dines argued, quite correctly, that the damage done to the market in 1974 was much more severe than was suggested by the Dow Jones Industrial Average and constituted an "invisible crash," the title of his 1975 book-length compendium of *TDL* comments. He derided all the market's forays above 1,000 as "a graveyard in the sky," and predicted a final downward "killer wave," combined with a catastrophic depression. The Dow, he said for years, would sooner or later cross the gold price. And in January 1980 it almost did: the Dow was in the 890s when gold peaked at around 850. Not until the stock market moved decisively above 1,000 in 1982 could the specter of a Dines disaster be said to have been finally exorcized.

As gold failed him after 1980, Dines grew increasingly emotional. *"The Numbering of TDL's Days"* began one issue in April 1982. Complaining piercingly that no one had listened to Dines and that therefore the world was now "headed straight for a depression that is unstoppable," it advised subscribers to "enjoy your monthly TDL now as someday this pointless exercise will disappear forever." Dines had made similar noises in the 1974–6 gold bear market, which he had also missed. But this time gold did not return to save him.

During this period, Dines' relentless insistence on his own prescience took some peculiar turns. In 1981, for instance, he recommended an incredible sixty-six call options in one of his several "Supervised Lists," and then, in his own monitoring, proceeded to credit himself with selling out at the high in each one, although he actually issued no further instructions until a final sell signal the following year. Not unnaturally, such maneuvers embroiled Dines in a number of altercations with Mark Hulbert. Eventually, Hulbert offered Dines the standard space to make his objections known to readers of the *Hulbert Financial Digest*. Dines' response was deeply revealing. "My research department," he announced in his space, "believes it has found numerous mathematical errors in Mr. Hulbert's ratings that are too tedious to relate here." As an example, he offered a detailed accounting of one of his Lists for part of 1983, which he said showed "quite precisely" that it was up 33 percent instead of up only 8.3 percent. But Hulbert argued in his response that this 33 percent increase had been achieved by (1) never putting more than 10 percent into any one stock, a limitation only mentioned in *TDL* after several months as an afterthought; (2) adding $3,000 to the hypothetical portfolio partway through the year, enabling it to buy new recommendations without losing profitable earlier ones; (3) to similar effect, showing in his treasury bill section something that Hulbert in his comments austerely described as "the phenomenon encountered after August 17 of 'negative cash.' " That Dines could seriously expect *Hulbert Financial Digest* readers to swallow this argument can only be regarded as an indication of a somewhat tenuous relationship to the external world.

But for Dines there was to be life after MVAOOAOGASSS. Later in 1982 he announced drastic changes. As he had been so abused and mistreated, he said, he was going to completely refocus *TDL* on the short term. Eventually he even dropped his heavily damaged precious metal model portfolio, while insisting all the while that catastrophe and a gold standard at a much higher gold price was coming yet—for a' that and a' that, so to speak.

The result has been spectacular. After an interlude of what presumably were preparations, Dines' portfolios took off from underwater like Poseidon missiles, trading fiercely, at times going entirely into options. All of them soared: at one point his Short-Term Trading List was up 373 percent. By the end of June 1985, some signs of flame-out were apparent. But Dines' Growth List ranked second of all those Hulbert has followed since 1980, with a gain of 241 percent against the dividend-reinvested S & P 500 gain of 114.6 percent. His Speculative List had fallen just behind the S & P, with 113.8 percent; his Short-Term Trading List was just ahead of the Dow, with a gain of 105.3 percent. Only his Moderate Risk List underperformed the market, self-destructing in early 1984 and finishing down 12.5 percent. Over this five-year period, the average performance of all Dines' portfolios, still weighted to adjust for two he abandoned in early 1984, is up 67.3 percent.

Dines' run of success with his top-performing Lists constitutes perhaps the most remarkable single feat in the *Hulbert Financial Digest* records. Annual gains for these Dines portfolios in this period have ranged up to 90 percent. This pace is completely out of line with anything that Hulbert's experience with other advisors would suggest is sustainable. Dines himself has advised clients that the most they can expect from professional money managers over five years is that they match the Dow in bull markets and break even in bear markets. Hulbert thinks that would be pretty good.

It is true that Dines' achievement has involved taking on a great deal of "risk" (as measured by volatility). But even when adjusted for risk, three out of four Dines portfolios were still positive through June 1985. By contrast, *The Option Advisor* 's Aggressive Portfolio, which has shared with Dines' Short-Term Trading List the distinction of being by far the riskiest in the Hulbert stable, did indeed top the chart in 1984 but suffered a crippling loss of more than 83.3 percent in 1983. Interestingly, although all Dines' Lists now consist of stocks and options, he has still been able to control their riskiness so that it varies according to their advertised speculative propensity.

Maybe it's all luck. But the Lists traded actively in these three years, which is equivalent to a lot of coin-tosses. At the very least, the feat might suggest that some skilled traders seem able to turn on bursts of speed for short periods, like Bob Prechter's similar sprint in 1984. And another significant aspect of Dines' record has been even less noted than his being Born Again in 1982. This is the fact that through mid-1985 his Speculative and Growth Lists, although occasionally underperforming the market, never had an actual loss in the five years Hulbert had been following them.

Dines now regularly cites Hulbert's ratings in his promotions. " . . . the discipline of the [Hulbert] competition will be good for all of us," he solemnly assured the 1984 Market Technicans Association Annual Conference in a keynote address, the tone of which was judged to be so condescending that his outraged listeners were sending acidly annotated copies to friendly journalists for months afterward.

"He's like a black box emitting signals," says Mark Hulbert sadly. It conflicts with his rationalistic world view. Dines has said, in his application to be registered as an investment advisor in New York State, that he watches some 200 technical indicators expressed in chart form, many of which he claims to have developed and a considerable number of which he has named after himself. Thus the Dines First Market Axiom: *"A trend in motion will continue until it actually ends."* (In technical analysis, this is not a tautology: it means Dines generally favors trend following over turn-calling.) And the Dines Second Market Axiom: *"When a trend is flat, dull, or unclear, assume that the previous clear trend is intact until proven otherwise."* And the Dines Theory of Positive Negativism ("DTPN"), which goes one step further than Humphrey Neill's Contrary Opinion Theory and asserts that not just stampedes but any consistent move by a crowd will be wrong. And the Dines Wolfpack Theory, stating that a move by some stocks in a group will be followed by all the stocks in that group. And . . . and . . . And, on the front page of every *TDL,* the Dines Prescience Index ("DPI"), a composite of Dines' 200 indicators. Any individual indicator can be wrong, Dines maintains, but rarely a consensus. In 1972 he self-published a highly regarded compendium of his technical theories, *How the Average Investor Can Use Technical Analysis for Stock Profits.* The text ran to over 400,000 words.

But Dines' investment method is not exclusively dependent on chart reading. He also mixes in some orthodox fundamental analysis. "The importance of each approach varies from situation to situation, from day to day, and sometimes from hour to hour," Dines told New York State. "This is a function of Mr. Dines' expert experience." As a young analyst, Dines' interest in gold was first sparked when he saw a number of bullish stock charts from the period of the Great Crash, and discovered on closer inspection that they were all gold mines. Over two decades later, MVAOOAOGASSS came when both gold and silver made new lows, confirming a bearish trend according to Dines' theory that the two metals move in tandem—an echo of the Dow Theory which he has (of course) named the Dines Theory. But in between, Dines' attitude to gold was really based on fundamentals: the economic consequences of profligate expansion of the money supply. In addition, Dines' method embraces psychology—his *Technical Analysis* draws on Freudian concepts and he has said that the stock market reflects a Jungian collective consciousness. And there are persistent reports from his peers that he is interested in astrology.

Bracketed with Dines' claim to be The Original Goldbug in each issue of *The Dines Letter* is the supplementary slogan: "Leader in Point & Figure." Dines has specialized in this particular type of charting, which is thought to date back to the Civil War and was popular in the 1960s. Stripped of refinement, Point & Figure charting takes no notice of time or volume, recording only price moves larger than a size judged to be significant— perhaps $1 or $5. A price rising through successive such increments would be plotted on graph paper as a vertical column ("box") of *X*'s. If the price then falls by the significant increment, another column or "box" is begun alongside the first, this time using *O*'s. These columns can extend for any period of time, as long as the price continues to move in that direction, and there are as many columns as there are changes in direction. The Point & Figure method gives distinctive formations, which are interpreted with normal charting rules. When a stock is moving up and down in a trading range, this appears on a Point & Figure chart as a series of boxes shuffling sideways across the page, and is known as a "congestion areas." Theories have been developed that relate the width of a congestion area to the distance a subsequent breakout is likely to carry the stock.

Point & Figure charts are designed to eliminate minor fluctuations, to compress information and to focus attention on resistance levels and breakouts. For example, Charles Stahl says he uses the method in combination with normal charts to confirm and assess new major moves. But other experienced technicians, like Bob Gross, are not attracted to Point & Figure at all, and in recent years it has been in eclipse as younger analysts explore other ideas like cycles or the application of ancillary trading statistics like volume and relative strength. This has certain aesthetic drawbacks, since Point & Figure is particularly rich in the delightful terminology of charting— Diatonic Uptrends, Spearhead Bottoms, Inverse Compound Fulcrums and so on. It seems appropriate to find Dines in such an esoteric, exotic and elliptical area.

Because Dines is now an active trader, holding very few positions longer than six months, his long-term views are no longer as central to his investment strategy. He still talks of

government monetary profligacy inexorably provoking a defla-
tionary nemesis and a "Second Great Depression," and periodically alludes to evidence that one or another of his long-standing
predictions is being borne out. But at other times he seems to
imply that the inflation of the late 1970s and the recession of the
early 1980s was vindication enough. He has said publicly that he
no longer expects a "horrendous crash" in the stock market, and
indeed by mid-1985 was one of the more prominent bulls. Despite MVAOOAOGASSS, he has gone back into the gold market on occasion, for example catching the March 1985 rally with
great precision.

In late 1976, Dines moved his operation from New York to
San Francisco. Now, when he addresses an investment conference there, he will pass out samples of his *Romantic Dining &
Travel Letter*, which covers restaurants in the Bay Area and
elsewhere. He also runs a model agency, but samples of this are
not distributed. Another Dines sideline has been his association
since 1979 with International Capital & Technology Corporation, formerly China Trade Corporation, the vehicle of an ex–
New York construction contractor and promoter, Charles
Abrams. In 1980, *Fortune* magazine described Abrams as "the P.
T. Barnum of the China Trade," pointing out that none of his
deals to date had really taken off. ICTC stock came down from
$9.50 in that year to below $1 in 1985. But Dines maintains that
China is in the grand historic process of turning away from
Marx. This will justify ICTC—and the involvement in it of a
self-proclaimed devotee of "missionary free-enterprise capital-
ism."

"I want to leave you with as much as possible," Dines told
the not-noticeably-grateful Market Technicians Association.
Like Joe Granville, he has been up and down many times, and
he now likes to say he is in his "sunset years." Far from East
Coast media attention, *The Dines Letter* has been quietly rebuild-
ing its circulation after the devastation of 1980–82, and is probably now around 2,000–3,000. But as the death-defying Dines
(DDD) prolongs his astonishing run of success, he threatens to
be almost as much a shock to the investment letter industry as
to the academic community.

CHAPTER SEVEN

The Winners: Technicians and Hybrids

The best of all tipsters, the most persuasive of salesmen, is the tape.

—"LARRY LIVINGSTONE" (JESSE LIVERMORE), IN EDWIN LEFEVRE'S *Reminiscences of a Stock Operator* (1923)

Charles Stahl insists that all technical analysis is really charting: it's just a question of whether or not you actually draw the chart. Not all those who study stock market action (a.k.a. "the tape," although nowadays it's a green screen) are in agreement with this subtle point. Some are quite concerned to disassociate themselves from what they see as a lunatic fringe. *Market Logic,* for example, regularly publishes chartist-baiting items, such as helpful demonstrations of how classic formations can be conjured up simply by altering a graph's scale.

In its most developed form, the technical analysis of market action can become formidably quantitative and scientific-looking, bearing a considerable resemblance to the models constructed by academic economists to forecast the economy. And this resemblance is more than printout-deep. Economists' models make basically the same assumption that the future direction of the economy can be predicted by measuring various of its twitches and extrapolating from them on the basis of historic trends and relationships. Indeed, one of the twitches frequently included is the stock market itself, which is viewed as a leading indicator of economic activity. Conversely, the Dow Theory was first developed by Charles Dow more as a barometer of business conditions than of forthcoming stock prices. Economists, of course, have not been exposed to the ridicule heaped upon technicians. Their professional prognostications, however, have not been noticeably more successful.

Besides this respectable complexity, moreover, some sophisticated technical systems do incorporate quantities of information about subjects like monetary policy or corporate earnings that would conventionally be regarded as fundamentalist. Few of the advisors in Mark Hulbert's handful of market-beaters are scrupulously pure in their methods. But in the interest of avoiding semantic dispute, some of these more analytical tape trackers could tactfully be described as hybrids.

ARNOLD J. BERNHARD AND *VALUE LINE*

The Value Line Investment Survey graduated from the kitchen table so long ago that today many investors don't realize it was ever there. Value Line, Inc., is now a 435-employee public company with a market capitalization of more than $200 million and floors of austerely furnished but expensive office space in midtown Manhattan. It publishes five different investment services including a recent addition aimed at institutional clients, manages some $2.5 billion, and is expanding into the computer software and data bank business. Its most celebrated product, the weekly *Value Line Investment Survey,* has more than 100,000 subscribers paying $390 a year, which means that its circulation revenues exceed that of established magazines like *Fortune.* Apart from regular market commentary and masses of statistical information, the *Value Line Investment Survey* quickly cumulates over three months into a single volume that provides an utterly exhaustive rolling review of some 1,700 individual stocks. This has become a standard reference work for Wall Streeters who would choke on their martinis at the thought that they were reading anything as déclassé as an investment letter.

Most of Value Line's activities are beyond the scope of this book, although its story is significant as an example of an investment letter that made good. But attention must be paid to the *Value Line Investment Survey*'s rating system as the first and best-attested case of an advisory service's exploiting an anomaly in the much-celebrated efficiency of the stock market. Moreover, according to the *Hulbert Financial Digest*'s count, this remarkable organization, although run by all accounts with the harsh discipline that the best business schools maintain is incompatible with employee creativity, nevertheless seems to have been able to foster yet another little-publicized and quite distinct method of beating the market. This is embodied in its $300-a-year bi-weekly *Value Line OTC Special Situations Service*.

There is a certain ceremony about lunch with Arnold J. Bernhard, founder, chairman and chief executive officer of Value Line, Inc. Bernhard was born in 1901. He is a bald, seemingly frail figure with a wispy white mustache who is recovering from hip surgery and moves with the aid of canes, slowly but purposefully. His shoulders are bowed but notably broad. Bernhard dominates his corporate dining room with courtly formality and a wry wit, gently but firmly supplementing the replies of a respectful retinue of top company officials to an interviewer's questions. Only Value Line's cheerful new president, Jean Bernhard Buttner, is sufficiently uninhibited to contradict him outright. She's his daughter.

The son of Jewish immigrants from Austria and Rumania, Bernhard grew up in Hoboken and Brooklyn, where his father was a cigar merchant and a retailer. His sister was to become a journalist; his brother a full-time union official who, when the executives of a company with which he was bargaining pointed out that Bernhard was on their board, blandly responded that he had always been the black sheep of the family. Bernhard himself graduated Phi Beta Kappa in English from Williams College, and won a fierce competition to be theater critic for the new *Time* magazine. Then he discovered that the pay was so low he had to double as critic for the New York *Post*. Some Value Line ex-employees are sufficiently jaundiced to say that this must have been a formative experience: certainly Bernhard retains a great admiration for *Time*'s founder Henry Luce. During this period, Bernhard wrote a play, *Bull Market*, which was optioned by two Broadway producers including the celebrated Jed Harris, although it was never performed. Just recently, however, there's been interest in a musical version.

Bernhard says he was attracted to Wall Street by Edwin Lefevre's 1923 classic *Reminiscences of a Stock Operator.* Eventually, he worked for the book's thinly disguised subject, the legendary speculator Jesse Livermore. He remembers writing a report recommending copper stocks, which Livermore promptly sold short, and being called in to identify an unknown stock symbol, while Livermore traded a large position on the strength of its tape action alone. Next, Bernhard joined Moody's Investors Service. He was employed first as an analyst in the Railroad Department and then as an account executive giving personal investment advice. In 1931, with the Depression gathering force and the stock market beginning its final paroxysm, a client of his from Georgia, a scion of the Coca-Cola fortune, sued Moody's, alleging mismanagement. "Truth to tell, Gerald Loeb and I had done some speculative trading for him," Bernhard recalled fifty years later in a speech accepting an award from the Newsletter Association, "but that part turned out all right. The 1930 deluge was what caused him to blow up. I don't think I was to blame for not being bearish in 1930. Moody's advice was to stay in good common stocks." He was fired anyway.

"You can have no idea what it meant to be out of a job in 1931," Bernhard continued. "My situation then was dire. I really didn't know which way to turn. I even contemplated some desperate remedies. But after some days of agony, my unpredictable friend from Georgia telephoned . . ." Despite the suit, which he eventually dropped, he wanted Bernhard to continue advising him. Other clients did the same. Bernhard had involuntarily become an independent investment counselor.

"I have always been and still am more than ordinarily gullible," Bernhard innocently assured the Newsletter Association. "So it is not surprising that the Great Crash came as a completely traumatic experience to me." But the total failure of Wall Street professionals to anticipate the debacle made a deep impression on him. His own mother lost the insurance money left by his father because she had bought Cities Services stock on margin. In retrospect, as always happens, it seemed obvious that the market had been overvalued. For example, the stocks comprising the Dow Jones index were selling at an average of well over twenty times earnings, as opposed to 6–7 at market lows (and 16.5 in mid-1985). Bernhard became convinced that there had to be some way of establishing the underlying intrinsic value of stocks. He began by eyeballing the relationship between a stock's monthly price over a twenty-year period and its concurrent annual earnings and book value—"taming the earnings curve with book value." This yielded an individual formula for each stock that when applied to future earnings estimates, produced a price goal—"the Value Line."

> I worked these equations out for 120 individual stocks . . . I bought a Multilith press and printed 1,000 copies of my book of Value Line Ratings of Normal Value. If you design, write, print and bind your product, you really get to love it. I took enormous pride in the book of Rating Charts that was to reveal to the world the normal and rational prices at which stocks should sell. It was to be a discipline that would control the market and I was going to give it to them—for $200 a book—which really wasn't too much even for those days, when you consider the cost of the irrational price fluctuations between 1925 and 1932.
>
> It was hard for me to realize how little the world would be interested. I called on banks and institutions without success. Only curious, although usually polite, stares greeted my presentations. I did make one sale to a reluctant and skeptical portfolio manager of the Phipps Estate, but that was all. And the selling effort was diverting time and energy from my investment counseling accounts. The inventory of 1,000 books took up an embarrassingly large percentage of my office space too.
>
> One day a noted man came to see me. I don't recall what caused him to drop in. His name was Major L.L.B. Angas. He was, you might say, the Joe Granville of his day . . . He showed some interest in my book and I avidly seized the opportunity to try to sell it to him. He didn't buy, but he did say he might be inclined to study it and perhaps mention it favorably in his enormously influential Bulletin. On hearing this, I urged him please to accept the book with my compliments, which he did. A couple of days later, he called to say that he found the stuff interesting and would comment favorably in his forthcoming Bulletin, which he did—sort of. He said in his Bulletin that "this young fellow Bernhard has published a book of ratings which show

when stocks are too high or too low. Everybody should own one. Write to Bernhard at 347 Madison Avenue, New York City—the price of the book is $55."

You can imagine my dismay on seeing my $200,000 inventory written down to $55,000 almost overnight. I was still more dismayed when I received a bill for $800 from the Major to cover the expense of printing the Bulletin in which the endorsement appeared. Not only did my inventory shrink, but my quick assets were at one stroke diminished by about 50 percent by the occurrence of this new, unexpected expense. The building manager of 347 Madison, who had been a friend of mine at college, was consulted on my unfortunate situation and he agreed to let the rent accumulate for some months until I could recover.

But again came good luck. A little while after this happened, some sixty $55 checks appeared on my desk in response to the Major's recommendation. That was how I learned that a service could be sold to the public by means other than direct, personal representation . . .

Value Line was now covering its costs, but it needed something more to make it a paying proposition:

One day, again by luck, a man from *Barron's* magazine called on me. I think his name was McQueen. I'm ashamed to say I can't really remember it as I should. For his advice turned out to be invaluable. He persuaded me to advertise in *Barron's* for two weeks. Each ad would cost $35 for a total commitment of $70. I bought the deal. The advertisements were designed to bring in leads of $5 each—that is to say, the reader of the ad would send me $5 and I would send him a sample . . . The two ads pulled nine leads for a total return of $45, which to my highly analytical mind was a poor way to spend $70. So when Mr. McQueen dropped by to get me to renew my ads I refused, pointing to the disappointing results. Mr. McQueen then patiently explained to me that this was not the end-all of the campaign, but only the beginning. I was to write seven or eight follow-up letters telling the "qualified leads," that is to say the people who put up the $5 as an earnest of their interest, more and more about what I regarded as my earthshaking revelation that there was such a thing as a normal value for stocks. Well, I wrote the eight or nine follow-up letters and sure enough three of the nine leads subscribed at $55. So it really did pay off, after all. The *Value Line* service has advertised in *Barron's* every week since that time, and the pattern Mr. McQueen showed me is still the pattern by which we get our sales

... we also use many other publications as well as direct mail, but nothing pulls for us like *Barron's*.

To this day, *Value Line*'s charts of its 1,700 stocks include a "value line" tracking the multiple of cash flow (earnings plus depreciation) that has best correlated with the past price of each individual stock.

Bernhard continued to tinker with his system, after 1946 with the aid of a freshly minted statistician from City College of New York, Samuel Eisenstadt, now sixty-two and director of statistical research. From 1947 to 1964, the two men tested and employed many much more complex combinations of variables for each stock in its expanding universe—"earnings, dividends, book value, interest rates, price lags, market yields and so forth." These methods did have some success in detecting years when a stock was undervalued in absolute terms, although unfortunately that condition might persist for years. But they said nothing about one stock's value relative to any other.

In April 1965, Value Line unveiled its ultimate weapon: "cross-sectional analysis." With minor alterations, this remains its approach today. Basically, cross-sectional analysis compares one stock against all others at a point in time, rather than against its own individual performance over time. Each stock is assigned a score, and then ranked. The top 100 stocks become Group 1; the next 300, Group 2; the middle 900, Group 3; the next 300, Group 4; the bottom 100, Group 5. Stocks within each group are published in alphabetical order, since *Value Line* is making a statement of cumulative probabilities rather than of individual certainty. But a portfolio of about 15 Group 1 stocks would probably be sufficiently diversified to duplicate its overall performance.

Each stock's score is 50 percent determined by three factors which are combined according to a common weighting formula that has been established by retrospective testing. The first two are (1) the stock's "relative earnings" and (2) its "relative price" —its earnings and average price over the latest twelve months, divided in each case by the average earnings and price of all Value Line stocks in the same period. These figures are compared with the stock's relative earnings and price for each of the last ten years and are ranked accordingly. Thus a stock that is doing very well might just have had its strongest earnings and price performance, compared to all other stocks, for the last ten years—a "10" in each category. A discrepancy between the stock's earnings and price ranks might suggest it was undervalued. The third factor, (3), is the stock's "price momentum." This is calculated by dividing its latest ten-week average relative price by its fifty-two-week relative price.

Some 25 percent of a stock's score is determined by "earnings momentum." This is the year-to-year change in quarterly earnings per share compared to that of all Value Line stocks. Thus the individual company's earnings increase is set in the context of all other companies' performances. Finally, in a refinement made in the late 1960s, the last 25 percent of the score is the "earnings surprise factor," an incremental amount that can be added or subtracted according to the extent to which the stock's quarterly earnings exceed or fall short of the projections of Value Line's analysts.

It is a paradox frequently remarked upon that Value Line employs a staff of over ninety securities analysts to report continuously upon its 1,700 stocks, more than most Wall Street firms —but does not allow them to contribute to its rating system. A three-year experiment of allowing some room for their opinions was abandoned in mid-1979. However, they do have an indirect impact. The "earnings momentum" figure is calculated after fairly sophisticated adjustments have been made for special factors like strikes, accounting changes and other nonrecurring items; and it may be modified if the relevant analyst is particularly confident that a marked change is looming. Additionally, the "surprise factor" obviously needs a straight-man analyst to discombobulate, although possibly the earnings estimate held by the consensus of analysts on the street would do.

Between April 1965 and April 1985, Group 1 stocks appreciated some 7,590 percent by Value Line's count, which does not include dividends or transaction costs. This compared with a S & P 500 gain of some 105 percent and a 365 percent average increase for all stocks in the Value Line survey. The other groups have moved, in duly descending order, +696 percent, +85 percent, −46 percent, and −91 percent respectively. This assumes that stocks were bought and sold as they entered and exited each Group. If the simpler course were adopted of buying the stocks in each Group as of January 1 and holding all year, the results would have been +1,386 percent, +763 percent, +363 percent, +131 percent, +28 percent. In all but three years, the Groups have performed in sequence, and in all but one Group 1 has come out on top.

That year was 1984, when Group 1 was down 2.1 percent against a S & P increase of 1.4 percent. This was a moment of particular crisis for Value Line, because it coincided with some serious stumbling in its generally successful money management effort, which is not wholly dictated by the rating system and prematurely gambled on a break in interest rates. (There was a similar stumble in the late 1960s and early 1970s, when a bearish Bernhard was finally converted to the bullish case just as the 1973–4 slide began.) "The Bernhards were worried," says Sam Eisenstadt, a short man with a mobile, expressive face and even more mobile, expressive hands. As director of statistical research, Eisenstadt is the official Keeper of the Rating System. He says that Value Line is constantly experimenting with its system, and sometimes it does emerge in retrospect that some alteration would have improved it, but only for brief periods. Thus the system's recent problems, actually confined to a few months in the winter of 1983–4, could have been avoided by a simple adjustment for asset values, which for some reason at that time suddenly intrigued investors more than earnings. But Eisenstadt resisted any change. He argued that the historical combination of factors would reassert itself in the long run. And this seems to have happened. Value Line's figures show that the system is now solidly back on track.

These figures are confirmed by the *Hulbert Financial Digest*, which does allow for dividends and commissions and also prices each recommendation not on the day of publication but when it receives its copy in the mail. Hulbert's count of the *Value Line* rating system's performance has been generally parallel to but about three percentage points below *Value Line*'s own reckoning. Both methods reflected a distinct upturn in 1984. Assuming that this difference is constant, Hulbert has projected that the Group 1 stocks would have appreciated 214.3 percent from June 1980 to June 1985.

Sam Eisenstadt will concede if pressed that the rating system might prove biodegradable over time. But, he says, it hasn't yet—and his own money is in one of the three Value Line mutual funds that follow a modified version of the system.

Some critics have suggested that the rating system is causing its own success: people buy because they know other investors will be bidding the price up. Actually any such effect would tend to be self-liquidating. Holders of the stock and the specialists who make markets on the floor of the stock exchange would adjust their asking price on the news of a recommendation, making it impossible to snap up cheap. Eventually the excitement would wear off, as subscribers realized they could be left holding the bag. A study conducted by the scholarly-minded *Market Logic* service suggests that this process is underway: several weeks after recommendation, *Value Line* stock picks are usually lower. Then they recover to beat the market. *Market Logic* also found that *Value Line* recommendations had an intriguing habit of appreciating *before* they were announced—and in 1985 the SEC duly brought insider trading charges against a group acting on information supplied by an employee of Value Line's contract printer. "*Value Line* itself is blameless; in fact, it is the ultimate victim of the scheme," commented *Market Logic*.

Curiously, Value Line has discovered that pretty much the same rating formula will work on the Tokyo Stock Exchange. The only exception: the weight assigned to price momentum has to be negative instead of positive. Apparently, the Japanese tend to buy on weakness, looking for a reversal. This is thought to be due to a short-term trading propensity that has developed because more individuals participate in the Japanese market, and because of the absence of a capital gains tax in Japan.

The *Value Line Survey* is famous for its quantities of fundamentalist fodder. But its rating system is actually largely technical in its assumptions: it focuses on price action and past trends rather than underlying assets and earnings projections. Sam Eisenstadt is unhappy with this observation ("any valuation system has to look at price"). But he concedes that relative price strength, which adds up to nearly 20 percent of a stock's score, is indisputably a traditional technical toy.

Perhaps this should not be a surprise. It's not widely known that Arnold Bernhard himself remains quietly but deeply interested in technical analysis, and uses it to reinforce his market judgments. He reads a wide range of investment letters and keeps his own hourly charts of the Dow Jones Industrial Average on a side table in his office. He thinks a contributing factor in his departure from Moody's was his being identified as a chartist at a time when right-thinking Wall Streeters regarded them all as witch doctors. "I've never been averse to any new way of predicting the market," he says. Once he had his troops spend two years checking the theory that stock prices are influenced by fluctuations in "sidereal radiation"—starlight. The results were inconclusive, but he recalls with a headshake approaching a prominent scientist for technical advice only to have him refuse even to consider the idea.

On the other hand, the Value Line organization is vast and contains multitudes. From a corner office up at the back of the building, a precise bespectacled young man called Peter A. Shraga and five analysts put out (among other things) the totally fundamentalist biweekly *Value Line OTC Special Situations Service.* Although little-publicized, and with a circulation that at low points in the market cycle is probably considerably below the 8,500 mentioned in the company's 1984 10–K form, Shraga's service is also among the handful followed by the *Hulbert Financial Digest* that have consistently outperformed the market averages on a cumulative basis over the 1980-to-1985 period. After five years it was up 131.2 percent against a dividend-reinvested S & P gain of 114.6 percent. It has done this despite absorbing a couple of heart-stopping down years, which probably come with the volatile territory—very few of Shraga's over-the-counter stocks are among Value Line's main 1,700.

OTC Special Situations' approach appears to be entirely fundamental. The object is the identification of sustained earning power to be bought and held for two or three years, rather than undervalued assets or any of the one-shot developments usually thought of as "special situations." This goal, of course, is hardly unusual. Quite how *OTC Special Situations* has achieved it so well is frankly difficult to fathom. Shraga himself, a Cornell engineering major who dropped out of New York University's MBA program to join Value Line in 1973, is inclined to attribute it to hard work and superior intelligence. He declines to draw parallels with other advisories, stoutly denying that he reads any. Asked if he employs Graham-and-Dodd methods, he replies, "I prefer to call them Peter Shraga methods." His analysts focus on published material and make no company visits, but they do talk to managements by phone and place a high pre-

mium on veracity and realism. Much of their work is detailed
financial analysis, "tearing apart" the annual report, "looking
for negatives," assessing financial strength, and monitoring ex-
pense trends. Financial institutions, oil companies and foreign
stocks are avoided, but otherwise there is no standard checklist
of factors to be considered.

Shraga blinks like an owl in unaccustomed daylight. He is
not used to being interviewed. Although he is technically both
editor and publisher of the *OTC Special Situations Service* and talks
with proprietary authority about what he requires from "my
analysts," he still appears in some ways to think like an employee himself. Asked why he favors a format that requires a
new recommendation each issue, which can create difficulties
when the market is being awkward, he responds quickly,
"That's not my decision to make." But when his defensiveness
is thawed by sufficient references to his record, he will eventually dissolve into a rare smile and insist with quiet determina-
tion that *OTC Special Situations* is destined to be not merely
superior but absolutely the best investment service. Whether
Shraga will continue to play a subordinate role in the Bernhard
drama is difficult to forecast. A previous editor of *OTC Special
Situations,* William T. Chidester, now puts out *Market Vantage,
Investment Values* and other Orion Publishing services. Whatever
happens, if Shraga can sustain his current performance he will
be at least as famous as Arnold Bernhard by the year 2032.

Value Line takes the corporate view that the stock market
will probably move much higher in the next several years. But
Bernhard regards market timing as a still unconquered field.
The *OTC Special Situations Service* says nothing about it at all, and
the *Value Line Investment Survey* offers essentially general comment. However, in a typical example of how investors can make
their own use of Value Line's volleys of information, Mark
Hulbert has examined the relationship between the overall market and the *Value Line Investment Survey*'s weekly list of stocks
selling below current asset value; and also between the market
and the number of stocks recommended in the *OTC Special Situations Survey.* He concluded in the May 1985 issue of the *Hulbert
Financial Digest* that both measures had some predictive power.
Fewer Value Line stocks sell below liquidation at market highs,
and more special situations are recommended at market lows.
Which is what was happening at the time—suggesting (cor-

rectly) that secondary stocks might be about to recoup the ground they lost in 1983–4 to the more seasoned issues.

Bernhard says with a sly smile that he has no plans to emulate Jesse Livermore and write his autobiography. He still works full time. His wife is now an invalid; his son, after some years in the business, now farms and pursues an interest in design. Bernhard's wife was a Protestant and the couple at one point converted to Unitarianism, but he has remained "an ardent Zionist," becoming a substantial benefactor of Israel and even giving money to Menachem Begin's Irgun private army when it was operating underground before Israel's independence. He says his motive was largely the desire to see something done to help Jewish refugees after World War II. But additionally he was attracted to the combination of nationalism and free-market capitalism advocated by Begin's mentor Vladimir Jabotinsky, who founded the Revisionist movement in opposition to the socialist tendencies of mainstream Zionism. Bernhard says he has always believed that capitalism and liberty are inextricable, even when the Depression was driving many of his friends to the left.

Bernhard does have a hobby: he backs plays, including David Mamet's *American Buffalo* and *Glengarry Glen Ross*. Asked how he's done, he responds instantly and with deep feeling: "Disastrously!" But Ms. Buttner will not let him get away with this. "Oh, come on, Dad!" she chides. Until the recent flop of the musical *Harrigan & Hart*, she says, Bernhard seriously maintained that he was doing better on Broadway than on Wall Street. He has never been short of imagination.

GLEN KING PARKER, NORMAN G. FOSBACK AND *MARKET LOGIC*

The Institute for Econometric Research lives in an ordinary-looking office building amid Fort Lauderdale's sunlit urban sprawl. There are no galley slaves chained to word processors or whip-wielding overseers, at any rate on first inspection. In fact, the atmosphere seems distinctly casual, with employees wearing T-shirts. Yet with a total staff of fewer than forty, the Institute churns out five full-scale investment services. Their combined circulation is a reported 75,000, with subscribers in some fifty countries. And the Institute's twice-monthly flagship letter, *Market Logic* (circulation 17,000, $195 a year), is one of the select group of services that the *Hulbert Financial Digest* says have cumulatively outperformed the broad market throughout the five years it has been monitoring them, appreciating 139.3 percent versus the dividend-reinvested S & P 500's 114.6 percent.

Despite its name, the Institute is actually a private company owned by its chairman, Glen King Parker, and run by him jointly with its president, Norman G. Fosback. Unlike most investment advisories, it has not just growed, but was a carefully planned act of will. Bob Gross at *Professional Investor* still likes to complain comically about the hours he spent on the phone with Glen Parker answering questions about the letter business before he realized he was helping create a competitor right next door. Parker responds tightly that Gross persuaded them to delay starting *Market Logic* at the bottom of the market in 1974, which in retrospect would have been an ideal time because they were bullish then. *Market Logic* was eventually begun in March 1975, with a print run and promotion campaign whose scale startled observers. It quickly established itself as a major factor in an industry that remains somewhat puzzled about Parker's motives: in recent years he has public-spiritedly channeled his combativeness into the Newsletter Association, of which he is a director, and into *Lowe* v. *SEC*, for which he raised funds and coordinated strategy.

At the end of the summer Glen Parker is perhaps the only man in southern Florida wearing a suit and tie. He is a well-groomed, indefinably dangerous-looking figure who smiles rarely, at least on first acquaintance, and is stubborn on points of fact. He wears the lapel pin of the Confrerie de la Chaine des Rotisseurs, the international gourmet society, knows the summer vacation schedules of Fort Lauderdale's chefs, and comments acidly on available lunch options. Parker was born in New York City in 1936. His father was a Canadian-born executive with a book wholesaler; his mother, a librarian. He was educated in Long Island public schools and spent a year at Johns Hopkins University, where he studied chemistry and physics.

According to a biography supplied by the Institute, Parker worked briefly as a newspaper writer and photographer and then entered the real estate business, becoming president of Cape Canaveral Corporation, a publicly owned Florida developer, at the early age of twenty-three. During this period he was also involved in the flotation of a number of small companies, including the predecessor of Caesar's World. From 1963 to 1974 he was managing director of the Bahama-based Pan American Mutual Funds. He still retains interests in both fields, as president of the general partner of Tucker Land Company, a Los Angeles–based public real estate firm, and managing director of Eurodollar Research Corporation, a Bahamian private investment company. He is divorced, with three children.

Norman Fosback is chubbier and more relaxed. He is scrupulously well-mannered and radiates the serene confidence of someone who loves his subject. Fosback was born in 1947 in Astoria, Oregon, and grew up in Portland, where his father had a construction business and his mother was a teacher. In 1982 he married and dragged to Florida a vivacious New York stockbroker, Myrna Liebowitz, now with Gruntal & Company in Fort Lauderdale. Outsiders suppose that Parker, who retains a deep scientific interest in the technicalities of the investment letter business, handles the commercial side of the Institute while Fosback conducts the research. They themselves insist they share all functions.

Fosback did his father's bookkeeping from the time he was in the seventh grade, and entered Portland State University intending to be an accountant. But then he answered an advertisement in *Financial World* magazine and was promptly inundated with investment letter solicitations. Fosback was intrigued. He even subscribed to one—*Indicator Digest*, which today is regularly quoted among several others on the Investor's Digest page of *Market Logic*. Ultimately, he switched to finance.

Fosback was happily studying finance when he met Parker, who had contributed money to the university's Investment Analysis Center. This was a pioneering organization invented by a particularly enterprising PSU professor called Shannon P. Pratt, coauthor of an early classic study on the predictive potential of insider trading reports. (Pratt has had a substantial impact on the investment industry in the Pacific Northwest, founding a money management firm, a regional investment letter and the

Insider Indicator letter now run by Michael Reid, before more recently refocusing his attention on the specialized problems of evaluating small businesses, about which he has written a standard text.) One thing led to another for Fosback, and in 1971 he abandoned academic life and drove across the country with all his belongings in effect to become the Institute for Econometric Research, leaving behind him an MBA that was within six credit hours of completion. For four years, Fosback pored alone over the market, utilizing Eastern Airline's computers in Miami and Parker's money. *Market Logic* was begun in 1975. The following year Fosback's findings were published by the Institute in *Stock Market Logic: A Sophisticated Approach to Profits on Wall Street,* a 384-page, $40.00 book now in its tenth printing with 150,000 copies in circulation, which is used as a promotional tool.

Stock Market Logic is a remarkable work that the advisory industry regards with a universal if rather uncomprehending respect. As a social phenomenon, it is the equivalent of Ohio farm boys building a space rocket in their backyard—or, perhaps, inventing the airplane. Fosback systematically tested dozens of Wall Street nostrums on the overall market and on stock selection. He then synthesized the results by using techniques employed in econometric model-building and placed them in the context of an integrated financial strategy. The *Market Logic* service is designed to follow suit. This feat demonstrated analytical and statistical skills of a very high order. But although Fosback continually scours the academic literature—in the Institute's library, there are over two hundred Ph.D. dissertations alone—he and Parker have yet to show Arnold Bernhard's interest in academic recognition. Outside of the investment letter industry, their work is virtually unknown.

Fosback's inclinations are clearly highly quantitative, but his work has turned out to be a direct challenge to the reigning academic orthodoxy of the Efficient Market Hypothesis. The Institute's official investment philosophy holds that it *is* possible to beat the market through the application of straightforward research techniques. "Basically, EMH has been ripped to shreds," Fosback says calmly. He believes his work has established several situations that can be relied upon, generally speaking, for superior performance. If stock prices moved entirely randomly, none of these patterns would persist. Among them are our old friends, stocks with low price-earnings ratios, which will beat stocks with high price-earnings ratios; and stocks with smaller capitalization, which will outperform stocks with larger capitalization. And most important are stocks that attract insider buying, which show the strongest tendency of all to superior performance.

This is not to say, however, that the Institute's conclusions would appeal to hands-on Wall Street types either. Fosback has concluded, for instance, that conventional chart reading ("windmills in the mind") simply won't stand up to rigorous testing. Either it is too nebulous to yield unambiguous (=unfudgable) prediction, he says, or it's simply wrong. His book is even skeptical of the venerable Dow Theory. On the other hand, *Stock Market Logic* and the *Market Logic* letter eschew fundamental analysis as a practical matter, arguing that earning power and commercial realities dominate a stock's action only over the really long, five-year-plus, haul. *Market Logic*'s focus is primarily technical in the sense of being concerned with price action. However, its regular Indicator Review includes in the "sentiment" category such indicators as margin debt and mutual fund cash reserves. It counts as "monetary" a variety of measures of Federal Reserve activity and interest rates, and as "fundamental" items like the median price-earnings ratio of New York Stock Exchange stocks and dividend yield.

Among the indicators tested by the Institute and now employed in *Market Logic* are the short-interest ratio; the value of common stock offerings; and average dividend yield—"the single indicator most highly correlated with market performance over a year or more," says Fosback. Exceptionally high dividend yield levels from the Dow Jones Industrial Average and the S & P 500 were among the factors that led *Market Logic* to predict the August 1982 rally, adding correctly that it would include 100 million share days, a call that deeply impressed Mark Hulbert, who reported that *Market Logic* had anticipated the 1982 move best of all the services he followed. A wide range of such measures is synthesized into *Market Logic*'s "Major Trend Indicator," which has been in bullish territory since late 1974, except for brief periods in 1979 and 1980. Once the major trend has been determined, *Market Logic* makes stock recommendations according to another synthesis that particularly weights insider trading, relative strength, substantial cash holdings, low price-earnings multiples (on historic earnings—the Institute makes no earnings estimates) and volatility—which in a bull market offers the bonus of sharp random gains.

Interestingly, Fosback's ferreting also turned up "dozens" of technical indicators that worked well, such as trend-following systems and measures of "overbought" and "oversold" status, but for which he could think of no theoretical rationale. So he rejected them. Without knowing why an indicator works, he argues, he would be "operating in a vacuum." Needless to say, eccentric techniques like astrology are absolutely O-U-T. If this is a deviation from inductive scientific method, he says with the asperity he sometimes displays off his home turf, "we'll have to live with it."

The Institute in fact is very good at living with difficulties from which most investment letters recoil. *Market Logic*'s Master Portfolio of recommended stocks is resolutely long-term—Fosback believes longer-run trends are easier to spot, and that fits just fine with Glen Parker's sensibilities as a much-churned mutual fund executive. In 1982, out of about thirty-five stocks, *Market Logic* sold only five, with an average holding period of over five years. In 1983 it sold only one. This strategy can work spectacularly well: in mid-1985 *Market Logic*'s lucid disclosure of its portfolio revealed that it had held Humana, then $30, since its first issue when it was purchased at an effective fifty-eight cents; American Express, then at $45.37, had been held since $1.08 in April 1978. But inevitably the more speculative-minded subscribers get bored. It seems a little late for them to buy Humana or American Express now. In fact, of the forty-five-odd stocks in the Master Portfolio at any one time, at least half are usually rated "holds." New subscribers are advised to build a diversified portfolio including "holds," but otherwise, if Parker and Fosback don't like the market, as they didn't in the late 1970s, there may be no current "buys" at all. *Market Logic* is crowded with material, including scholarly articles on questions of importance to investors, an Option Portfolio and advice to mutual fund telephone switch traders. But ultimately Parker and Fosback's response to unsatisfied speculators is, go someplace else.

Equally, *Market Logic* remained stoically bullish right through the sloppy markets of 1984. Parker and Fosback believe that near-term market movements are much more random than price levels a year or so out, but they do methodically list on

Market Logic's front page their capsulized opinion on the course of the S & P 500 over intervals up to the next five years. Their one-year forecast as of January 6, 1984 ("14% HIGHER"), was simply wrong. So were their stock picks: Mark Hulbert showed the *Market Logic* portfolio down 13.7 percent in 1984, by far its worst performance and only down year, whereas its market timing alone would have eked a gain in tandem with the lackluster averages. (*Market Logic* bounced back sharply in the January 1985 rally.) It just happened that *Market Logic*'s system had simply steered it into dangerous areas like high technology, and into one stock, Storage Technology, which dropped 95 percent and eventually went bankrupt. (Marty Zweig was shorting it. But, as Fosback points out wryly, it was in *Value Line*'s Group 1 when *Market Logic* first bought it.) Unlike the Bernhards, however, Parker and Fosback did not worry about their system. They believed that with diversification and patience, this too would pass.

It should be noted, moreover, that Fosback is contemptuous of most commonly accepted market measures—particularly the venerable Dow Jones Industrial Average. This is a widespread opinion in the investment letter community. Of the inhabitants of this chapter, both *Value Line* and *The Zweig Forecast* have developed their own indexes, in both cases aimed at a broader spectrum than the Dow. Fosback prefers *Market Logic*'s even more ambitious approach: an unweighted "Total Return" New York Stock Exchange Index, including both price gains and dividends, which he believes more accurately reflects investors' experience. This shows that what he regards as a primary bull market starting from 1974 is essentially unbroken by recent corrections. Projected by complicated calculations back to 1871 and adjusted for inflation, the Total Return Index shows that stocks have been the best investment of all over the last century— which is perhaps merely a measure of the U.S. economy's remarkable success.

Market Logic is expecting this primary bull market to continue. In mid-1985 it was coolly predicting that the S & P 500, then at a new all-time high of about 190, would be "57% HIGHER" in five years. It also felt that there would be a correction in two years so that by mid-1987 the market would be only 2 percent above its mid-1985 level.

"That's what our model suggests," said Fosback at the time.

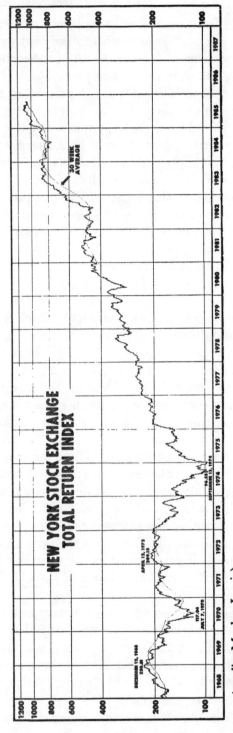

(credit: Market Logic)

"But we'll wait until it's closer and see what the twelve-month forecast says before we make our minds up for sure. There's really no parallel in the last half century for the bull market that began in 1974. It's had no deep corrections. The bull market that began in 1949 lasted for nearly twenty years, but there were several occasions when the market was off sharply, in 1953, 1956–7, 1966. So I'm hesitant. But I'm not saying this bull market can't last for twenty years either."

As a matter of corporate strategy, the Institute has backed its own predictions and philosophy. It acts on its own recommendations. And in 1978, as the bull market began to snort with underwritings, it also began *New Issues,* a letter reviewing and recommending initial public offerings. In 1980 the Institute began *The Insiders,* expanding its monitoring of insider trading. But although the Institute is committed to the view that common stocks are the best investment in the long run, it remained sufficiently flexible to initiate *Money Fund Safety Ratings* in 1981, exploiting the money market fund boom and ballooning interest rates. Not untypically, this service began by picking a public brawl with William Donoghue, publisher of *Donoghue's Money Fund Report* and *Donoghue's Moneyletter* and author of the best-selling *Complete Money Fund Guide.* Glen Parker described Donoghue as a spokesman for the industry who ignored the issue of the funds' relative safety. Donoghue protested the charge. In 1985 the Institute also began a monthly $100-a-year mutual fund rating and telephone-switch timing letter, the *Mutual Fund Forecaster,* which in terms of circulation—over 30,000 within six months—seems likely to be their most successful yet.

DR. MARTIN E. ZWEIG AND *THE ZWEIG FORECAST*

Given that Charles Allmon is a terrier and Al Frank is a Saint Bernard, it comes as no surprise to discover that Dr. Martin E. Zweig has the refined, soulful look of a red setter. Zweig is a tall, conservatively dressed man with glasses, cropped hair and a friendly but worried expression. Appearances are not deceptive. Zweig is renowned throughout the investment letter industry for his straightforward and sweet disposition. He does not bite or even snarl except under extreme provocation. He is even good with children: his delight in the two young sons he has with his wife Mollie, an ex-schoolteacher, is patent and touching. And he worries. When the market goes against him, he has been known to become so distressed that he has to switch off the monitor screen on his desk, and to throw down his chopsticks with a grimace in mid–Chinese meal because his digestion is off chasing the Dow.

With Norman Fosback, Marty Zweig is one of the most sophisticated statisticians currently publishing an investment letter. Zweig's *The Zweig Forecast* and Fosback's *Market Logic* are both based on a substantial foundation of independent research into market indicators, which—fortunately for the two men's peace of mind—has reached broadly similar conclusions. But the investment morals they have drawn could hardly be more different. *Market Logic*'s tortoiselike strategy is almost embarrassingly close to buy-and-hold. By contrast, Zweig is a hare: a hyperactive trader, who during the time Mark Hulbert has been monitoring him has completed as many as 136 transactions in a single year, with an average holding period as low as fifty-three days. Nevertheless, Zweig is a hare that stays the course: he has been able to outperform the market cumulatively over the last five years, up 146.2 percent against the dividend-reinvested S & P 500's 114.6 percent. Still more remarkably, Zweig's naps barely amount to nervous yawns: although he has failed to beat the market in individual years, he has never actually lost money.

Zweig was born in Cleveland, Ohio, in 1942. He grew up in Miami, Florida, where his mother moved when he was nine upon her remarriage to a doctor after the death of Zweig's father, a lawyer-accountant who was active in the real estate business. Zweig says he was always anxious to get into the investment industry. He dates his experience from 1961 when, as a college student, he opened his first account and thereby earned the right to spend an entire summer hanging around a local broker's office. His reputation among Miami brokers eventually grew to the point where three of them offered him jobs after graduation. He joined Bache as a trainee. Later he was a consultant to another New York Stock Exchange member firm, Axelrod & Company.

Zweig's academic career was one of the unintended consequences of the Vietnam war. In 1965, in fact, some days before the date they had originally set for their wedding, the Zweigs and a friendly Florida judge improvised a hurried midnight ceremony after hearing that in a speech that evening Lyndon Johnson had announced the end of the marriage deferment effective the next day. Zweig then went to bed, and his wife spent her wedding night studying for an examination the following morning. Subsequently they repeated their vows before a rabbi. By 1969, in addition to his BSE from the University of Pennsylvania's Wharton School, Zweig had acquired an MBA from the University of Miami and a Ph.D. from Michigan State University, where his dissertation topic was an analysis of option trading strategies.

Being such a nice fellow naturally recommended Zweig to *Barron's,* and he published his first article in the magazine in 1970 while teaching finance at the City University of New York's Baruch College. It was on the use of option trading volume as an indicator of future stock market action, with high levels meaning speculative excess and an imminent slump in stocks and low levels the reverse. Zweig used this device to predict the 1970 upturn successfully, attracting so much attention that in 1971, after the abrupt implosion of Axelrod, he began to circulate his opinions in letter form. For three years he published *The Zweig Forecast* from the living room of the couple's one-bedroom Manhattan apartment, simultaneously continuing his series of *Barron's* articles, which has now extended to the point where some of his industry peers, always willing to believe the best of a colleague, insist that he's related to *Barron's* editor Alan Abelson. (*Firmly* denied—nor is Zweig related to *Wall Street Week*'s Louis Rukeyser, although he is a regular guest panelist. For the record, Richard Russell's *Dow Theory Letters* began amid a similar burst of *Barron's* articles over a decade earlier, and *Grant's Interest Rate Observer* is the work of *Barron's* former bond columnist, James Grant.)

Zweig's service grew rapidly. He won particular acclaim for steadfast skepticism at the end of 1972, based on the condition of the broad market and contrary opinion at a time when the

rest of Wall Street was marching with almost unanimous enthusiasm off the cliff into the 1973–4 market abyss. But then Zweig
three times tried to call the bottom, finally succeeding by dint
of toughing it out for several months at the end of 1974. His
indicators were apparently disoriented by unprecedentedly
high interest rates. "You're talking to a guy who's been wrong,"
Zweig was quoted by Andrew Tobias in an epochal *New York*
magazine article published in October 1974, two months before
the the bear market ended, and starkly entitled "The Bulls of
Wall Street (Both of Them)." (The other was Kenneth B.
Smilen, the technically oriented proprietor of Smilen Investment Management, Inc., in Manhattan.) The experience was
devastating. *The Zweig Forecast*'s circulation collapsed, to well
below 1,000. It is perhaps not surprising that Zweig kept one
foot in academe, teaching part time at New Rochelle's Iona
College until 1981.

As Zweig rebuilt his service, he displayed the responsive-
ness to his audience that is one of his most notable characteristics. At first he had commented only on overall markets, but by
popular demand he soon began to recommend specific stocks.
(Successfully too—his portfolio usually does better than his
market timing alone.) Gradually his focus became more and
more short-term, as he discovered that any attempt to ride out
a market correction brought bloodcurdling screams from terrified subscribers regardless of eventual vindication. Other services like *Market Logic* sternly disregard this pressure, and it's
tempting to believe that Zweig has allowed himself to be in-
timidated into an investment style quite unsuited to his basic
personality. In support of this theory is the fact that he hardly
socializes at all with Wall Street's professional traders, an otherwise tightly knit fraternity that generally lacks his intellectual
approach to the market, or to anything else for that matter. But
for all his wailing, Zweig hangs in there tenaciously. And, as Joe
Granville has said in another context, there are no accidents.

When the *Hulbert Financial Digest* appeared on the scene,
Zweig reacted with typical alacrity. He at once included his
telephone hotline in his basic subscription price, thus making it
eligible for monitoring under Mark Hulbert's rules. In the next
few years, by updating his recorded messages as much as several
times a week, Zweig became virtually an electronic service.
Zweig said ruefully that Hulbert's mid-1980 start-up date just

missed one of his hottest streaks, but nevertheless he was well ahead of the market in the last half of 1980, and was reported to be top performer in 1981 and 1982. He tended to make his gains in short, sharp bursts, such as during 1981's fall rally. "It looks like Zweig can hold you even in a down market, plus make some multiple [of the market's gain] in an up market," said Mark Hulbert in 1982. "He's an honest guy," said Zweig of Hulbert at the same time. "He's doing something that needed to be done. I won't like it if I have a bad year, but . . ."

Zweig was right. He didn't like it. To be fair, however, the rules were changed on him. In 1983, Mark Hulbert heeded the ceaseless complaints of those letters that traded infrequently, and began to make allowances for commissions and dividends. Additionally, he altered his method of establishing the hypothetical buying price for each recommendation so as to take account of the "next-day effect"—the tendency for a stock's price to jump up the day following its recommendation on a popular service's telephone hotline as eager subscribers piled into the market. This effect meant that the closing price on the evening of the recommendation, which Hulbert had previously been using, was an unsatisfactory proxy for the price obtainable as a practical matter by most investors. As with *Value Line*, the effect had also led to allegations that Zweig's forecasts were self-fulfilling prophecies, particularly because Zweig frequently selected thinly traded issues where his followers' impact was often dramatic.

To the extent that a Zweig forecast had a self-fulfilling effect, of course, it would also be self-liquidating because of the response of other investors and the specialists who make the market. Indeed, this phenomenon once caused Zweig to denounce publicly the indignant American Stock Exchange as "a horror show" where "the specialists absolutely demolish my subscribers." In any case, Hulbert found that Zweig's choices tended to appreciate after the next-day spasm subsided.

Hulbert's new, improved method of establishing a hotline recommendation's price was to average the next day's high and low. This may have reproduced more accurately the experience of the average subscriber, and for most letters it made little difference anyway. But it was undeniably hard on Zweig. It meant that the next-day effect was now harming instead of helping his performance, which was calculated after the effect had been absorbed. And, while the average subscriber may not have been able to get a lower price, this could hardly be described as a flaw in Zweig's stock-picking ability as such. *The Zweig Forecast*'s circulation had soared to some 20,000 and Zweig had moved into vast new offices in Manhattan at least partly on the strength of Hulbert-generated publicity. He was launching ancillary services, developing a money management arm and clearly preparing to mutate into a full-blown financial institution. It was indicative of the extreme pressure he came under in 1984, when his circulation probably halved, that he was quoted in the press sharply criticizing Hulbert and the whole idea of performance measurement. Hulbert, who genuinely likes Zweig and respects his intellectual integrity, was quite forlorn. But firm.

The change in Hulbert's rules happened to coincide with one of Zweig's periodic streaks of stock market coolth. His techniques are essentially trend following, and are most successful when prices are headed purposefully in one direction or another. After May 1983 they declined to do this for nearly eighteen months. But the real problem was that Hulbert, in his scholarly way and against the advice of his more politic friends, had gone back and revised his earlier ratings. (The tables in this book reflect all such second thoughts.) Zweig, whose niceness does not preclude a fair degree of competitiveness and ambition, had quite reasonably been very proud of his Hulbert standings. He had advertised them widely. After publishing the revisions, Hulbert actually began to have nightmares about Zweig's committing suicide in a fit of despair. Fortunately this did not occur, but Zweig's reaction was no doubt quite dramatic enough to send some rather intense vibrations into the ether.

It should be noted, however, that even after revision Zweig's performance was impressive. His 1980 result actually improved slightly. He still came first in 1981, although his portfolio's appreciation was reduced from 37.8 percent to 23.2 percent. In 1982 his appreciation was cut more sharply, from 80.3 percent to 24.6 percent (and his rank was affected by the subsequent addition of other letters), but he still beat the market in a very bullish year. By contrast, the 1981 reading of Stan Weinstein's *Professional Tape Reader*, which is perhaps the closest equivalent of *The Zweig Forecast* in frenetic trading although relying much more on traditional chart-reading methods, went from up 6.9 percent to down 6.7 percent.

Zweig's innate fair-mindedness and his sheer abilities seem to have eventually combined to calm things down. By the end of 1984 he edged ahead of the market, although it was a trendless year. And his was the most accurate of all the letters Hulbert follows in calling the January 1985 rally, one of the strongest in history. At the same time, Zweig began obvious efforts to slow down his trading, urging his subscribers not to buy his recommendations at the next day's opening, holding his selections longer, and hedging with index futures, where he would earlier have sold outright and paid commissions. "I'll play your game," he told Hulbert wryly. Hulbert told himself that to the extent that his game represented reality, this was a Good Thing.

Zweig describes his investment philosophy as a hybrid. Every three weeks *The Zweig Forecast* reports on the world according to a few of the scores of separate indicators developed, smoothed out and continuously monitored by Zweig. Most of these indicators are also aggregated together in various combinations to give readings on key aspects of the market. Zweig says he has three basic maxims: "Don't Fight the Fed," "Don't Fight the Tape" and "Beware of the Crowd." Accordingly, he has built a "Monetary Model" comprising some thirteen discrete indicators of interest rate activity and Federal Reserve policy, three multicomponent "Momentum Models" trained on the tape over differing time periods and a "Sentiment Composite," made up of various measures of investor optimism. Three dozen of the momentum, sentiment and other indicators are then stirred together and refried to form Zweig's "Intermediate Index."

Despite his statistical bent, however, Zweig's handling of his material does not seem to be dictated by a fixed formula like that of *Value Line*. He constantly makes evaluative aha-ing noises about individual indicators, like advance/decline lines (Momentum) and institutional investor cash levels (Sentiment). Quite often he does not specifically report all his proprietary aggregates. Indeed, in 1982 he decided that his twelve-item daily Momentum Model, which, indulging his taste for verbal confections, he used to call "MO," had become so widely followed that it was getting distorted. So he stopped reporting its status altogether, although he still employs it.

An example of Zweig's approach was his December 3, 1984, article in *Barron's* announcing a revision in one of his monetary measures, the "Fed Indicator," which he had first unveiled in another *Barron's* article nearly ten years earlier. Essentially, Zweig's Fed Indicator assigns a numerical value to any move in the Federal Reserve Board's discount rate (the rate at which member banks can borrow from the Fed) and in its reserve requirement (which controls the ability of the member banks to make loans). Tightening in either can choke off bull markets. The values are weighted to emphasize changes in policy and moves toward easing rather than tightening, because these seem to have more effect. Having developed these rules by studying one period of Fed history, Zweig tested them in another, a standard procedure to confirm predictive power. Reviewing the record, he concluded that the then current Fed Indicator reading was at a level that on ten of twelve occasions since 1958 had presaged sharp rallies. The January 1985 rally duly appeared on cue.

The Federal Reserve's influence on the stock market is one of the areas where there are distinct parallels between Zweig's views and those of *Market Logic*. Both agree, for example, that when two successive easings by the Fed occur, there is a strong tendency for a subsequent market surge—a phenomenon that Norman Fosback in 1973 christened "two tumbles and a jump."

But no single technique can be depended upon, Zweig says. And although he will predict interest rates, they are much more important to him as a leading indicator to which he will respond regardless of his previous opinion. "That's the way I am." Overriding his three market maxims, he says, is a fourth—"Be flexible, always." It served him well when the great August 1982 rally erupted: his Model Portfolio was actually in a net short position, anticipating a further decline, but within one day he was 70 percent long and was fully invested soon afterward. Zweig says he suffers so intensely during market corrections that he would really rather get out before one occurs, even if he suspected that stocks would eventually recover. That way he can sleep in the interim. Many different treatments work in the stock market: Dr. Zweig's prescription is for nervous temperaments like his own.

A similar self-knowledge underlies Zweig's chosen methods of selecting individual stocks. Once when he was associated with Axelrod, he says, he saw an analyst trick the unwary management of a small public company into revealing their private earnings expectations by asking a cunning question about dilution—the amount that earnings would fall if some additional stock were issued. Zweig instantly decided he just wasn't devious or psychologically acute enough to compete in the company interview business. Instead, he has evolved elaborate formulas to rate stocks based on their published results and trading patterns. The results form the basis of his stock selection in *The Zweig Forecast*, are utilized in his companion service, *The Zweig Performance Ratings Report*, and are published in full in another service, *The Zweig Security Screen*. Although Zweig's performance ratings have not attracted the same academic attention as those of *Value Line*, his own figures show that portfolios managed according to them since their inception in May 1976 would have marched upward in a similarly sequential fashion, with this Group 1 appreciating 984 percent by late 1985, not counting transaction costs.

Many of the elements of Zweig's rating system are familiar. He is deeply interested in a stock's volatility—its "beta." He looks for low price-earnings ratios, insider trading, earnings surprises and stocks that are subject to heavy short selling, although he cautions that this last technique can backfire unless handled with care. He studies earnings trends, price-earnings ratios relative to the market currently and in the past; and, in order to gauge the interaction of supply and demand, volume trends measured both in share turnover and in dollars. He also factors in some balance sheet fundamentals, such as the debt-equity ratio and book value per share; and dividend information, such as yield, payout ratio and growth rate. One unusual consideration is the promptness with which a company reports its earnings. Tardiness often spells trouble.

Zweig's eclectic attitude to stock selection emerged clearly in a talk with *Barron's* on May 23, 1984:

BARRON'S: What's a reasonable P/E these days?

ZWEIG: I try to relate it gut-wise to what's going on in the market. I might be more than willing to pay 12 times earn-

ings for a certain stock today, whereas nine months ago I would
have thought that was exorbitant . . . My best stock in this cycle
was a computer stock called Emulex, which I bought last August. About a month ago, I sold it with about a 340 percent
profit. The stock was still doing okay, although it was looking a
little tired on the tape, but maybe I was looking too hard. The
earnings were still great, but the P/E reached 50. And I mean,
enough's enough . . .

BARRON'S: What does it do?

ZWEIG: They sell a gizmo to IBM. I'm not that involved
with the products. I don't contact a company, or very rarely. I
don't tear apart a company. If somebody can show nice consistent
earnings for four of five years, I don't care if they make broom-
sticks or computer parts.

Zweig is a hybrid, not merely of technical and fundamental
analysis, but of the rational and intuitive. It is hard to tell precisely how large a role what he calls his "gut" plays in what
otherwise appears to be, at least potentially, a highly systematic
approach to the market. But it is noticeable that the *Zweig Forecast*'s stock selections are by no means restricted to those with
a top Zweig Performance Rating. (Zweig will discuss his investment philosophy further in his forthcoming book, *Martin
Zweig's Winning on Wall Street.*)

Zweig says he goes where his formulas lead him. But his gut
intervenes. In mid-1985 it was resisting being led into high-technology stocks. Zweig's highly numerate mind seems to be simultaneously unusually open to the numinous. For example, like all
investment academics, he says he doesn't believe in charting.
Before recommending a stock, however, he still glances at its
chart "to see if it looks good." *Looks good?* What does he mean,
looks good? Zweig hesitates. Then he laughs. A contradiction, he
admits with a shrug.

CHAPTER EIGHT

Contending, Placing, Showing: The Telephone Switch Letters and Others

It matters not who won or lost
But how you played the game.

—SIR HENRY NEWBOLT

Americans are not noted for their enthusiastic espousal of the Victorian view that playing well is its own reward (nor, for most of their history, were the British). But the way the investment letters have played in the last few years is worth studying. Some have come so close to outpacing the cumulative performance of the broad market over a five-year period in which it has, after all, appreciated quite appreciably, that their exclusion from the winners' circle would be somewhat arbitrary. This is a particular problem with Standard & Poor's *Outlook* and the *Dow Theory Forecasts*. Both offer stables of portfolios that have variously beaten and been beaten by the overall market.

Another difficulty is posed by the telephone switch services, in recent years the fastest-growing segment of the investment letter industry. Mark Hulbert has been able to reconstruct a five-year record for only one, Richard J. Fabian's *Telephone Switch Newsletter*. However, the evidence is sufficient to suggest that combined with their revolutionary simplicity and practicality, especially for small investors, the investment strategies offered by the telephone switch letters have been successful enough to ensure that they will be a permanent addition to the investment scene.

RICHARD J. FABIAN AND THE *TELEPHONE SWITCH NEWSLETTER*

It's eight-twenty in the morning at the Annual Investment Conference of Jim Blanchard's National Committee for Monetary Reform in New Orleans, and Dick Fabian, a small, bald, intense man of fifty-nine, plunges with undiminished energy and many exclamation points into his second presentation of the day. Despite the hour, he has attracted a crowd so large and attentive that no reasonable IRS agent could deny the conference's tax deductibility.

Fabian tells the crowd that his monthly $117-a-year *Telephone Switch Newsletter*, published from Huntington Beach, California, does not make predictions. It is devoted entirely to one single trend-following indicator covering the overall stock market. This indicator has generated on average only 1.2 buy or sell signals per year for the last several years. It is so simple that anyone can calculate it for himself in a few minutes every week —and if that's too much, Fabian can suggest a computer program that will do it in seconds. Yet, Fabian says, his letter has over 27,000 subscribers. ("I'm making so much money it's sinful.") He manages money, and, although he does for his clients only what he recommends to his subscribers in his letter, can charge a steep 3 percent annual fee. ("I'm greedy.")

Fabian's frankness only just inflames his audience. At the end of his speech, he is mobbed by enthusiasts. It's proof that his service is indeed, as it asserts at the end of each letter in stentorian tones, <u>first investor oriented, then investment oriented</u>. Fabian explicitly ministers to the psychological pressures that afflict investors—above all, the destabilizing feeling that "there must be *someone* out there making money. (BUT THERE AIN'T!)" Fabian believes it is impossible to call market turns, pick stocks or even choose high-performing mutual funds in advance. He says nine out of ten investors lose money in the long run, echoing one of old Roger Babson's favorite observations. But never mind. To subscribe to Fabian's letter is to be embraced by a family (it employs four of his five children, his wife and his seventy-eight-year-old mother, who stuffs envelopes) or perhaps even a religious cult. Initiates are expected to study extensive scriptures laying out Fabian's simple market philosophy in hellfire prose. He will not even consider accepting managed-account clients who are under forty-five and thus too antsy to submit to his discipline.

Fabian's is the largest and arguably the oldest of the telephone switch services. These have sprouted to help individuals exploit the telephone switch privilege now offered by many mutual funds, which makes it possible to buy into and sell out of the fund with a simple phone call. Mutual funds generally travel in herds, or "families," under the guidance of a single management company. The management companies adopted telephone switching in the late 1970s, originally as a defensive measure. They hoped to retain the business of investors who had become disillusioned with any one fund in the family by making it easy for them to transfer into another. In that era of high inflation, investors were particularly anxious to switch out of mutual funds that purchased stocks and into those that purchased money market instruments, which offered both safety of principal and high yield. Before deregulation, of course, these "money market funds" were the only way small savers could get a competitive rate of interest on their money. Soon, every respectable mutual fund family included one.

But the ability to switch instantly without onerous paperwork or fees sharply enhanced the original rationale behind mutual funds: to offer small investors the opportunity to participate in the market with the protection of diversification and the benefit of a portfolio manager's professional investment judgment. Most of the telephone switch mutual funds were "open-ended" and "no-load." They sold and repurchased unlimited numbers of their shares to and from the public without any initial sales charge, levying only a small annual management fee. By using these mutual funds, small investors could trade in amounts as low as a couple of thousand dollars without facing any brokerage commissions or other transaction costs, even going into "cash"—the fund family's money market fund—whenever they felt like second-guessing the portfolio manager's opinions about stocks. Indeed, by alternating between a fund that reflected the broad market and a money market fund, individual investors could act purely on their beliefs about the overall direction of stocks—"market timing"—rendering obsolete the old Wall Street maxim that "you can't buy the market," you have to buy a specific stock, which might go bad. Of course, the maxim wasn't quite obsolete. It was just fading away. Few small investors were satisfied with an "index fund" that just bought the 30 stocks comprising the Dow or the 500 stocks favored by S & P. Most still looked for a fund that would do a little better. But telephone switching meant that they could run with the experts in bull markets, and, when bears were prowling, could take shelter in high-yielding money market funds. In theory, at least, their capital would be steadily ratcheted upward. The mutual fund industry had significantly improved its product. Largely as a result, assets under its care tripled between 1979 and 1984 to a total of $138 billion, after nearly ten years of stagnation.

"I was in the right place at the right time," says Fabian. He was born in Brooklyn in 1925. His father died when he was young and his mother worked as a waitress. He was a radio operator on a Liberty ship in World War II and studied economics and accounting at Colgate and New York Universities. Subsequently, he worked as assistant to the controller at an engineering firm and then sold computers for Univac for sixteen years. In 1959 ("the year after the Dodgers") he gave up on East Coast winters and moved to California. He was so delighted with the development where he bought his house—and where he now lives on the waterfront, with a 27-foot sailboat—that he became a salesman for it. "I sell what I believe—I'm selling me." Fabian next believed in mutual funds. They were just entering their late-1960s boom period, when the fashion was for actively managed load funds with a high initial fee to be marketed, often in combination with life insurance, through salesmen on commission. Fabian became a registered representative working, among others, for Equity Funding.

In 1969 the stock market sneezed and the mutual funds collapsed. It was the end of the go-go years. For Fabian, the experience was devastating. "All the money I had was in the stock market. I sold all my relatives [mutual funds]." One of his main vehicles, Fred Carr's Enterprise Fund, was down 25 percent in that one year (and by 1974 had lost two-thirds of its value). Disillusioned, Fabian changed careers and became a Registered Financial Advisor, helping private clients with their money in return for a straight fee rather than a commission. He developed a program for investing in the no-load funds then appearing on the scene, recommending retreat to a bank savings account when he judged that the market was about to decline.

Fabian traces the origin of telephone switching to 1974, when it was first offered by the Franklin Group of funds. The first money market fund, the Reserve Fund, had begun three years earlier. Fabian was electrified by the combination. But he found so much resistance to the new idea that in early 1977 he self-published an explanatory manual, *How to Be Your Own Investment Counselor*, now much reprinted and still his fundamental doctrinal expression. On the strength of a vague reference in the manual to a possible newsletter for telephone switchers, readers began sending Fabian subscription checks in the mail. So, obligingly, he began one later that year. In 1984, he says, mutual fund managers told him that one of his switch signals had generated transfer orders from the public amounting to some $600 million.

Every telephone switch letter has to address two basic questions: firstly, when do you switch? secondly, what do you switch into? Fabian is scathingly derisive of services that claim to generate their switch signals by proprietary methods. He says they're just trying to intimidate credulous subscribers. His own switch signals are given entirely mechanically. He maintains simple 39-week moving averages of the Dow Jones Industrial Average, the Transportation Index, and what he calls his "Mutual Fund Composite" index, which is the aggregate he has constructed from what he considers to be the current five top-performing funds. When the Mutual Fund Composite rises above its 39-week moving average and is followed by one or other of the Dow indexes also breaking through its 39-week moving average, a buy signal has been given. It remains in effect until the Mutual Fund Composite goes below its 39-week moving average and is similarly confirmed by either of the Dow indexes, constituting a sell signal. The 39-week moving average, Fabian maintains, is a happy medium: moving averages based on shorter periods generate too many signals and potential "whipsaws"—signals following each other almost immediately, with no time in between for a significant market move. Fabian says a 52-week period works even better—but no investor can stand the strain of watching passively during major market moves. "If people aren't going to do it—why talk about it?"

It seems astonishing that the market can be mastered by such a simple trick. It's pure charting and completely antithetical to the Random Walk view that price trends do not persist. Norman Fosback in his book *Stock Market Logic* investigated several moving average systems and concluded that they did indeed have some predictive value, although the gains could be small, perhaps not always enough to outweigh commission costs. Investors in no-load mutual funds, of course, do not pay commission. But not everyone—even when over forty-five—is patient enough to stick with Fabian's slow if sure system. In fact, he says he picked up the idea at an investment seminar held by Curtis R. Richmond, a Beverly Hills money manager and publisher of the *Richmond Outlook* letter. Richmond never capitalized on his idea, and in 1984 at the age of fifty-three he was jailed for running bogus tax shelters. Fabian thinks Richmond chose a 39-week moving average simply because a popular chart service had conveniently computed it.

"Every morning I say to the market, *Howya doing, Market?*" Fabian proclaims. "And the market tells me. It says, *Flat.* Or, *Up ten points—feeling good.*" Fabian's method is entirely reactive. Like any moving average system, it follows trends rather than predicts them. It can never catch tops and bottoms. Fabian has to content himself with only a portion of market moves. He does this happily. Small gains, he says, are quite enough when allied to the power of compound interest. Fabian is an evangelical advocate of compound interest. Given time and patience, he points out insistently, it steadily builds remarkable sums that hyperactive trading cannot easily match. His moving average system, he says, will get him out of bear markets and into bull markets. In poor years it may do no better than money market rates, but in good years it can easily recoup: three of his five buy signals generated between 1976 and 1984 resulted in gains of over 45 percent while they were in effect. Which adds up. What he's aiming for, he says, is a return of 20 percent, compounded over a five-year period.

As of March 1984, in fact, Fabian's switch strategy added up to a gain of 179 percent since January 1, 1977, according to a study done for the *Wall Street Journal*'s Karen Slater by Lipper Analytical Services, Inc., a New Jersey firm that monitors mutual fund performance. This was significantly better than the 129 percent performance of the Lipper Growth Fund Index, which reflects typical fund experience. But Fabian was not pleased. He wrote a special supplement to *Telephone Switch Newsletter* complaining bitterly that the *Wall Street Journal* study was not taking into account his answer to Basic Question Number Two—which fund you should buy. It merely calculated his performance as if he had traded in and out of the Lipper Index, rather than the thirty-five mutual funds he monitors and ranks. Thus it tested only his market timing and not his fund selection.

In April 1985, Fabian claimed that his five-year cumulative appreciation, investing in the Mutual Fund Composite on buy signals and factoring in the very high yield received from money market funds in this period whenever he was out of the market, amounted to 21 percent compounded annually. This came to a total of over 150 percent, appreciably better than the market. But Mark Hulbert showed him up only 101.8 percent in the five-year period to June 28, 1985, against the dividend-reinvested Dow's 100.8 percent and the dividend-reinvested S & P 500's 114.6 percent. Hulbert says that Fabian's own numbers are not inaccurate, but that for about a year after 1984 the *Hulbert Financial Digest* was following Fabian's newly introduced "Model Portfolio," which recommended only one fund, Fidelity Select Technology. Fabian abandoned his Model Portfolio in July 1985, and Hulbert went back to monitoring the entire Mutual Fund Composite, downgrading Fabian's Clarity Rating from *A* to *C* because of the resulting complications.

Fabian is not particularly pleased by Hulbert's numbers either. His complaint about them is that the Hulbert rating system gives no indication of the suitability of various advisory letters for investors. People subscribe blindly to the top-performing letters, he says, and then find out that these letters use options, or margin, or trade actively, or employ some other sophisticated technique that is simply out of the ordinary investor's league. By contrast, telephone switching offers both performance and unrivaled practicality. There is no doubt that Fabian is right about this, nor that there is little Hulbert can do about it.

Fabian follows all suitable funds through specific market phases (a "meaningful market move"). He then recommends shifting into superior performers as they emerge. Thus he believes his subscribers can respond (slightly after the fact, once again) to any tendency for market leadership to change as the bull market proceeds. Thus in mid-1985 the five funds in Fabian's Mutual Fund Composite were mainly invested in over-the-counter stocks, since this area had led the 1982-3 rally. Some pundits were claiming that New York Stock Exchange stocks were now going to forge ahead: if so, Fabian argued at the time, funds specializing in them would rise to the top and be selected. Additionally, in 1980 he adapted his 39-week moving average system to both the newly hatched telephone switch gold funds and the funds specializing in foreign securities. (He hadn't found confirming indicators, however, and so used conventional technical analysis to assess the importance of each signal.) Each subscriber was supposed to make up his own mind about whether to use the gold and international funds; the *Hulbert Financial Digest* follows each separately. Fabian said he was experimenting with rules allocating assets between these options —an investment equivalent of the search for the elusive unified field theory in physics. But still, he argued, his subscribers were already positioned to take advantage of every conceivable future development: inflation (gold), deflation (cash), devaluation (foreign stocks), even steady economic growth (U.S. stocks). "It's an investment policy for all seasons," he claims.

There is a school of thought among investors that regards the stock market as an actively malevolent force, constantly plotting to lure in victims and rob them of their capital. Fabian has cause to agree. At the time of his optimistic presentation to the National Committee for Monetary Reform conference in the fall of 1984, the market was unerringly exposing a weakness in the moving average technique. That year's summer rally had been all packed into just a few days, too fast for Fabian's system to catch. When he did get a buy signal, on August 3, stocks promptly stopped going up and began a prolonged sideways movement. Fabian was mortified. He said his calculations showed this was the first time a buy signal had been followed by such sidewinding for many years. As the indices' current prices converged on their moving averages, Fabian grew increasingly worried about being whipsawed. In September, for the first time, he advised second-guessing his system, allowing for a Mutual Fund Composite decline through its moving average to a point where he thought he detected technical support. But eventually he had to give up, and advised selling out in December for his first recorded loss. Within days, his Mutual Fund Composite went back up through its 39-week moving average, giving a buy signal that was confirmed by the Dow Indicators. Fearing another whipsaw, Fabian second-guessed his system again—and missed the start of the January rally. This time, however, the rise was sustained enough for him to catch up with it a few days later via a buy recommendation on his telephone hotline.

The *Telephone Switch Newsletter* finished 1984 down 12.1 percent according to Mark Hulbert's record-keeping, its first losing year. It's important to note, though, that Hulbert showed it up 4.7 percent on timing alone—using Fabian's signals to trade the NYSE Composite Index rather than the fund he actually chose. With this score, *Telephone Switch Newsletter* would have beaten the Dow and most other newsletters. Ironically, in view of his complaints about the *Wall Street Journal* study, Fabian was having trouble with his fund selection. Trend following as usual, he had used Fidelity Select Technology fund in his Mutual Fund Composite index and in his model portfolio because of its high performance in the 1982-3 rally. But in 1984, high-technology stocks in particular and junior stocks in general just lay down and died. They barely twitched even in the January 1985 rally, so that Fabian's model portfolio did not really benefit from it.

In 1985, Fabian made adjustments in his investing methods. He replaced Fidelity Select Technology, berating himself for having employed such a narrowly based fund in a role that required a more diversified general equity fund like Fidelity Magellan, which he substituted. At the same time, he announced a new program to utilize the large numbers of "sector funds" that were being invented and sold by major fund families, and of which Fidelity Select Technology—and the gold funds—were really harbingers. These offered investors the opportunity to buy into specific segments of the market. Such segments can move independently of the general market, as gold did in 1973-4 (up) and technology in 1984-5 (down).

Sector funds were fashionable in the 1930s and 1940s, when

they were known as "serial" funds and focused on areas like agricultural equipment and tobacco. But they were necessarily volatile, and eventually investors got vertiginous. With telephone switching, however, it is easy to escape to another sector, or a money market fund. Fabian proposed that investors should rotate between sectors according to the extent to which the apposite sector fund's relative strength computed against the New York Composite Index is above its 20-week moving average ("Relative Strength Differential"); and also the extent to which the fund's price is above its 39-week moving average ("39-Week Differential"). These and many other statistics about the funds are reported each month in *Telephone Switch Newsletter*.

"We are again completely comfortable with each of our investment plans," Fabian said in June 1985, "and are eagerly looking forward to fulfilling our goals with each in the months and years ahead." Once again he was preaching the virtues of trend following rather than predicting the market. "I don't know what's going to happen in five years, and I don't care." He would follow his nose—and his system. And he was backing his words with his own money. "The *only investment* I ever use are the mutual funds we monitor in the Newsletter. I have *no money* in any other investment area."

Interestingly, however, Fabian is still a devoted reader of many other investment letters that do try to make predictions. It's partly self-defense. "I fear the unknown," he says. He has been particularly impressed by Bob Prechter's *Elliott Wave Theorist*, although Prechter follows the diametrically opposed strategy of trying to call market turns with a method of universally feared complexity. "But you know what?" he asked on the convention floor in New Orleans. "*Prechter keeps all his own money in mutual funds!*" He lunged into the crowd and retrieved a passing Prechter, who, while cautiously noting that much of the *Elliott Wave Theorist*'s advice is designed to be appropriate only for risk-taking professional traders, confirmed that it was true.

JAMES M. SCHABACKER AND *SWITCH FUND ADVISORY*

In her *Wall Street Journal* article that so much excited Dick Fabian's indignation, Karen Slater reported on another telephone switch service that, although less prominent, had nevertheless apparently achieved an even better record: James M. Schabacker's *Switch Fund Advisory*. Trading the Lipper Growth Fund Index according to Schabacker's signals for "inactive traders/investors" between January 1, 1977, and March 6, 1984, would have resulted in an appreciation of 197 percent, compared to *Telephone Switch Newsletter*'s 179 percent and 129 percent for the index itself. Subsequently, Schabacker happily updated the figures to the end of 1984: *Switch Fund Advisory* was up 217 percent, *Telephone Switch Newsletter* was up 186 percent, and the Lipper Index was up 145 percent. Mark Hulbert follows Schabacker's inactive trader/investor signals in his Timing Scoreboard section, and shows it up 148.4 percent in the five years ending June 1985, versus the dividend-reinvested S & P 500's 114.6 percent.

(*Forbes* magazine, in its amiable way, had a comment on Slater's article too. It said slightingly that it had "set a personal computer to guessing market timing over the same period, selecting 5,000 sequences of switch dates at random. One in twelve of these random strategies beat the market by a third [matching Schabacker's score]." This is an example of the difficulty of applying scientific standards of proof to ordinary life. An event that has a one-in-twelve chance of occurring randomly has a 92.666 percent probability of happening nonrandomly. Most statisticians would accept a 95 percent probability, or a one-in-twenty chance of the event occurring randomly as effectively establishing that a result was no accident; many would be satisfied with 90 percent. In addition to which, of course, Schabacker might reasonably ask what more, beyond beating the market, he was expected to do.)

Schabacker's $135-a-year letter also features a "$100,000 Model Portfolio" consisting of a conservative selection of diversified general equity mutual funds and a small position in gold mutual funds. Mark Hulbert has tracked this in his Performance Rating section since 1983. Cumulatively it increased 92.6 percent to June 1985. But it did so with some 36 percent less "risk" than the dividend-reinvested S & P 500 so that it actually outperformed the market according to the academic "risk-adjusted" criteria. And Hulbert's numbers confirm *Switch Fund Advisory*'s own record-keeping in this period almost exactly, lending credibility to Schabacker's claim that his Model Portfolio has appreciated 158.7 percent since he began it in June 1979. This constitutes the highly respectable rate of over 17 percent compounded annually.

JAY SCHABACKER—AN "ARISTOCRAT" OF THE INVESTMENT WORLD, FROM A "FIRST FAMILY" OF STOCK MARKET ADVISORS said the promotional literature for *Mutual Fund Investing*, a less technical companion letter that Schabacker began publishing in a joint venture with Phillips Publishing, Inc., in March 1985. It went on:

> You see, his father was R. W. Schabacker, the famous financial editor of *Forbes* who wrote the classic *Stock Market Theory and Practice*, the Wall Street bible of its day. His uncle, Robert D. Edwards, was the first man to spell out chart patterns in the early years of Wall Street, and his text on *Technical Analysis of Stock Market Trends* [co-authored with John Magee] is likewise a classic that's gone through 14 printings.
>
> But the ablest pupil either of these Wall Street giants ever taught was R. W. Schabacker's own son, Jay . . .

On this testimony Schabacker's abilities extend considerably beyond the investment world, since he was born in 1935, two months after his father's death. He studied mechanical engineering at Cornell and worked for many years for firms such as Douglas Aircraft and General Electric on projects ranging from the Titan missile to the Apollo moon shot, all the time actively following the stock market. Latterly, he says, he was a consultant to the aerospace industry in Washington while completing an MBA degree at George Washington University, with a thesis on market timing and a heavy emphasis on starting his own business. He began *Switch Fund Advisory* in 1977. Schabacker Investment Management now employs thirteen people in Gaithersburg, Maryland, publishes two other mutual fund letters, *Weekly Advisory Bulletin* and *Retirement Fund Advisory*, and has $35 million under management.

As it happens, Schabacker makes comparatively little use of the chart formation theories favored by his father and his uncle. His market timing signals are dictated by his own proprietary "Stock Market Forecaster." He describes it as a model that includes technical factors like the short interest ratio, net upside volume, mutual fund cash holdings and some cycle work; fundamental factors like the intrinsic value of stocks in the Dow Jones Industrial Average; and macroeconomic factors such as interest rates, money supply growth, credit conditions and business activity figures. From this Stock Market Forecaster, Schabacker derives his strategy for inactive traders/investors and another one for "typical investors." The former entails being either completely in or out of the market; the latter often involves incremental commitment, with varying reserves retained in cash.

Schabacker also offers advice on sector funds and on gold. He has invented a proprietary Gold Equity Forecaster, a model similar to his Stock Market Forecaster, whose components include interest rates, futures prices, unemployment, national debt and bankruptcy figures. In 1985, Mark Hulbert had not begun to follow these comments. In addition, Schabacker systematically rates and recommends mutual funds according to a wide variety of possible investment objectives. His coverage of the mutual fund scene, in fact, is so extensive and exhaustive that it really qualifies his service as a standard reference resource. His data base is used by *Money* magazine in its monthly "Fund Watch" feature and in its semiannual survey of mutual fund performance; he had provided the statistical backing for *Consumer Reports'* coverage of mutual funds.

The success of Schabaker's inactive trader/investor strategy is a triumphant demonstration of Dick Fabian's encomiums to market timing and excoriation of frequent trading . . . although he possibly does not appreciate it. During the five years ending in June 1985, Schabacker gave a grand total of two switch signals. He went out of the market in 1981 as it sagged downward and reentered it on August 24, 1982, three days before *Telephone Switch Newsletter* and twelve days after the low. (These are the dates on which subscribers would have been able to act.) After this, Schabacker sailed on for the next three years with majestic indifference to short-term alarums and excursions, keeping his inactive traders fully invested. By contrast, Fabian signaled a sell in January 1984, after which the market did decline and many advisors began to think the bull market had expired. But it hadn't, and by mid-1985 the Dow was almost 500 points higher than it had been in mid-1982, effectively vindicating Schabacker's cool strategy.

Mark Hulbert's analysis appears to confirm that market timing can work. In April 1985, for example, he reviewed the switch signals given since mid-1980 by nine letters in his roster and found that all except one had outperformed a completely passive buy-and-hold strategy. Interestingly, the best results, Schabacker's and Fabian's, had been achieved with the fewest switches. The worst, Stan Weinstein's in *Professional Tape Reader*, involved an incredible 25.33 switches—the fraction representing a partial commitment to the market.

Many long-established investment letters are now tailoring their advice to telephone switch traders. Other letters are specifically directed at them. An indication of changing realities in the industry was the Seattle-based *Fund Exchange Report*, founded in 1983 by former stockbroker and manufacturer Paul Merriman. This purposefully set out to bite into Dick Fabian's audience by offering intensive customer support, even undertaking to administer switch orders for money management clients in their Individual Retirement Accounts, no matter how small. With equal purpose, it insistently brought itself to Hulbert's attention, eventually offering proof of its 1984 record independently audited by a Big 8 accounting firm. *Fund Exchange Report* has established eight different model portfolios, varying according to investment objectives and risk preference. "People will not accept even five or ten percent losses," says Merriman. His switch signals are generated by trend-following models that combine weighted and unweighted moving price averages with some point-and-figure charting.

A slightly different response came from *Mutual Fund Strategist*, published by Charlie Hooper of Burlington, Vermont. Hooper's service features an extensive review of the opinions of his fellow specialists in the mutual fund area, and at one point he set out to rate their performance. They greeted this endeavor quite unenthusiastically. Hooper's own service rates funds and employs a long-term and short-term timing model. Hulbert's monitoring of *Mutual Fund Strategist* began only in 1985. But his numbers have paralleled its own records, which Hooper says demonstrate a superior performance extending back to 1982.

Some other older services focus more on rating the funds than on market timing. These include *Growth Fund Guide*, published from Rapid City, South Dakota, and *No Load Fund-X*, which follows a "Follow the Stars Strategy" recommending that investors rotate each month into the highest-performing fund categorized by investment objective.

Mutual-fund switching is here to stay, but it will probably not stay in the same place. It is already altering the way mutual funds are run. Previously, the portfolio managers had the option of going into cash when they didn't like the stock market: now their clients expect them to stay fully invested at all times. Moreover, in order to ride out the tidal wave of redemptions whenever a major service like *Telephone Switch Newsletter* gives a switch signal, the mutual funds have to build up the cash reserves they keep permanently on hand, reducing their participation in the market. In the long run, their consequent lack of maneuverability will tend to reduce their average performance. Indeed, even an index fund might have trouble keeping up with the averages because of cash needs and other complications. A further problem is that even the best-run fund cannot always liquidate its stock positions fast enough to accommodate massive redemptions without breaking down the market. In 1984–5 this problem was particularly acute for Fidelity Select Technology, which was heavily invested in thinly traded issues, and it was a factor behind Fabian's reluctance to accept his system's signals.

Some funds have resisted telephone switching for these reasons. Some investors, in the market for the long haul, prefer funds without telephone switching. But the pressure of competition is wearing the funds down. Simultaneously, however, a tendency is developing for switch funds to impose a small redemption fee, perhaps $50, to discourage promiscuous switching. The switch letter editors generally think this will not impede serious investors. Another new development is the trading of mutual funds on margin, putting up only a fraction of their worth. This facility was first offered by the San Francisco discount broker Charles Schwab & Company and was instantly the object of intensely thoughtful perusal from the switch services.

Paradoxically, market timing and mutual-fund switching are particularly useful to two opposed categories of investors: small and large. For small investors, the combination offers a safer, systematic approach to the market, where limited amounts of attention and knowledge can pay off. It is especially suited to long-term tax-exempt portfolios like IRAs, where the relatively small gains can compound without interference. For large institutional investors, disillusioned with the cost and bureaucracy of a traditional investment department and the results of detailed security analysis and active portfolio management, a diversified, or index, fund offers the comforting guarantee of an average performance, and timing extends the hope that this average can be improved upon by concentrating attention on the simpler question of what assets will be allocated where.

This is the sort of humble conclusion that investors are prepared to accept only while they remember losses. And the gains of the early 1980s have not yet repaired the damage done by the catastrophe of the 1970s. But already, with sector funds and funds that can be bought on margin, the temptation to seek performance is making itself felt. Indeed, it may not be wholly unreasonable—not that it ever is. To the extent that investors concentrate their monies with a small number of managements and in index funds, the market will grow less efficient at recognizing value. New companies will go undiscovered; established but improving companies will go unappreciated. In short, exactly the situation will be created where stock pickers—and their investment letters—will once again flourish.

THE EVANS FAMILY AND *DOW THEORY FORECASTS*

"One of the big ones circulation-wise," wrote Bob Gross about the *Dow Theory Forecasts,* in one of his periodic critiques of the investment letter industry that appeared way back in 1971. "It carries a consensus of other market letters which is useful, a market commentary, special reports, follows Dow Theory, and has a Trader's page. It's the kind of service you can't really knock, and yet it's hard to get excited about."

Dow Theory Forecasts is so hard to get excited about, in fact, that it has almost no press clippings to show for over forty years in business. Being based in Hammond, Indiana, probably hasn't recommended it to junketing New York journalists. And its format, which does not appear to have altered much since Gross pronounced his considered yawn a decade and a half ago, is undeniably staid by the glitzy standard of Wall Street publications. But this total neglect must be regarded as another example of metropolitan parochialism. The investment letter community has long known that a serious eruption has been in progress in Hammond, Indiana, because of discernible tremors on its competition Richter scale and the extraordinary quantities of direct-mail solicitations hurtling across the landscape. *Dow Theory Forecasts* has perfected a strategy of promoting heavily a very cheap and very short-term trial, generating a vast number of responses of which only a fraction will convert to a long-term subscription, but with a very high proportion of that fraction reliably renewing. By contrast, most investment letters offer more expensive trials of which a high proportion convert but a much lower proportion renew. Select Information Exchange's George Wein has estimated that in the boom year of 1968, *Dow Theory Forecasts* inspired the incredible total of nearly 600,000 one-dollar single-issue trials. Recently, with a slightly more expensive $3 eight-issue trial, *Dow Theory Forecasts* has been entertaining up to 75,000 subscribers in a year, including over 22,000 who currently receive the full $163-a-year weekly service.

Another reason for *Dow Theory Forecasts'* lack of public acclaim is the unobtrusive nature of its record. It recommends several lists of stocks attuned to different investment objectives. Mark Hulbert constructs his model portfolios for the *Hulbert Financial Digest* from those selections highlighted as "especially promising." None of the portfolios has ever performed particularly spectacularly in either direction. But over the June 1980–June 1985 five-year period, *Dow Theory Forecasts'* Income Stocks and Investment Stocks both outperformed the Dow, with gains of 112 percent and 104.9 percent respectively. And its Growth Stocks portfolio, which finished at only 90.5 percent, had kept ahead of the market for three years until mid-1983. The weakest portfolio was Speculative Stocks, which finished at 70.1 percent. The average performance of *Dow Theory Forecasts'* portfolios was thus 94.8 percent, as opposed to the dividend-reinvested Dow's 100.8 percent. This record would probably be somewhat stronger had Hulbert followed *Dow Theory Forecasts'* list of low-priced stocks. At one time these stocks were categorized by investment objective, and Hulbert assigned them to the appropriate portfolio. When *Dow Theory Forecasts* ceased this practice in 1981, he hesitated to set up yet a fifth portfolio.

Dow Theory Forecasts is the creation of LeRoy B. Evans, a cheerful septuagenarian who, according to his son Richard, now president of Dow Theory Forecasts, Inc., "still comes into the office every morning and raises Cain—takes us the rest of the day to straighten things out." Another son, Robert, runs the production side of the business, which does all its own printing and mailing. It employs over fifty people and also publishes *The Low-Priced Stock Survey, Emerging Growth Stocks* and *Special Situations Under $5.*

LeRoy Evans was born in Iowa in 1911. He studied to be a schoolteacher at what is now the University of Northern Iowa in Cedar Falls and briefly contemplated journalism, but was rescued from this fate by a friend who steered him into advertising in Chicago. In 1938, while working for LaSalle Steel in Hammond, Evans invested $700 of his savings in Curtis Publishing at 7; it went to seventy-five cents. He discussed his experience with a LaSalle engineer, who advised him to study Dow Theory, then being refined by Robert Rhea. Evans became a believer, but after Rhea's death in 1939 he felt that no available service was fully worthy of Dow's mantle. He began mimeographing his own opinions, started publishing *Dow Theory Forecasts* in 1945, and after successfully predicting the 1946 crash, made it his full-time career.

Despite this long-standing interest in Dow Theory, the space devoted to market timing in *Dow Theory Forecasts* is relatively limited. Critics say the comments are sometimes vague, with a slightly bullish tendency, and never recommend specific levels of exposure to the market. As always in such cases, Mark Hulbert accordingly calculates *Dow Theory Forecasts'* portfolios on the assumption that they are always 100 percent invested. The core of *Dow Theory Forecasts* is its selection of stocks, where, of course, Dow is no help. Instead, stocks are picked according to "current prices in relation to past price-earnings multiples, present technical and fundamental outlooks and the prospects for industry groups in general." "We look for companies with a lock on their markets," says Richard Evans. "We like to see increasing net margins, good earnings trends." *Dow Theory Forecasts'* five-man research staff makes no company visits and works entirely from published information, even using publicly available earnings estimates. Technical analysis comes into play with lower-priced and speculative stocks. *Dow Theory Forecasts'* director of research, Chuck Carlson, who, like Richard Evans, is a graduate of Northwestern University, has qualified as a Chartered Financial Analyst, the union card of fundamental analysts, which requires a grueling obstacle race of night school courses that few Wall Streeters ever complete.

The list of stocks selected by *Dow Theory Forecasts* is stable. Its size never fluctuates in response to the market and most of its recommendations will be held for the long term. This conservative approach and calmly plodding performance is obviously attractive to a certain class of investors. *Dow Theory Forecasts*, perhaps because of its regular rating of nearly 800 stocks, seems also to have a particular appeal to reference libraries.

And its charms are more than meet the eye. Uniquely in the investment letter industry, *Dow Theory Forecasts* encourages subscribers to write or call for free consultation on their portfolio problems. If they do not, it will actually send them a letter urging them to do so.

ARNOLD M. KAUFMAN AND STANDARD & POOR'S *OUTLOOK*

Unlike the Evans family, Arnie Kaufman of *Outlook* is often quoted in the press, and his employer, Standard & Poor's Corporation, is universally accepted as a Wall Street landmark. But Kaufman's comments are usually on current market conditions or specific ingenious ideas he thought up, such as his listing of "Stocks you should avoid" or surveys of dividend changes. The weekly $185-a-year *Outlook* itself remains a relatively unknown dimension of Standard & Poor's, albeit, with its approximately 50,000 circulation, quite a large one.

Mark Hulbert has followed the stocks noted as "best situated" in *Outlook*'s four Master Lists: Foundation Stocks for long-term gain, Growth Stocks, Cyclical/Speculative Stocks and Income Stocks. After 1982, *Outlook* no longer made specific allocation recommendations between cash and the market, so Hulbert began to treat all these portfolios as fully invested. In late 1984, however, *Outlook* began a "Master Portfolio" including allocation advice: Hulbert has followed it since 1985.

Outlook's performance has been like that of *Dow Theory Forecasts:* plodding, persistent and—possibly—passable. Of the two, *Outlook* has been the stronger. Between June 1980 and June 1985, its Foundation Stocks portfolio appreciated 61.5 percent, its Growth Stocks Portfolio 90.5 percent, its Speculative Stocks 132.4 percent and its Income Stocks 142.6 percent, opposed to the total-return Dow's 100.8 percent and the S & P 500's 114.6 percent. All had enjoyed quite long periods where they had kept ahead of the market on a cumulative basis; none had slipped below it until mid-1983. Even the average performance of *Outlook*'s portfolios, up 108.2 percent, beat the Dow.

Outlook's approach to stock selection appears to be entirely fundamental. And Kaufman's educational background would fit a Wall Street analyst: he is a graduate of Baruch College and has an MBA from New York University. In addition to editing *Outlook*, he is the chairman of Standard & Poor's stock selection committee and vice chairman of the company's investment policy committee. But Kaufman obviously keeps an eye on the tape. In late 1984, *Outlook* was pessimistic about stocks based on its expectation of an economic slowdown in the first half of the new year. But the January rally caused *Outlook* to change its mind in a hurry. Kaufman cited the release of favorable GNP and inflation figures for 1984—and "the superb technical action of the market." He added, lapsing into technicians' language, "We are now in the second leg of the bull market that began in August 1982."

CHAPTER NINE

Conclusions

There are nine and sixty ways of constructing tribal lays,
And-every-single-one-of-them-is-right!

—RUDYARD KIPLING

Or wrong. As the case may be.

The first conclusion to emerge from any study of the *Hulbert Financial Digest*'s list of successful investment letters is that while the market can be beaten, there is no uniquely successful way of beating it. The techniques used by this group are quite divergent and in fact frequently incompatible. Some favor fundamental analysis (Charles Allmon, Al Frank), others are chartists (Bob Gross, Jim Dines, Charles Stahl). Some are tortoiselike long-term holders (Glen Parker and Norman Fosback), others are hare-ier active traders (Marty Zweig). Some prefer mutual funds (the telephone switch letters), others pick stocks (everyone else except Charles Stahl). The key seems to be that each of the advisors has found an approach that suits his personality. And they are generally prepared to do a little methodological poaching when they feel like it.

The second conclusion is that regardless of their methods, the best that advisors of all stripes can be expected to do over the long term falls into roughly the same range. And at first sight the range may not boggle anybody's calculator. The five years from June 30, 1980 to June 28, 1985 included one strong bull market and two fairly distressing declines, ending with the dividend-reinvested averages up some 100 percent to 115 percent, or an annual rate of 15 percent to 16 percent compounded. In that period the top investment letter performances were turned in by Al Frank's fundamentalist *The Prudent Speculator*, up 272.9 percent, and by James Dines' chart-reading *The Dines Letter*, whose Growth Portfolio gained 241 percent. This works out at 27 percent to 30 percent compounded annually. Their pace may well slow: Frank's growing portfolio will be less maneuverable, and Dines' volatility is alarming. The top four portfolios in the market-beating group all appreciated at an annual compound rate of 25 percent or more. The others straggled behind, with an eclectic cluster in the 130 percent to 140 percent range: *The Zweig Forecast* (hybrid-technical), *Market Logic* (hybrid-technical), *Outlook*'s Income Stocks (fundamental), Value Line's *OTC Special Situations Service* (fundamental) and *Professional Investor*'s OTC Scan (cheerfully undogmatic chartist). The annual compounded growth rate of this cluster was around 18 percent to 20 percent.

It seems reasonable to say that somewhere around 20 percent to 25 percent compounded annually seems to be the maximum practical return in the market over the long term. This conclusion is reinforced from other sources. In 1985, for example, PIPER—*Pension & Investment Age*'s quarterly Performance Evaluation Report of bank and insurance company commingled equity funds—peeped that over the previous ten years the top-performing manager had achieved an annual return of 25.7 percent compounded; the next five—including Citizens Bank of Chillicothe—were all between 21.1 percent and 19.2 percent. And this was coming off the 1974 bottom. In the last five years the same top-performing money manager, Toronto's Manufacturers Life Insurance Company, achieved an appreciation equivalent to 32.5 percent compounded annually; the next five ranged from 27.2 percent to 24.9 percent. In neither case did much more than a quarter of these professional money managers beat the averages, not notably a better performance than that of the investment letters, which embraced a much wider range of investment objectives.

Warren Buffett provides further reinforcement. When he began his famous family partnership in 1956, he said his goal was to beat the Dow by ten percentage points each year. The upward trend of stocks, counting dividends and capital appreciation, has, of course, been somewhere over 9 percent. Thus Buffett's ambition was to achieve about 20 percent compounded annually. This is sometimes regarded as demonstrating great moderation of character. But it was actually coolly audacious.

That it is practically impossible to get more than 20 percent or 25 percent compounded on your money on a sustained basis is such important information that no one will remember it. It will be wiped out by just one or two years in which friends, or friends of friends, are making, or are rumored to be making, triple-digit returns. Which is what happened in the go-go years of the late 1960s. A collector's item in the financial community is the 1969 coffee-table book *New Breed on Wall Street,* in which Cornell Capa photographed and Martin Mayer cleverly interviewed some five dozen of the hot young money managers who personified the era's cult of performance. Mayer quoted Fidelity Management's Edward C. Johnson II, universally known as "Mr. Johnson" and one of the industry's most respected elder statesmen, on the prevailing mood: "I have known supposedly conservative investors to come in and say, 'I'd like to leave a few hundred thousand with you for a couple of years. I don't want you to do anything spectacular with it, just make 20 percent to 30 percent a year for me.'" The implied point: 20 percent to 30 percent *was* spectacular. Within five years, of course, most of the cult's personalities had ended up on the sacrificial altar.

At this point many investors will be tempted to take their money and withdraw gracefully to Las Vegas. At least there's a slight chance of instant wealth. And they would get to see naked girls. But this desperate step is unneccessary. To echo *Telephone Switch Newsletter*'s Dick Fabian: small gains are fine *when allied to the power of compound interest.* Compound interest is emphatically not the same as simple interest. Although the arithmetic of compound interest is elementary, its effect is all too frequently overlooked even by investment professionals. Many Wall Streeters are frankly incredulous, for example, when they hear that a model portfolio made up of *Value Line*'s Group 1 stocks would have appreciated 7,590 percent between 1964 and 1984. But this is merely what happens when 24.2 percent is compounded over twenty years. *Value Line,* needless to say, did not make 24.2 percent smoothly every year, but that was the trend underlying its gains and losses. And as Mr. Johnson says, Wall Streeters in their euphoric mode brush off a 20 percent to 30 percent annual return as mundane.

Compound interest possesses a crucial statistical quirk: each additional year, and each additional percentage point, makes the end result exponentially more spectacular. A thousand dollars compounded at 20 percent will more than double in four years, increase over sixfold in ten years—and at the end of thirty years it will be worth $237,376.31. Thirty years, of course, is less than a working lifetime. If in 1626 the Manhattan Indians had taken the 60 guilders given them by the Dutch in exchange for Manhattan Island—some $22.20 by Norman Fosback's count in Stock Market Logic—and invested it in bonds at 7 percent, by 1976 they would have had $427 billion. Had they invested in stocks and got 9 percent, they would have had $300 trillion.

The harsh reality of investing exposed by Mark Hulbert's work compels one rational response: because the market can be beaten, but not by much, relatively small gains must be eked out wherever possible and then compounded over many years. The fact that this appears to be the only really feasible route to riches explains why inflation is such a mortal threat. The investment calculus is so finely balanced, with each percentage point so vital, that it simply cannot accept changes in the value of money of even 1 or 2 percent a year, let alone 15 percent to 20 percent. Moreover, any minor inflation in the general price level is refracted through the system to produce vast inflation in specific prices—real estate, perhaps, and the securities of public companies that deal in it. Naturally, this dismays investors who have been eking patiently away in other areas, and quickly destabilizes the market. Both of the stock market's great speculative blow-offs of this century, in 1928 to 1929 and 1966 to 1968, left a telltale whiff of monetary inflation hanging above the wreckage.

Equally, the reality of investment life raises disturbing questions about the profound and pervasive effects of taxation. Compound interest works both ways. If the government taxes the 20 percent yield on that $1,000 at the top marginal rate of 50 percent, it will take not thirty but fifty-eight years to grow into $237,000. The federal income tax is a relatively recent import to the United States. It has been around only since 1913, and in that year a mere 0.4 percent of Americans earned enough to file any return at all. Even as late as 1930, only 1.4 percent of Americans' total personal income was claimed by income tax. By 1981 it was 12 percent. Moreover, the effect of inflation in the 1960s and 1970s was to push ordinary people whose purchasing power hadn't increased at all into tax brackets that were originally intended only for the very rich in the days when a dollar was a dollar. This has resulted in the phenomenon, wholly new in peacetime, of large numbers of middle-class Americans facing high marginal rates of taxation—the amount of each additional dollar of their income that is claimed by taxes, the decisive factor controlling their incentive to invest or consume. In 1961, only about 12 percent of American taxpayers faced marginal rates above 23 percent. By 1979, over 45 percent did. The tax reforms of the 1980s served merely to arrest this "bracket creep," not roll it back.

The long-term effect of financing current government needs in this way is quite simply unknown. It might be unexpectedly awful, like felling trees in an arid area. Certainly, the investment industry is only beginning to adapt its overall thinking on behalf of the individual investor to the problem of taxes, despite some considerable experience on the more detailed level of estate-planning and tax-loss selling. Some advisory letters worry vaguely about qualifying their profits as capital gains, but in the period under review few reflected that the tax incursion sharply detracted from one of the more profitable strategies: staying in cash. Many probably hope the advent of tax-exempt trading for Keogh Plans, IRAs and the like will save them from having to think about this unpleasant topic. No one has yet attempted the complex task of allowing for taxes in calculating the dividend-reinvested S & P or Dow indexes, in the way that the Gross National Product is routinely adjusted for inflation.

If someone really knew how to beat the market, they wouldn't sell the secret in a newsletter for a lousy few hundred bucks. The fallacy behind this assertion is now clear. Investing is more like farming than mining. The regular reaping of small gains is more important than the occasional lucky strike. It takes a lot of manure-shoveling and mosquito bites to accumulate a store of wealth in the market. You can starve to death in the interim. In

1983, for example, seven years into an investing career that can only be described as phenomenal, Al Frank told *Barron's* Jaye Scholl that his *Prudent Speculator* portfolio would yield him some $7,000 in dividend income that year. This was almost as much as his entire capital commitment in 1976, but it was still considerably less than Frank earned as a journeyman college teacher (and of course he has drawn upon his capital during this period, complicating his track record). However, by helping large numbers of others to similar small gains, the investment letter editor in effect spreads the benefit of his knowledge, and thereby multiplies its total value. He performs a legitimate economic function —and receives that lousy few hundred bucks from enough people to add up to a sum upon which there are no flies at all.

The strategy of reaping small gains, moreover, can require the planting of large amounts of capital. Only then can the risk-reducing effects of diversification be obtained. For example, Charles Allmon's model portfolio in *Growth Stock Outlook* began with a hypothetical $50,000. Of course, Al Frank started with less, but in more recent years a subscriber wishing to mimic his approach would have had to deploy over a quarter of a million dollars' worth of stock margined to the maximum, a maneuver requiring some $125,000 in cash backed by a sufficiently substantial net worth to soothe the skittish brokerage house handling the transaction. No matter how good an advisor's investment ideas, he may just not have this sort of money. Additionally, he may feel inspired to give advice in some especially dangerous market, like options or commodities, which can be played only by those prepared to lose their initial stake, and which are therefore restricted to professionals, the rich and the suicidal.

There is no doubt that some investment advisors are peddling illusions. But publishing an investment letter is not in itself conclusive evidence of guilt.

The advisors who have beaten the market in the five years under review are an odd lot. They have few obviously common traits. Most received no formal education in investments or economics, but a few did. A majority displayed some predilection for figures, such as studying accounting or a hard science, but none is highly quantitative—even Marty Zweig says modestly that he isn't particularly numerate by comparison with his academic colleagues—and a couple have experimented with distinctly artistic careers. Some of the advisors are dedicated family men, but others are sexually promiscuous. In apparent confirmation of Wall Street folk wisdom about successful traders, a high proportion are either Irish or Jewish. Or, in Bob Gross's case, both.

There is, however, a marked tendency for them to be older men, with years of experience in the market that include periods of loss. An exception is Peter Shraga at *Value Line OTC Special Situations Service,* but he is operating within a long-established tradition and may be benefiting from institutional memory. Marty Zweig is in his early forties, but he has been publishing *The Zweig Forecast* since 1971. Glen King Parker and Norman Fosback, respectively in their late forties and late thirties, have also been publishing *Market Logic* for an appreciable period, since 1975. Both *The Zweig Forecast* and *Market Logic* have highly analytical approaches to the market, suggesting that science, in some circumstances, may be a partial substitute for scars.

Not only are the other advisors older and battle-scarred, but they also tend to have changed careers. Often they came to investments relatively late in life, having worked in completely different areas. Sometimes their lives at the point they entered the field must have looked quite unimpressive. Yet, occasionally after a purgatorial phase of losing money and suffering, they were apparently equipped for a significant run of investment success.

Age—experience—patience—small gains, compounded over long periods. These, with the possible addition of a capacity for open-mindedness, are the apparent morals to be drawn from the *Hulbert Financial Digest*'s monitoring of the investment letter industry.

But journalists have a habit of reporting events that have ended. It must have something to do with sticking to the facts, which limits them to what's already happened. In mid-1985 the stock market was at a new high, but the conservative message coming through loud and clear from Mark Hulbert's numbers was far more typical of a market low than a market top. So was the advisors' incessant moaning about circulation. There are times, in war and in speculative markets, when the virtues of youth are actually more valuable than those of age. The gunslingers of the 1960s really did make money, for a while. Those times have not yet returned to Wall Streets. But they will. And when they do, there will be investment letters—among this present group of successes and elsewhere—that will be able to profit from them.*

---

*No doubt inspired by these words, the stock market aroused itself late in 1985 and lunged sharply higher, breaking through 1,600 on the Dow in February 1986. The results through December 1985 are reflected in the *Hulbert Financial Digest* tables on pages 68 to 75. Naturally, the top performing letters of 1985 were up spectacularly. The *McKeever Strategy Letter*, a commodities service, was up 99.3 percent; *Medical Technology Stock Letter* gained 83.3 percent; *High Technology Investments* was able to rebound 77.1 percent; *OTC Insight* and *BI Research* were up 66.3 percent and 65.9 percent respectively. This partly reflected continued rotation among sectors, but speculative skills were also in evidence. Without neccessarily topping the charts or even beating the dividend-reinvested averages in this very strong year, all the Hulbert long-term winners did well enough to remain long-term winners. Al Frank (up 62.2 percent) lengthened his lead over Charles Allmon (up 24.7 percent) but assumed significantly more risk, Marty Zweig (up 41.8 percent) had his best-ever year, and James Dines' cumulative performance continued to subside to more human proportions. Other confirmed patterns included the nonmaterialization of Howard Ruff's Phantom Investor, despite some premonitions after *Lowe* v. *SEC*, and Joe Granville's refusal to extend diplomatic recognition to the bull market.

Risk-Adjusted Return

The topic of risk-adjusted performance is inherently numbing, and it has been therefore quarantined below.

A portfolio's "risk-adjusted" performance is based upon a comparison with the performance of a similar portfolio invested entirely in treasury bills. The theory is that the yield from treasury bills is certain, and is in effect what the investor could have achieved without taking any investment risk at all.

Many investment strategies can outperform the T-bill return by assuming differing amounts of risk. So the key issue is: *how efficient is each strategy's use of risk?*

The *Hulbert Financial Digest* calculates this in a two-stage process. Firstly, accepting the academic identification of risk with volatility, it finds the standard deviation of each investment letter's monthly preformance. This constitutes the "risk-rating" of each letter, telling readers, for example, that the *Option Advisor*'s portfolio in late 1985 was over twenty times more volatile than that of *Kinsman's Low-Risk Advisory*. Secondly, the *Hulbert Financial Digest* divides each letter's premium above the treasury bill return by its "risk-rating." This reveals how much each investment letter has been able to earn per unit of risk.

The table below covers the five-year period from June 30, 1980, to June 28, 1985. It shows the *average monthly return* that each letter has been able to achieve for the same amount of risk. Thus the most efficient, *Growth Stock Outlook,* has been able to appreciate 0.28 percent per month, or 3.3 percent a year above the T-bill rate per unit of risk. Several letters actually performed worse than the T-bill rate as they took on more risk, and thus are shown with negative scores.

1. Growth Stock Outlook
   0.292

2. The Dines Letter List #2
   0.206

3. Professional Investor—Amex Scan
   0.185

4. Outlook—Income Stocks
   0.181

5. The Prudent Speculator
   0.174

6. The Zweig Forecast
   0.158

7. Green's Commodity Market Comments
   0.154

8. Professional Investor—OTC Scan
   0.145

9. Market Logic—Master Portfolio
   0.143

10. Market Logic—Option Portfolio
    0.138

11. Outlook—Speculative Stocks
    0.133

12. Chartist—Actual Cash Account
    0.126

13. S & P 500—Total Return
    0.124

14. Dow Theory Forecasts—Income Stocks
    0.118

15. Dow Theory Forecasts—Investment Stocks
    0.105

16. Value Line OTC Special Situations Service
    0.104

17. Telephone Switch Newsletter—Equities
    0.092

18. Dines Letter List #6
    0.088

19. Dines Letter List #2
    0.076

20. Outlook—Growth Stocks
    0.069

21. Dow Theory Forecasts—Growth
    0.054

22. Dow Theory Forecasts—Speculative
    0.032

23. Kinsman's Low-Risk Advisory
    0.014

24. Outlook—Foundation Stocks
    0.006

25. T-bill Only Portfolio
    0.000

26. United Business Service—Income Stocks
    −0.007

27. Professional Investor—NYSE Scan
    −0.028

28. Professional Investor—Investment Grade
    −0.031

29. United Business Service—Cyclical Stocks
    −0.051

30. International Harry Schultz Letter
    −0.060

31. Howard Ruff's Financial Success Report
    −0.097

32. United Business Service—Growth Stocks
    −0.108

33. Dines Letter List #1
    —0.109

34. Professional Tape Reader
    —0.134

35. Holt Investment Advisory
    —0.190

36. The Granville Market Letter—Aggressive Traders
    —0.305

37. Heim Investment Letter
    —0.311

Where to Find Newsletters and Books

At press time, the newsletters mentioned in this book were at approximately the latitudes and longitudes given below. Investment letters pass across the map faster than the proverbial speeding bullet, and no list of them can pretend to be definitive. In particular, prices are to be regarded as merely approximate. Investment letters regularly offer special discount subscription rates, sometimes on a semipermanent basis. Many thoughtfully refrain from printing any price at all on individual issues of their publications in order to spare the subscriber who has paid the full rate unnecessary suffering at the sight of subsequent radical reductions. Others prefer to maintain a theoretical price as a sort of inspirational ideal, while in practice settling for much less.

Needless to say, investment letter editors are much too individualistic to name their creations in the consistent style copy editors like to see. This complicates the task of ordering them alphabetically. It has been simplified here by (1) ignoring definite articles when they appear in newsletter titles, and (2) ignoring initials and first names in those cases where the letters are named in celebration of their proprietors.

Several of the investment letters listed here are part of larger families. Their siblings are not mentioned unless they appear in the book. Modern direct-mail techniques are such, however, that an inquiry about one letter virtually guarantees the arrival of helpful information about the others in due course.

The individuals mentioned with each of the letters are those most prominently associated with them, although they are not in all cases the editors.

Some important investment letters escaped without mention in this book, and their names therefore do not appear below.

The Addison Report (Andrew Addison)
P.O. Box 402, Franklin, MA 02038
$140/year

The Aden Analysis (Mary Anne Aden, Pamela Aden)
(see *Market Alert*)
$250/year

The Astute Investor (Robert J. Nurock)
P.O. Box 988, Paoli, PA 19301
$195/year

Babson's Reports
Wellesley Hills, MA 02181
$96/year

The Bank Credit Analyst (J. Anthony Boeckh)
3463 Peel Street, Montreal, Quebec H3A 1W7, CANADA
$475/year

BI Research (Thomas C. Bishop)
P.O. Box 301, South Salem, NY 10590
$80/year

The Bowser Report (R. Max Bowser)
Box 6278, Newport News, VA 23606
$39/year

Harry Browne's Special Reports (Harry Browne)
P.O. Box 5586, Austin, TX 78763
$225/ten issues

The Cabot Market Letter (Carlton G. Lutts)
P.O. Box 3044, Salem, MA 01970
$150/year

California Technology Stock Letter (Mike Murphy)
155 Montgomery Street, San Francisco, CA 94104
$220/year

Canadian Business Service
133 Richmond St. West #700, Toronto, Ontario M5H 3M8,
  CANADA
C$175/year

The Charted Course (Carl A. Cascella)
P.O. Box 88, Westport, CT 06881
$195/year

The Chartist (Dan Sullivan)
P.O. Box 3160, Long Beach, CA 90803
$115/year

Commodity Traders Consumer Report (Bruce Babcock, Jr.)
1731 Howe Street, Sacramento, CA 95825
$150/year

The Contest Newsletter (Roger Tyndall)
P.O. Box 1059, Fernandino Beach, FL 32034
$12/year

The Contrary Investor (James L. Fraser)
309 South Willard Street, Burlington, VT 05402
$70/year

Crawford Perspectives (Arch Crawford)
250 East 77 Street, New York, NY 10021
$250/year

Daily Graphs (William O'Neil)
Box 24933, Los Angeles, CA 90024
$540/year

Dick Davis Digest (Dick Davis)
Box 2828, Miami Beach, FL 33140
$95/year

Deliberations (Ian McAvity)
P.O. Box 182, Adelaide St. Station, Toronto, Ontario, M5C 2J1
  CANADA
$215/year

Dessauer's Journal (John P. Dessauer)
P.O. Box 1718, Orleans, MA 02653
$150/year

The Dines Letter (James Dines)
P.O. Box 22, Belvedere, CA 94920
$195/year

Donoghue's Money Fund Report (William E. Donoghue)
Box 540, Holliston, MA 01746
$595/year

Donoghue's Moneyletter
(see *Donoghue's Money Fund Report*)
$87/year

Dow Theory Comment (Michael MacGuire)
10 Upland Rd., Colorado Springs, CO 80906
$100/year

Dow Theory Forecasts, (L. B. Evans & clan)
7412 Calumet Avenue, Hammond, IN 46324
$163/year

Dow Theory Letters (Richard Russell)
P.O. Box 1759, La Jolla, CA 92038
$225/year

Lynn Elgert Report (Lynn Elgert)
P.O. Box 1283, Grand Island, NE 68802
$225/year

Elliott Wave Theorist (Robert R. Prechter)
P.O. Box 1618, Gainesville, GA 30503
$233/year

Emerging & Special Situations
(see *The Outlook*)
$130/year

Emerging Growth Stocks
(see *Dow Theory Forecasts*)
$125/year

Financial World
P.O. Box 10750, Des Moines, IA 50340
$41.95/year

The Fund Exchange Report (Paul Merriman)
AGC Building, 1200 Westlake Ave. North, Ste. 507, Seattle, WA
   98109-3530
$195/year

Gann Angles (Phyllis Kahn)
245-A Washington St., Monterey, CA 93940
$360/year

W. D. Gann Weekly Technical Commodity Letter (Joseph L. Lederer)
Box 8508, St. Louis, MO 63126
$125/year

The Garside Forecast (Ben C. Garside)
P.O. Box 1812, Santa Ana, CA 92702
$125/year

Kenneth J. Gerbino Investment Letter (Ken Gerbino)
9595 Wilshire Blvd, Suite 200, Beverly Hills, CA 90212
$295/year

Good Money (Susan Meeker-Lowry, Peter Lowry, Richard Lowry)
28 Main Street, Montpelier, VT 05602
$49/year

Grant's Interest Rate Observer (James C. Grant)
233 Broadway, Suite 1216, New York NY 10279
$250/year

The Granville Market Letter (Joseph E. Granville)
P.O. Box Drawer 23006, Kansas City, MO 64141
$250/year

Green's Commodity Market Comments (Charles Stahl)
P.O. Box 174, Princeton, NJ 08540
$240/year

Growth Fund Guide
Growth Fund Research Bldg., Box 6600, Rapid City, SD 57709
$175/year

Growth Stock Outlook (Charles Allmon)
P.O. Box 15381, Chevy Chase, MD 20815
$175/year

Hard Money Digest (Royal Krieger)
3608 Grand Ave., Oakland, CA 94610
$152/year

Heim Investment Letter (Lawrence H. Heim, Truman C. Pagh)
720 SW Washington St., Portland, OR 97205
$150/year

Tony Henfrey's Gold Letter (Tony Henfrey)
P.O. Box 9137, Allentown, PA 18105
$185/year

High Technology Growth Stocks (Bud Anderson)
14 Nason St., Maynard, MA 01754
$165/year

High Technology Investments (Michael C. Gianturco)
5925 Kirby Drive, Ste. 219, Houston, TX 77005
$119/year

The Holt Investment Advisory (Thomas J. Holt)
290 Post Road West, Westport, CT 06880
$225/year

Hotline (Frederick D. Goss)
Colorado Building, Ste. 700, 1341 G Street N.W., Washington, D.C.
   20005
(Newsletter Association—membership $225/year)

The Donald J. Hoppe Business and Investment Analysis (Donald J.
   Hoppe)
Box 997, Crystal Lake, IL 60014
$125/year

The Hulbert Financial Digest (Mark Hulbert)
643 South Carolina Avenue S.E., Washington, D.C. 20003
$135/year

Indicator Digest (Jack Mohrer)
451 Grand Ave., Palisades Park, NJ 07650
$175/year

Insider Indicator (J. Michael Reid)
2230 N.E. Brazee St., Portland, OR 97212
$145/year

Insiders
(see *Market Logic*)
$100/year

International Harry Schultz Letter (Harry Schultz)
FERC P.O. Box 381, CH-1001, Lausanne, Switzerland
$260/year

The Investech Market Letter (James B. Stack)
522 Crestview Drive, Kalispell, MT 59901
$150/year

Investment Values (William T. Chidester)
P.O. Box 517, Mt. Kisco, NY 10549
$80/year

Investment Quality Trends (Geraldine Weiss)
7440 Girard Avenue, La Jolla, CA 92037
$175/year

Investors Intelligence (Michael L. Burke)
1 West Ave., Larchmont, NY 10538
$84/year

The Janeway Letter (Eliot Janeway)
15 East 80th Street, New York, NY 10021
$250/year

Robert Kinsman's Low-Risk Growth Letter (Robert Kinsman)
70 Mitchell Blvd., San Rafael, CA 94903
$125/year

The Kiplinger Washington Letter
1729 H Street N.W., Washington, D.C. 20006
$42/year

Kondratyev Wave Theory
Box 1675, Sausalito, CA 94965
$150/year

LaLoggia's Special Situations Report (Charles M. LaLoggia)
P.O. Box 167, Rochester. NY 14601
$230/year

Lambda Financial Advisor (Julius J. Spohn)
P.O. Box 3569, Jersey City, NJ 07303-3569
$36/year

Harry Lankford Charts
Box 213–A, Wichita, KS 67201
up to $900/year

Let's Talk . . . Silver & Gold (James H. Sibbet)
61 South Lake Avenue, Ste. 301, Pasadena, CA 91101
$77/year

Lowe Investment & Financial Letter (Christopher L. Lowe)
P.O. Box 6, Jersey City, NJ 07303-0006
$195/year

The Low-Priced Stock Survey
(see *Dow Theory Forecasts*)
$75/year

Justin Mamis' Insights (Justin Mamis)
P.O. Box 907, Peck Slip Station, NY 10272
$145

Mansfield Stock Chart Service
2173 Kennedy Blvd., Jersey City, NJ 07306
up to $1,365 /year

Margo's Market Monitor ("Margo")
P.O. Box 642, Lexington, MA 02173
$125/year

Market Alert (James U. Blanchard III)
4425 West Napoleon Street, Metairie, LA 70001
$60/year

Market Logic (Glen King Parker, Norman Fosback)
3471 N. Federal Highway, Fort Lauderdale, FL 33306
$135/year

Market Mania (Glenn Cutler)
P.O. Box 1234, Pacifica, CA 94044
$85/year

Market Vantage
(see *Investment Values*)
$80/year

The McKeever Strategy Letter (Jim McKeever)
P.O. Box 4130, Medford, OR 97501
$195/year

Medical Technology Stock Letter (Jim McCamant)
155 Montgomery St., Suite 1401, San Francisco, CA 94104
$220/year

Money Fund Safety Ratings
(see *Market Logic*)
$100/year

The Money Letter (Ron Hume)
4141 Yonge Street, Willowdale, Ontario, Canada
$95/year

Mutual Fund Forecaster
(see *Market Logic*)
$49/year

Mutual Fund Investing (Jay Schabacker/Phillips Publishing, Inc.)
(see *The Retirement Letter*)
$145/year

Mutual Fund Strategist (Charles Hooper)
P.O. Box 446, Burlington, VT 05402
$87.50/year

Myers' Finance & Energy (C. Vernon Myers)
N. 7307 Division, Suite 204, Spokane, WA 99208
$200/year

New Issues
(see *Market Logic*)
$200/year

Newsletter Digest (Dr. Al Owen)
2335 Pansy Street, Huntsville, AL 35801
$75/year

The Newsletter on Newsletters (Howard Penn Hudson)
44 West Market Street, P.O. Box 311, Rhinebeck, NY 12572
$66/year [The Newsletter Clearinghouse]

Maxwell Newton's Daily New York Money Market Report (Maxwell
   Newton)
Box 1246, Darien, CT 06820
$7,500/year

The Ney Report (Richard Ney)
Box 90215, Pasadena, CA 91109
$295/year

The Nicholson Report (Robert Nicholson)
7550 Red Road, Coral Gables, FL 33143
$200/year

No-Load Fund-X (Burton Berry)
235 Montgomery Street, San Francisco, CA 94104
$95/year

Northwest Investment Review (Shannon P. Pratt)
400 Williamette Bldg., 534 S.W. Third Avenue, Portland, OR 97204
$195/year

Nourse Investor Reports (Tom Nourse)
P.O. Box 28039, San Diego, CA 92128
$175/year

Oil/Energy Statistics Bulletin (Roger E. Spear, Jr.)
P.O. Box 127, Babson Park, MA 02157
$185/year

The Option Advisor (Robert D. Bergen, Bernard G. Schaeffer)
P.O. Box 46709, Cincinnati, OH 45246
$225/year

OTC Insight (Louis G. Navellier)
P.O. Box 1329, El Cerrito, CA 94530
$100/year

The Outlook (Arnold Kaufman)
Standard & Poor's Co., 25 Broadway, New York, NY 10004
$195/year

The Patient Investor (John W. Rogers, Jr., Jessica E. Berger)
307 N. Michigan Ave., Suite 2014, Chicago, IL 60601
$125/year

The L.T. Patterson Strategy Letter (Lawrence T. Patterson)
105 West Fourth Street, Suite 633, Cincinnati, OH 45202
$149.95/year

The Ron Paul Investment Letter (Dr. Ron Paul)
9001 Airport Boulevard, Suite 302, Houston, TX 77061
$150/year

Penny Stock Newsletter (Jerome Wenger)
8930 Route 108, Ste. J., Columbia, MD 21045
$50/year

Personal Finance (Richard Band)
1300 N. 17th St., Arlington, Va. 22209
$94/year

The Peter Dag Investment Letter (Peter Dag)
65 Lakefront Drive, Akron, OH 44319
$250/year

Plain Talk Investor (Fred Gordon)
801 Skokie Blvd., Suite 218, Northbrook IL 60062
$95/year

The Polymetric Report (Picton Davies)
P.O. Box 1428, Williamsville, NY 14221 (NYSE Edition)
84 Valentine Drive, Don Mills, Ontario CANADA (TSE Edition)
$195 each/year

Powell Monetary Analyst
181 State St., Portland, ME 04101
$285/year

The Predictor & Tillman Survey
P.O. Drawer 22008, Santa Barbara, CA 93121
$195/year

Pring Market Review (Martin J. Pring)
P.O. Box 338, Washington Depot, CT 06794
$295/year

The Professional Investor (Robert T. Gross)
P.O. Box 2144, Pompano Beach, FL 33061
$200/year

The Professional Tape Reader (Stan Weinstein)
P.O. Box 2407, Hollywood, FL 33022
$250/year

Professional Timing Service (Curtis J. Hesler)
P.O. Box 7483, Missoula, MT 59807
$150/year

The Prudent Speculator (Al Frank)
P.O. Box 1767, Santa Monica, CA 90406
$150/year

PSR Stockwatch (Ken Fisher)
433 Airport Blvd., Suite 106, Burlingame, CA 94010
$250/year

The Puryear Money Report (Milton Puryear)
45 John Street, New York, NY 10038
$65/year

Rating the Stock Selectors (Mannie Webb)
8949 La Riviera Drive, Sacramento, CA 95826
$180/year

Retirement Fund Advisory
(see *Switch Fund Advisory*)
$59/year

The Retirement Letter (Thomas L. Phillips)
7315 Wisconsin Ave., Suite 1200N, Bethesda, MD 20814
$60/year

The RHM Survey of Warrants, Options & Low-Price Stocks (Sidney
    Fried)
172 Forest Avenue, Glen Cove, NY 11542
$155/year

Howard Ruff's Financial Success Report (Howard J. Ruff)
6612 Owens Drive, Pleasanton, CA 94566
$99/year

Scientific Market Analysis (Dr. Irving Reich)
Box 28261, Rancho Bernardo, San Diego, CA 92128
$55/year

Smart Money (Yale Hirsch)
6 Deer Trail, Old Tappan, NJ 07675
$98/year

Special Situations Under $5
(see *Dow Theory Forecasts*)
$97/year

The Speculator (Stephen Leeb)
37 Van Reipen, Jersey City, NJ 07306
$175/year

Stockmarket Cycles (Peter G. Eliades)
2260 Cahuenga Blvd., Suite 305, Los Angeles, CA 90068
$198/year

Stock Market Performance Digest (Joel Nadel)
10076 Boca Entrada Blvd., P.O. Box 30007, Boca Raton, FL
   33431-0907
$96/year

Street Smart Investing (Kiril Sokoloff)
Box 173, Katonah, NY 10536
$195/year

Switch Fund Advisory (Jay Schabacker)
8943 Shady Grove Court
Gaithersburg, MD 20877
$129/year

Systems & Forecasts (Gerald Appel)
150 Great Neck Road, Great Neck, NY 11021
$160/year

Technical Stock Advisory Service (Dr. David G. Funk)
103 State Street, Boston, MA 02109
$720/year

Telephone Switch Newsletter (Richard J. Fabian)
P.O. Box 2538, Huntington Beach, CA 92647
$117/year

Timer Digest (Robert E. James)
P.O. Box 030247, Fort Lauderdale, FL 33303
$150/year

The Tortoise Report (Robert J. Ringer)
(see *Market Alert*)
$96/year

United Business & Investment Report
210 Newbury Street, Boston, MA 02116
$170/year

Value Investing (John C. Boland)
P.O. Box 38125, Baltimore, MD 21231
$139/year

Value Line Investment Survey (Arnold Bernhard)
711 Third Avenue, New York, NY 10017
$395/year

Value Line New Issue Service
(see *Value Line*)
$330/year

Value Line OTC Special Situations Service (Peter A. Shraga)
(see *Value Line*)
$300/year

Wall Street Digest (Donald H. Rowe)
101 Carnegie Center, Princeton, NJ 08540
$150/year

Wall Street Transcript (Richard A. Holman)
99 Wall Street, New York, NY 10005
$860/year

Weber's Fund Advisor (Ken Weber)
P.O. Box 92, Bellerose, NY 11426
$79/year

Weekly Advisory Bulletin
(see *Switch Fund Advisory*)
$129/year

The Wellington Letter (Bert Dohmen-Ramirez)
733 Bishop Street, #1800, Honolulu, HI 96813
$132/year

Wellington's Worry-Free Investing
(see *The Wellington Letter*)
$96/year

The Worden Report (Don Worden)
P.O. Box 3458, Chapel Hill, NC 27515
$100/year

World Market Perspectives (Diego Veitia)
2211 Lee Rd., Ste. 103, Winter Park, FL 32789
$96/year

The Zweig Forecast (Dr. Martin E. Zweig)
P.O. Box 5345, New York, NY 10150
$245/year

Zweig Performance Ratings Report (Joe DiMenna, Carol Whitehead)
(see *The Zweig Forecast*)
$150/year

Although many of the books mentioned in the text are now out of print, they can often be obtained through two mail-order book sellers specializing in the investment area:

Fraser Publishing
Box 494
Burlington, VT 05402-9990
(802) 658-0322

The Investment Center Bookstore
2124 S. Sepulveda Blvd.
Los Angeles, CA 90025
(213) 478-5263

Also:

Technical Trends (Arthur A. Merrill)
P.O. Box 228, Chappaqua, NY 10514
$60/year

Select Index
to Advisory
Organizations

H

I

J

K

O

P

R

S

T

About the Author

PETER BRIMELOW is a graduate of the University of Sussex in England and of Stanford University Graduate School of Business, where he studied on a Fulbright Award. He has been an Associate Editor of *Barron's* and *Fortune* magazine, and Business Editor of *Maclean's* magazine and a columnist for the *Financial Post* in Canada. He and his wife live in New York City and northwestern Connecticut.